Sociology Transformed

Series Editors
John Holmwood
School of Sociology and Social Policy
University of Nottingham
Nottingham, UK

Stephen Turner
Department of Philosophy
University of South Florida
Tampa, FL, USA

The field of sociology has changed rapidly over the last few decades. Sociology Transformed seeks to map these changes on a country by country basis and to contribute to the discussion of the future of the subject. The series is concerned not only with the traditional centres of the discipline, but with its many variant forms across the globe.

Spiros Gangas • Georgia Lagoumitzi

Sociology in Greece

Its History and Development

Spiros Gangas
American College of Greece
Athens, Greece

Georgia Lagoumitzi
American College of Greece
Athens, Greece

ISSN 2947-5023 ISSN 2947-5031 (electronic)
Sociology Transformed
ISBN 978-3-031-16189-6 ISBN 978-3-031-16190-2 (eBook)
https://doi.org/10.1007/978-3-031-16190-2

© The Author(s), under exclusive licence to Springer Nature Switzerland AG 2022
This work is subject to copyright. All rights are solely and exclusively licensed by the Publisher, whether the whole or part of the material is concerned, specifically the rights of translation, reprinting, reuse of illustrations, recitation, broadcasting, reproduction on microfilms or in any other physical way, and transmission or information storage and retrieval, electronic adaptation, computer software, or by similar or dissimilar methodology now known or hereafter developed.
The use of general descriptive names, registered names, trademarks, service marks, etc. in this publication does not imply, even in the absence of a specific statement, that such names are exempt from the relevant protective laws and regulations and therefore free for general use.
The publisher, the authors, and the editors are safe to assume that the advice and information in this book are believed to be true and accurate at the date of publication. Neither the publisher nor the authors or the editors give a warranty, expressed or implied, with respect to the material contained herein or for any errors or omissions that may have been made. The publisher remains neutral with regard to jurisdictional claims in published maps and institutional affiliations.

This Palgrave Macmillan imprint is published by the registered company Springer Nature Switzerland AG.
The registered company address is: Gewerbestrasse 11, 6330 Cham, Switzerland

PREFACE

This is the first monograph about sociology in Greece to appear in English since 1974. The nearly 50 years that elapsed were not years of total silence about Greek sociology. Important articles (which we use and discuss in the book) chronicled and assessed Greek sociology and its development amid social change. Our book is a concise account and overview of sociology in Greece and its impact in the international division of sociological labour. Although particular sociologists stand out, the book is more than a condensed account of their ideas. Rather, it provides a wider scope and exposition placement of these ideas in specific to Greece cultural resources and barriers, ideological paradigms, discipline boundary challenges and scientific controversies. The achievements of Greek sociology are by no means limited and negligible to be contained in a journal article or book chapter; nor are they so diverse and globally impactful as to justify a longer monograph. We write this book in this light and with the firm belief that sociology in Greece deserves an updated re-examination which will hopefully lead to a re-evaluation of its potential for becoming an active participant in the discipline's adaptation to the challenges that lie ahead. Thus, beyond providing a concise history and genealogy of sociology in Greece, our book addresses social, cultural, political and institutional factors that affected sociology's development in Greece in parallel to key sociologists' patterns of thought and major works. It also highlights some of Greek sociology's institutional features in the field of the discipline's organizational foundations to its adaptive mechanisms in face of challenges that stem from the wider field of education, politics, the mass media, the economy, global processes and not least from sociology's own international dynamics. Fora for sociology's growth and dissemination are addressed (some for the first time), and student demographics cap the discipline's current state and degree of appeal.

Drawing on this niche of ideas, scholars, institutions, fora and networks, our book hopes to heighten sociological consciousness in Greece, among Greek diaspora sociologists and academics from other fields and among the wider Greek public.

A compact monograph did not permit an exhaustive investigation of subtler processes in sociology's difficult period of emergence and growth in Greece. Paradoxically, we came to encounter a sociological tradition the intellectual labour of which revealed myriad hidden paths that could have led this narrative astray. Thus, by and large, irrelevant back region narratives that afflict sociology in Greece, like anywhere in the world, were beyond our intentions and aims. Moreover, a lexical list of all Greek sociologists was also evidently outside the aims and rationale of this book. We have tried instead to cite work that is indicative of Greek sociology's trajectory through its inception, selecting where appropriate work by Greek sociologists that has been published in English to relax the language barrier for readers who cannot read Greek. We hope that such decision indicates the breadth of Greek sociology without occluding the significance and originality of work that is available only in Greek which we also amply use and cite. For quoted passages from Greek publications or interviews that appear in this book, we made the respective translations.

We thank John Holmwood and Stephen P. Turner for accepting our book proposal in the *Sociology Transformed* series. Sujatha Mani, Elizabeth Graber and Brian Halm at Palgrave/Springer responded to all our queries with speed and clarity.

We have held enlightening and fruitful discussions about Greek sociology, its history and current state of affairs with Alexandros-Andreas Kyrtsis, Sokratis Koniordos and Nicholas Tatsis. We are grateful for their feedback and knowledge. We also thank Nota Kyriazi, Maria Kousi and Kostas Kalfopoulos for useful communication and help.

Demetra Papaconstantinou, College Archivist at the ACG Archives and Special Collections, gave us access to important ACG archival material. The library staff at Deree, particularly Angeliki Palaiogopoulou, and the Pierce library staff have made available to us in impressive document delivery speed hard to find bibliographical sources. Olga Karadimou at the very hospitable archives sector of the *Hellenic Broadcasting Corporation* (ERT) proved an invaluable resource, and Vassilis Alexopoulos, the Director of the ERT archives, showed support and enthusiasm in our project. Eleni Kovaiou and the library staff at the Archives Collection of the University of Crete at Rethymno provided swift and valuable access to digitalized archival material. The Panteion University library staff helped us with relevant guidance and practical help in consulting important books held at the collection, and we had useful communication with the *Greek Ministry of Education and Religious Affairs*. We are thankful and grateful to all.

We are indebted to Loren J. Samons, ACG CAO and Founding Executive Director of *the Institute of Hellenic Culture and the Liberal Arts*, for securing funding and for embracing the project under the Institute's contribution to the broader ACG 150 strategic plan to leverage education for an economic and social impact in Greece. Michalis Psalidopoulos, ACG 150 Director at the *Institute for Hellenic Growth and Prosperity*, was also very supportive of the project, and we are grateful to him for additional help under urgent circumstances. The views expressed in this book are those of the authors and do not necessarily express those of ACG.

Last but not least, we warmly thank our Department Head Chryssa Zachou who provided precious administrative support and helped us access important information about the *Hellenic Sociological Society* (HSS).

Of course, such a great company of individuals who helped in various ways has no bearing on the book's limitations and omissions for which we have the entire responsibility.

Athens, Greece	Spiros Gangas
Athens, Greece	Georgia Lagoumitzi

CHRONOLOGY OF EVENTS IN MODERN GREEK POLITICAL HISTORY[1]

1821	The Greek War of Independence begins.
1828	Count Ioannis Kapodistrias arrives in Greece as its first president aiming at the reconstruction of the country.
1830	France, England and Russia recognize the independence of Greece under the London Protocol of 3 February 1830.
1831	Kapodistrias assassinated and the reconstruction project is jeopardized through further factionalism and political party intrigue.
1833	Arrival of Prince Otto of Bavaria in Greece as its first king Greece. A period of royal absolutism begins.
1834	Athens becomes the capital of Greece.
1843	King Otto grants a constitution under the pressure of revolt.
1844	Birth of the Grand Idea through which the state was acquiring a destiny to expand the nation beyond the current borders while holding on to a fundamental 'national character'.
1862	King Otto is forced to abdicate after an uprising against his rule.
1863	Prince George of Denmark becomes 'King of the Hellenes'.
1864	The new constitution defines the political system as a 'crowned democracy', and a period of oligarchic parliamentarism begins marked by the exclusion of the masses from politics.
1871	Alexandros Koumoundouros' land reform further profits small landholdings.

---

[1] This chronology consulted, but is not limited to, Koliopoulos, J.S., Th.M. Veremis, (2002). *Greece, The modern sequel: From 1831 to the present.* Hurst & Company.

1875	Introduction of the 'principle of declared majority' into parliamentary life. The leader of a party enjoying majority support in parliament should be given the mandate to form a government.
1881	Annexation of the province of Thessaly by Greece.
1883–1893	The consolidation of a two-party system (Trikoupis-Deligiannis) is often considered to be the beginning of the battle between the 'modernizing' and the 'underdog' cultures.
1893	Prime Minister Charilaos Trikoupis declares bankruptcy.
1896	Cretan rebellion against Ottoman rule engages Greece in the Cretan liberation and inflates nationalist feelings.
1897	Secret societies fuel nationalist feelings and lead to the 'ignominious' Greco-Turkish war which ends with the defeat of Greece and a growing sense for the necessity of social and political change.
1908	Alexandros Papanastasiou establishes the 'Sociological Society' to spearhead social reforms relating to workers' rights.
1909	A group of officers organize the Military League which demands reforms in the army and the civil service. Revolt at Goudi, Venizelos is appointed by the officers as their political advisor.
1910	Venizelos launches extensive reforms, and the old political oligarchy is forced to share power with ascending middle-class strata.
1912–1913	The triumph of the Grand Idea during the Balkan Wars and territorial gains.
1915	National Schism. Clash between Venizelos and King Constantine over Greece's stance during World War I, Venizelos proposes an alliance with the Entente, while the king opts for neutrality. Venizelos twice was forced to resign.
1922	The end of the Grand Idea in Asia Minor.
1923	Treaty of Lausanne, 1,500,000 refugees arrive in Greece and provide an electoral basis for Venizelos but also for subsequent radical political parties like KKE (Greek Communist Party).
1924	Greece becomes a republic following a referendum.
1924–1926	Successive coups mark the intervention of the military into Greek politics. Growing frustration of the working classes is met by punitive measures.
1928–1932	Last term of Venizelos' liberal government in office. Rising unemployment and the shocks of the global financial crisis. Idionym law, mainly targeting Communists is used to suppress social protest.
1932	Default on debts.

CHRONOLOGY OF EVENTS IN MODERN GREEK POLITICAL HISTORY xi

1935	Failed anti-royalist pre-emptive coup speeds up King George's restoration.
1936–1937	Metaxas' dictatorial rule enabled by the King's endorsement of the suspension of certain articles of the constitution, sociology chairs in Thessaloniki and Athens are suspended for about 40 years.
1941–1944	German occupation and resistance. Castoriadis writes for the newly launched *Archive of Sociology and Ethics*.
1944	The 'December events', an armed conflict between EAM-ELAS (National Liberation Front and its military wing) and government forces supported by the British.
1946–1949	A full-fledged civil war between Communist-controlled Democratic Army in Northern Greece and the National Army under a coalition government of 'Populists' (right-wingers and royalists). The Communist forces are defeated in 1949.
1947–1952	Under the Truman doctrine massive aid is granted to Greece. A reconstruction programme is under way which finds its expression in sociology as social welfare.
1955–1967	A fragile democracy. Repressive parliamentarism.
1959–1967	Athens Social Sciences Centre (KKEA) led by John Peristiany is established, and the first steps of social research in Greece are taken. The first sociology undergraduate curriculum in the American College of Greece.
1960	Cyprus becomes an independent republic with Archbishop Makarios as President and Dr Fazil Kütchük as Vice-President.
1967–1974	Military dictatorship led by a group of colonels, flight of Greek intelligentsia to Europe, closing of the Athens Social Sciences Centre (KKEA).
1968	Historic split of the Communist party of Greece prompted by the Soviet invasion of Czechoslovakia into two factions, an 'orthodox' Marxist-Leninist and a pluralist, social democratic, Euro-communist. Nicos Poulantzas becomes the leading ideologue and member of the Communist party of the Interior denouncing Stalinist orthodoxy.
1968–1974s	National Centre of Social Research (EKKE) in Athens re-opens under junta surveillance, Polytechneion (Polytechnic) student uprising spells the beginning of the end for the military regime. Peristiany heads a new Centre of Social Research in Cyprus.
1974	*Metapolitefsi*, restoration of democracy. Turkish invasion of Cyprus and collapse of the junta. Karamanlis returns as prime minister from exile in Paris.

1979	Karamanlis signs the treaty of accession to the European Community with nine EC members.
1981	Greece joins the EC. Victory of PA.SO. K. (Panhellenic Socialist Movement) in the October election, the rise of populism.
1984–1990	Institutionalization of sociology, first public university sociology departments in Panteion University and the University of Crete.
1990–2000	Further consolidation of tri-partite politics, a new sociology department in the University of the Aegean. Initiation of postgraduate programmes.
2010–2015	Economic crisis and the rise of political extremes (e.g. Golden Dawn), austerity politics.
2015–2019	SYRIZA in power, July 2015 referendum, cultural and political identities on a collision course.
2019–2022	Between crisis and recovery

About the Book

Sociology in Greece: Its History and Development revisits a major source of cultural capital for modern and contemporary Greece which is no other than the profile and accomplishments of a vanguard and prolific discipline: sociology. The book provides a compelling chronicle of the discipline's inception in the early twentieth century, its post-war vision amid World War II aftermath and civil war and its path toward institutionalization as it grappled, like Greece, with modernization and dependency. It extends this narrative to Greek sociology's adaptation and struggle for voice during the dictatorship years and charts its post-1974 fruition in multiple trajectories even if crises like the Great Recession and the Covid-19 pandemic posed additional challenges and setbacks. Beyond making known to a global audience hidden but valuable profiles, individual works and institutional processes of Greek sociology's history, development and current state, the book recognizes and rehabilitates the work of seminal thinkers like Castoriadis and Poulantzas in Greek sociology along with other sociological literates that come from other disciplines. Its organization in clearly demarcated chronological chapters enables readers to retain a sense of historical continuity and change without conceding theoretical rigor. Along with the discipline's and its major representatives' contributions, what also emerges is a history of modern and contemporary Greece through the lens of sociology's institutional features and explanation of modern Greece. Hence, the book's appeal is not limited to the community of sociologists in Greece and abroad; it stretches to social scientists from neighbouring disciplines and to the vibrant Greek diaspora. It is an essential resource for students of sociology in Greece that aims not only to enrich the discipline's historiography but also to sustain and restore confidence and honour in its legacy and accomplishments.

Praise for *Sociology in Greece*

"This book opens entirely new perspectives for the study of sociological thought in countries which do not belong to the birthplaces of classical sociology. The authors reveal the interplay between transfers of ideas often originating from the work of renowned Greek intellectuals working abroad, the dynamics of nationally shaped networks of sociologists and the social and political history of Greece. This is a fascinating piece of history of academic ideas and their public perception."
—Alexandros-Andreas Kyrtsis, *Professor of Sociology, Emeritus, Department of Political Science and Public Administration, National and Kapodistrian University of Athens*

"At last, Greek sociology becomes accessible to the international social science community through this book. The authors have superbly succeeded in linking the development of sociology in Greece with the country's political and intellectual history and the precipitated course of Greek society from feudalism to modernity. The complex relationship between sociology and social change appears in fascinating detail."
—Michalis Lianos, *Professor of Sociology at the University of Rouen*

Contents

1	**An Incubation Era: 1900–1944**	1
	Sociology as Social Reform: Alexandros Papanastasiou and 'the Sociologists'	2
	The Sociological Society	2
	The Sociologists' Theoretical Aspirations	5
	'Protosociologists' Avrotelis Eleftheropoulos (1869–1963), Panagiotis Kanellopoulos (1902–1986) and Evangelos Lembesis (1904–1968)	7
	Avrotelis Eleftheropoulos: Extolling Individualism	8
	The Heidelberg Circle and Kanellopoulos' Idea of Sociology	9
	Evangelos Lembesis: Sociologist of 'Ressentiment'	15
	References	19
2	**From Academic Uncertainty to the Birth of Empirical Research: 1944–1974**	25
	From Social Welfare to Sociology: 1945–1962	26
	The Emergence of Social Research and Greek Modernization	30
	The Athens Social Sciences Centre: 1959–1967	30
	The National Centre of Social Research: 1968–1974	39
	References	41

3 Institutionalization and Re-politicization Amid Modernization and Dependency: 1974–1990 47
The Debate on the Greek Social Formation After 1974:
The Turn to Dependency and Underdevelopment 48
   International Capitalism as the Decisive Element in
   Underdevelopment: Vergopoulos and Poulantzas 51
   Vassilis Filias: Social Classes in Underdevelopment 52
   Constantinos Tsoukalas: Periphery and Underdevelopment—
   From Class Structure to Class Relations 53
   Nicos Mouzelis and the Capitalist Mode of Production as an
   Enclave Form 54
Institutional Developments: 1974–1990 55
References 59

4 Boundary Challenges from Abroad and from Neighbouring Disciplines 63
'Sociology in Greece': Prolegomena on Re-classification Issues 64
Cornelius Castoriadis: Sociological Contribution and Legacy in Greece 66
   The 1944 Writings 67
   The Imaginary Institution of Society (1975) 69
   Influence and Presence in Greece 73
Nicos Poulantzas: Sociological Contribution and Legacy in Greece 77
   The 'Miliband-Poulantzas' Debate 79
   The 1966 'Class and the State' Lectures/Seminars and the 1976–1977 Lectures at Panteion University 81
   The 'Poulantzas-Castoriadis' Polemic 87
Sociological Theory Input from Neighbouring Disciplines and Scholars 88
   Panagiotis Kondylis 89
   Kondylis' Sociologically Informed and Incomplete The Political and Man 89
   Kondylis' Sociological Diagnostics 93
   The Kosmas Psychopedis Axiologika *Interdisciplinary Group* 95
References 97

5	**Greek Sociology's Interdisciplinary and Multi-paradigmatic Shift: 1990–2000**	105
	Reconstructing Sociological Theory: Nicos Mouzelis	106
	Interdisciplinarity: Sociology's Identity Already in Doubt?	108
	Sociology in Public and Virtual Spaces	111
	Sociology Journals and Research Centres	112
	Greek TV's Mission Impossible: Disseminating Sociology to a Wider public Public (1)	114
	Multi-paradigmatic Post-Modernism: Veltsos' Non-sociology	122
	Greek Sociology's Steady Growth	123
	References	128
6	**Sociology in Greece After 2000: The Discipline in Face of Crises**	135
	The Crisis in Greece and the Crisis of Sociology?	136
	Greece's Crises: In Search of the 'Intermediate' Way?	137
	Greek Sociology's Struggle for a Public Audience	139
	The Journals Landscape	139
	The Translations Landscape	140
	Greek TV's Mission Impossible: Disseminating Sociology to a Wider Public (2)	142
	Recent Developments and Mouzelis' and Tsoukalas' Latest Works	143
	Mouzelis' Late Works	147
	Tsoukalas' Recent Diagnostic Sociology	149
	The Sociology of Sociology in Greece: The Work of Lambiri-Dimaki	151
	Further International Reach	153
	The 'Hellenic Sociological Society'	155
	The Current Profile of Sociology Departments in Greece	156
	References	160

Conclusion — 171

Index — 173

About the Author

Spiros Gangas is Associate Professor of Sociology at Deree—the American College of Greece. His major research focuses on classical and contemporary sociological theory, capability approach and value theory. He is the author of *Sociological Theory and the Capability Approach* (2020) and has published journals, articles and book chapters in sociological theory in Greece and abroad.

Georgia Lagoumitzi is Full-Time Lecturer in Sociology at Deree—the American College of Greece. Her current research interests include areas like globalization, modern Greek diasporas and collective memory.

List of Figures

Fig. 6.1 Total degrees in sociology (Bachelors, MScs, PhDs) 157
Fig. 6.2 Breakdown by degree 158

List of Tables

Table 6.1   Degrees in sociology per university and degree   158
Table 6.2   Change in the no. of students of sociology per university and degree   159

CHAPTER 1

An Incubation Era: 1900–1944

Abstract Greece's slow encounter with modernity takes place against a background of dramatic socio-political events that coincide with the birth of sociology in Greece. The first sociological interventions attempt to blend scientific reasoning and social reform and culminate in the founding of the *Sociological Society* in 1908 by Alexandros Papanastasiou. The 1916 renaming of the *Sociological Society* into *Society for the Social and Political Sciences* marks a sincere but abortive attempt to privilege science rather than politics. The cooperation between the *Society* and the journal *Archive of Economic and Social Sciences* (1921–1971) introduces sociological and economic approaches to social problems and hosts the work of 'protosociologists', that is, Avrotelis Eleftheropoulos, Panagiotis Kanellopoulos and Evangelos Lembesis. The establishment of two sociology chairs, one at the University of Thessaloniki (1929) and the other at the University of Athens (1930), marks the academic turn, which is short-lived, as both chairs operate outside the logic of a department until they are suspended after 1935. Attempts to establish professional sociology conclude with the Panteion School which Eleftherios Venizelos himself inaugurates in 1930. The idealization of the past and the criticism of early twentieth century attempt to move to what was interpreted as a mechanistic and impersonal *Gesellschaft* leaves the study of modernity as a distinctly sociological project unfinished.

© The Author(s), under exclusive license to Springer Nature Switzerland AG 2022
S. Gangas, G. Lagoumitzi, *Sociology in Greece*, Sociology Transformed, https://doi.org/10.1007/978-3-031-16190-2_1

Keywords Idealism • Individualism • 'Protosociologists' •
Ressentiment • Social reform • Sociology

SOCIOLOGY AS SOCIAL REFORM: ALEXANDROS PAPANASTASIOU AND 'THE SOCIOLOGISTS'

Greece's transition from the nineteenth to the early twentieth century was an anguishing one. The close of the nineteenth century was marked by the 'unfortunate' and 'ignominious' Greco-Turkish war of 1897.[1] While this was the first devastating defeat of the nationalist 'Grand Idea'[2] (Beaton, 2020, pp. 127–29), it also paved the way for a new era that generated opportunities to remedy the country's political system and provide a reconstitution of the Greek nation (Maroniti, 1997, p. 215). A 'healing' of the collective trauma of defeat was sought through the introduction of a new rhetoric of social reform, without necessarily abandoning the 'myths' that had brought Greece to bankruptcy and international economic control. In one of the pioneering efforts to chart sociology in Greece, John Peristiany notes that 'sociology was introduced as a scientific-sounding name for a movement of social reform' (1968, p. 272) whose origins lay in the founding of the first *Sociological Society* in 1908 by the prominent politician Alexandros Papanastasiou (1876–1936). Other founding members included Thrasyvoulos Petmezas (1874–1939), Panagiotis Aravantinos (1882–1932) and Konstantinos Triantafyllopoulos (1881–1966), all of whom had studied law in Athens and had later met again as students in Berlin. Subsequently, the *Society* was joined by Alexandros Delmouzos, Thalis Koutoupis and Alexandros Mylonas, who had varying degrees of intellectual affiliation with the *Society*.

The Sociological Society

The *Sociological Society* had a twofold aim, theoretical and political. On the one hand, the 'popularization' of philosophical, sociological and economic studies became a central pursuit. On the other, the re-definition of the role of the state in a paternalistic direction to ensure the end of exploitation

---

[1] A thirty-day war between Greece and the Ottoman Empires that ended in Greece's total defeat.
[2] Here, we adopt Roderick Beaton's terminology for the Greek nationalist ideology that informed Greek politics from 1844 to 1922 as opposed to the prevailing one named 'Great Idea'.

and the empowerment of the working class acquired the status of a missionary idea. To achieve the latter goal, it was deemed necessary not only for the working people to organize in cooperative associations but also around a new political party that would address workers' issues. In an early, short reference to sociology in Greece, Maus informs us that within the context of reform, 'traditional German "academic socialism" was taken as a guide. This early Greek sociology sought to secure the passing of labor legislation and helped to found the trade-union movement' (Maus, 1962, p. 175). Addressing the development of democratic institutions and the reconstruction of the working classes in a way that would integrate them into politics followed the German revisionist tradition of Eduard Bernstein and Fabianism.[3] Kyrtsis argues that, as it is often the case, the introduction of such ideas into the Greek political reality preceded any framework for their ideological use. For example, 'even before a crisis of the working-class movement appeared, indeed before the very formation of a movement, revisionist socialism was introduced as a branch of theoretical schemas belonging to the statist-corporatist tradition of the *Kathedersozialisten* (or 'armchair socialists') and of other moderate reformist perspectives that influenced the wider Venizelist circles' (Kyrtsis, 1996a, pp. 157–158). Moreover, the blend of reformist socialism and Fabianism constituted the crux of Papanastasiou's often quixotic efforts to cooperate with working-class representatives and liberal elements alike in the promotion of social policy measures. Such measures included, among others, a land settlement regarding landless peasants and refugees (post-1922); interventions furthering workers' rights, for example, the introduction of the 1911 parliamentary bill on women's and children's working rights; a vision for a more equitable electoral system; the defence of the demotic language as a political project;[4] and an education open to all Greeks, freed from scholasticism and prejudice. Indeed, the language question in Greece (the battle between a 'pure' form—*katharevousa*, which captures the continuity and immutability of the nation itself, as opposed to a popular—*demotic*—form that is a codified and normalized form of the 'natural', spoken language constitutes the first field in which

---

[3] For an extensive discussion of the two models on which the organization of the *Sociological Society* was based, see Kyrtsis (1996a, b, 1998, pp. 315–316). Also, see Marketos (2000, pp. 70–84).

[4] For an analysis of the connection between the *demoticist* movement and Papanastasiou's 'Sociologists' see Stavridi-Patrikiou (1988, pp. 353–370). For a full history of the language question see Mackridge (2009).

various sociological theories are ideologically tested in early socialist journals such as *Noumas, to Mellon* (The Future) and *O Laos* (The People). In fact, the 'crude' socialist ideas of *O Laos* are lamented by one of the foremost literary figures of Greece, Penelope Delta, who sees efforts to discover a non-existent proletariat in the country as foreign-born and intending to 'put out the last sparks of patriotism' (Bournazos, 1999, p. 279). Papanastasiou never saw socialism and patriotism as two irreconcilable ideologies; in fact, he believed and actively demonstrated that one entails the other. Of course, his brand of socialism was that of a benevolent, ethical state which assumes the responsibility of social reform. His social reform programme is already drafted by 1910, and its democratic-socialist principles are reflected in the creation of the Popular Party in the same year. The party's political manifesto, tellingly titled 'What Is to Be Done', was submitted to the leader of the Military League, the group of officers who in 1909, recognizing the need for the Greek political system to emerge out of the political, economic and moral gridlock, had carried out the so-called Goudi coup.[5] This was an action of high symbolic value that helped consolidate Papanastasiou's reputation as a democrat and modernizer. Moreover, Papanastasiou's democratic legacy during the interwar period finds its clearest expression in the February 1922 *Democratic Manifesto* published in *Eleftheros Typos* and *Patris* newspapers and which openly declared the monarchy an 'enemy of social cohesion' and 'harbinger of further calamities for the nation'.[6] Two years later, his opposition to the institution of the monarchy culminated in him heading the first government in what became a stillborn Republic 'characterized by intense political and social conflict, the emergence of class parties and recurrent military intervention which eventually led to its downfall and monarchical restoration in 1935 and subsequently to the suppression of competitive politics in 1936' (Mavrogordatos, 1983, p. xv). The Greek political system and especially conservative elites turned their back on Papanastasiou's legacy of reformist socialism, and by 1936 his struggles for the implementation of a social security system and agrarian reform

[5] In 1909, a group of young officers known as the Military League demanding reform in the army and within the civil service set up camp at the Goudi area at the foothills of Mount Hymettus. They then proceeded to deliver their ultimatum to the government. It was a bloodless coup whose demands were quickly met, yet it was the first involvement of the army into politics. (Gerolymatos, 2021, p. 15).

[6] See: Το Δημοκρατικό Μανιφέστο και ο τύπος (The Democratic Manifesto and the Press of the Interwar Period), Appendix in Anastasiadis, G (2008, pp. 265–288).

were either appropriated by other parties or forgotten (Marketos, 2000, p. 12). For example, many of the Popular Party's political goals were integrated into Venizelos' liberal programme. On the other hand, Papanastasiou's political weight derived from the adaptability of his proposals to the new political climate that Venizelos' ascendancy created after 1910. It is perhaps for this reason that Greek historiography has largely ignored political-ideological nuances, subsuming a variety of local ideological currents and their European origins under all-inclusive categories such as 'Venizelism' (Marketos, 2000, p. 13).[7] Despite the substantial contributions of modern Greek historiographers and historians of ideas, only recently has a clear understanding of the intellectual and political achievements of the period between 1909 and 1936 been produced (Kyrtsis, 1996a, b; Marketos, 2000; Kourahanis, 2014).

The *Sociologists*' Theoretical Aspirations

One question that tends to dominate current analyses is whether Papanastasiou's insistence on political reforms 'weakened' the more scientific aspects of the *Sociological Society*. It may well have done so. This was certainly the case for the *Sociologists*' German counterparts where 'scholarship became increasingly subservient to political argument; and this worked to erode that reputation for objectivity that forms the scientist's primary claim to authority in public affairs' (Offer, 1984, 22). Koniordos states that 'the identification of science (sociology) with a politically tinged social reform meant that the necessary autonomy from extra-scientific interventions was suppressed from the start' (Koniordos, 2010, p. 231).

The first journal reflecting mainly the intellectual pursuits of the Papanastasiou circle was the *Review of Social and Legal Sciences* (Epitheorisis ton Koinonikon kai Nomikon Epistimon 1908–09 and 1916–17), a short-lived endeavour in which sociological articles were sparse (Nikolaou, 1974,

---

[7] Papanastasiou's influence on Greek politics left an indelible mark as is clear in the formation of *Omilos Papanastasiou* (Papanastasiou Society) in 1965 by ex-Prime Minister of Greece, Kostas Simitis. Apart from Kostas Simitis, Sakis Karagiorgas and Vasilis Filias contributed to the drafting of the Declaration for its creation. Upon the imposition of the military dictatorship, Papanastasiou Society was renamed into *Dimokratiki Amina* (Democratic Defense) and carried out a struggle against the junta. Journalist P. Papadopoulos finds many common points between the Papanastasiou Society and the Declaration of the 3rd of September 1974 which coined the birth of PA.SO.K (Panhellenic Socialist Movement) (2006).

pp. 25–26). It was perhaps this realization, but more importantly the idea that deeper knowledge of the conditions of social and economic *malaise* should be a precondition for any state action that led to the 1916 renaming of *Sociological Society* into *Society for the Social and Political Sciences* in the tradition of the German *Verein für Socialpolitik*. One can assume that one of the intentions behind this development was the 'rediscovery' of one of the original aims of the *Sociological Society*, namely, 'the support and popularization of the philosophical, sociological, and economic studies', which was also a sign of the members' commitment to multidisciplinarity (Lambiri-Dimaki, 1987, p. 19). Yet, as John Peristiany, later the first director of the Athens Social Sciences Centre, remarks, 'what was to be popularized was, in Greece, as yet unborn' (Peristiany, 1968, p. 273). Indeed, sociology in Greece has had such a 'checkered career' (Peristiany, 1968, p. 275) that more than half a century later, Nikolaou refers to sociology as being 'relatively underdeveloped as a social science' (Nikolaou, 1974, p. v), while in 1996, Kyrtsis wonders about Greek sociology: 'Does it really exist?' (Kyrtsis, 1996b, p. 10). Yet, after 1920, there were a number of efforts that exemplify the scientific aspirations of a new community of social scientists. One such effort was the cooperation between the *Society for the Social and Political Sciences* and the journal *Archive of Economic and Social Sciences* (1921–1971) edited by political economist Dimitrios Kalitsounakis whose contribution to the social sciences was so significant that he received the National Academy award for this journal (Kourvetaris & Dobratz, 1971, pp. 47–48). The journal focuses on analyses of historical phenomena and problems facing European societies after the Great War, approached from sociological, economic and political science perspectives. It also includes the first translations-*cum*-interpretations of classical sociologists like Émile Durkheim; Max Weber; Alfred Weber's 'Societies, Civilization and Culture' (translated by Georgios Haritakis); or Alfred Weber's idea of progress (1930) presented by Kanellopoulos. One cannot but notice the initial absence of Max Weber, whose 'Science as A Vocation' was first presented in the journal by a non-sociologist, I. Sikoutris.[8] The journal, moreover, includes the first discussions about Greece's potential paths to modernity through the creation of agricultural cooperatives as a potential answer to the agrarian question, workers' groups, social classes and class conflict.

---

[8] This is in fact a free translation of Weber's work embellished with details from Sikoutris' own experiences from Greek higher education institutions (Sikoutris, 1933, pp. 205–286).

'PROTOSOCIOLOGISTS'[9] AVROTELIS ELEFTHEROPOULOS (1869–1963), PANAGIOTIS KANELLOPOULOS (1902–1986) AND EVANGELOS LEMBESIS (1904–1968)

The creation of a second university[10] in Thessaloniki in 1925 reflected the ideological and political tensions of the time. Greece was emerging from the traumas of the National Schism of 1915 which was actually another civil war[11] and the collapse of the *Grand Idea* in the ruins of Asia Minor. The violent aftermath of the National Schism turned the University of Athens into an ideological battleground between Venizelists and anti-Venizelists where the latter seemed to prevail. It was obvious that there was a pressing need for a second university, and in 1924, as Alexandros Papanastasiou became prime minister (March–July) not only the will but also the opportunity for the University of Thessaloniki emerged, and in 1925 the new university was inaugurated (Marketos, 2007, pp. 1–9).

It was there that the first Chair in sociology was established (1926–1935). The other followed shortly in Athens (1929–1935), and thus, the first serious attempt to address sociology as an academic discipline was born. Their incumbents were Avrotelis Eleftheropoulos, a philosophy professor in Zurich at the time of his appointment, and Panagiotis Kanellopoulos, heir to a prominent political family, who was appointed as Professor Extraordinary first and as full Professor in 1933, only to give up the post three years later to found his own political party. Finally, the initial attempts to establish sociology as an academic field were concluded with the inauguration of the Panteion School of Political Sciences in 1930 (renamed as Panteion University of Political and Social Sciences since 1989).

---

[9] There are two senses in which the term is used here: (a) First, in the sense that sociology is in a pre-paradigmatic stage and tinged by politics, and (b) second, in Habermas' sense where a 'protosociology would explicate a unified transcendental preunderstanding of its object domain' (Habermas, 1988, p. 98). It seems that sociology in Greece in this first period is characterized by both.

[10] The first was Athens University founded in 1837.

[11] This is the approach of historian G.B. Dertilis (2016) who discusses the two fatal decisions taken by the political camps at the time, namely, the 1920 referendum conducted by anti-Venizelists which re-instated the Germanophile King Constantine and provided the Great Powers with the pretext for withdrawing their support from Greece in the Asia Minor expedition, and the 'Execution of the Six' anti-Venizelist prominent political and military leaders who were blamed for the 1922 Smyrna catastrophe. These two events are rightly regarded by Dertilis as fatal for the perpetuation of the civil war far beyond the original National Schism in 1915 (pp. 71–86).

Avrotelis Eleftheropoulos: Extolling Individualism

By all accounts, Eleftheropoulos was not a systematic thinker, much less a sociologist as we understand the term today.[12] Yet, we discern some sociological areas which dominated his thinking, the most important of which was his unbridled belief in the individual over the group. Echoing his 1904 work published originally in German, *Man in Himself and Society: preliminary clarifications* appeared in Greek translation in 1930. In this work, he alerts the reader to the fashionable but erroneous position that the collectivity precedes and constitutes the individual (1926, p. 97, 1939, p. 47). Society is emphatically not greater than the sum of its parts, but rather 'an organized co-existence of individual units'. As a result, the task of sociology, at least Eleftheropoulos' sociology, becomes to discover the structure or mechanism behind such co-existence and analyse the constraint that society exerts on the individual. This sounds Durkheimian enough, yet the author at no point mentions the classical sociologist. Even in his *Positivism in Philosophy* (Eleftheropoulos, 1924), Durkheim's name remains conspicuously absent, and the essay concludes with a discussion of Comte's positivism. The unravelling of the relationship between the individual and 'the whole', that is, society, is used as a polemic against those who deridingly called his sociology 'the classical work of 17th century liberalism' (Eleftheropoulos, 1926, p. 97). It is intriguing that while he openly states that he will seek a sociological explanation of the relationship, he resorts to an unqualified individualism postulating the individual as a reality sui generis (100). It follows that sociality is synonymous to the pursuit of one's personal fulfilment in society. Individuals have no reason to be social, unless society and personality, the latter being defined through natural (biological) dispositions, correspond to one another (103). He concludes his exegesis by positing that the sui generis individual creates society through his thought and empathy. To defend the opposite, that is, the idea that society creates, individuals would be nothing short of a chimera. On the other hand, such is the strength of biological and psychological dispositions that even phenomena like social inequality are regarded as 'natural' (Eleftheropoulos, 1921, p. 4). No socialist revolution could impede the human proclivity to inequality since it is based primarily on natural differences in intelligence and, secondarily, on inherited wealth

---

[12] He is however described as an outstanding professor of sociology in Zürich where he taught before his arrival in Greece. Among his audience was Vladimir Lenin (Meletopoulos, 2021, p. 102).

(6–7). Today, he states the latter which is presented as a social cause tends to obliterate the former that has the status of a natural cause. Moreover, natural and social inequalities are reflected in social classes which find their representation, although never exact, in political parties. Do political parties aim at progress for all? Yes, if they are driven by principles, ideas and not by personal pursuits (16). On this point, Eleftheropoulos' analysis is reminiscent of Comte's when he states that social reform, predicated on party politics, depends to a considerable degree on the citizens' partisanship which in turn reflects their intellectual reform (19).

Eleftheropoulos' ideas were vehemently opposed and indeed derided by Panagiotis Kanellopoulos who had just been elected assistant professor of sociology at the University of Athens. In an article that he is subsequently reported to have regretted writing (Meletopoulos, 2021, p. 103), he attacks Eleftheropoulos' professional ethos and accuses him of discrediting sociology's status, while his work is dismissed as irrelevant, worthy of the public's disregard (Kanellopoulos, 1931, pp. 634–636). Kanellopoulos is joined by a chorus of critics against a work that is written by a sociologist, and yet it wards off sociological explanation (Vezanis, 1927, p. 69). Is Eleftheropoulos trying to 'save' social action from what he believes to be a mechanistic positivist approach? If so, he does it by adopting a stance *contra* sociology which is a paradox given his institutional position. As we will see below, such incongruity characterizes to varying degrees all 'protosociologists' who seem to pay lip service to the discipline while in reality distancing themselves from it.

The Heidelberg Circle and Kanellopoulos' Idea of Sociology

In 1929, three German-trained graduates that became known as the Heidelberg circle[13] decided to collaborate towards a renaissance of philosophy in Greece. To this end, they published together the *Archive of Philosophy and Theory of Science*, a quarterly journal that ran from 1929 to 1940. As is evident in an unsigned appraisal of the goals of the journal upon entering its fourth year of publication, the tone of the journal was

---

[13] A group of young neo-Kantian Idealists (Panagiotis K. Kanellopoulos (1902–1986), Ioannis Theodorakopoulos (1900–1981) and Konstantinos Tsatsos (1899–1987) who had studied in Heidelberg, then a centre for philosophy studies, in the decade from 1920 to 1929. In 1980, Kanellopoulos objected to both labels, the neo-Kantian and the Idealist (Meletopoulos, 2021, p. 82).

always meant to be polemical against both 'pseudo-idealists' and historical materialists. Being branded either as empiricist or psychologistic, ideas from both camps are rejected in tandem as having little if any relevance to philosophy (three years of the archive, 1993, p. i).[14] A synopsis of the journal's contribution to Greek intellectual life should include (a) its commitment to scientific analysis; (b) the introduction of a Greek audience into the works of Rickert, Jaspers, Alfred Weber, Dilthey and the latter's distinction between explanatory (*erklärende*) and interpretative (*verstehende*) methods, Leopold von Wiese, but also Ferdinand Tönnies, Karl Marx, Max Weber and Georg Simmel; (c) the few but important commentaries on various questions that continued to dominate the interwar years, such as the language question (see note 4) and its relation to social classes, (Kanellopoulos, 1933b, pp. 265–276); and (d) the promotion of a set of 'ideologies and value orientations' (Kyrtsis, 1998, p. 312) that ultimately seem to have inhibited rather than facilitated social change in Greece.

Of all members of the Heidelberg circle, the focus is inevitably placed on Kanellopoulos' ideas on sociology since he was the academic elected to the second Chair of sociology in the University of Athens. His inaugural speech in 1933 traces the birth of sociology in the intellectual and political battles of the nineteenth century, emphasizing that its 'alliance' with various secular elements does not deprive it from its scientific status (Kanellopoulos, 1933a, pp. 372–373). Its subject-matter, society, became the new 'idol' of bourgeois consciousness after the fall of the idols of the *ancient regime* (p. 375), yet when the bourgeois class finally triumphed, it turned against the idea of progress which was now threatening its very existence. To contain social dynamics, Auguste Comte enters the stage as a mediator between the present and the unknown and much-feared future and introduces a law to the idea of progress. Furthermore, Hegel's rationalism is seen as representing the ultimate battle between civil society, which is now seen as evil, and the state which encapsulates reason. Kanellopoulos' history of sociology continues with Marx's contribution through which the state is re-defined as an instrument of inequality and injustice. Abandoning Marx's teleological implications about the 'end of history', and criticizing the non-rational, mystical content of the 'old'

---

[14] The first volume of the *Archive of Philosophy and Theory of Science* was published under the editorship of Ioannis Theodorakopoulos. After that, it is published by an editorial board, which explains why the short appraisal is not signed.

German Romanticism, partly 'purged' by Hegel himself (Kanellopoulos, 1933d, pp. 382–383), he embraces Ferdinand Tönnies' new romanticism expressed in the dualism of *Gemeinschaft* and *Gesellschaft* with the former being the apotheosis of the dominance of culture and German values (*Kultur*), while the latter standing for civilization (*Zivilisation*), that is, reason as depicted in contractual relations, material culture, technology and cosmopolitanism. In identifying *Gemeinschaft* with *Kultur* and *Gesellschaft* with *Zivilisation*, Kanellopoulos draws inspiration from the culturalist tradition of Alfred Weber (Kanellopoulos, 1930, p. 92), but also from Savigny the main exponent of the historicist school who posed the idea of an 'organic community' against the idea of a 'mechanical society' (Kanellopoulos, 1929, pp. 191–192). It is no accident that Kanellopoulos is attracted to Tönnies, as the latter is seen to restore the definition of sociology as a '*scientific* philosophy of history' in the tradition of Lorentz von Stein and Comte (Heberle, 1937, p. 12). In Tönnies, he sees not only a plausible history of the evolution of society but also a method, in which individual phenomena are mirrored in repetitive types or generalizations, that is, they acquire formal characteristics (Kanellopoulos, 1928, pp. 332–333). Such is his insistence for the need of a method that is exclusive to sociology that one wonders whether method and subject-matter may in fact be synonymous.[15] If Ferdinand Tönnies provided Kanellopoulos with a 'method' unique to sociology, after all, there was 'no sociological research before Tonnies' (Kanellopoulos, 1926, p. 319), Karl Mannheim's *Ideology and Utopia* offered him the opportunity to attack the idea of continuous, uninterrupted progress driven by the ever-changing consciousness that corresponds to changing social conditions. The lecture ends pessimistically with the assertion of the impossibility of the new science which demands stern asceticism and objectivity, rationalization and disenchantment (Weber, 1958, p. 133), while life and politics, one might say, impose their own demands (Kanellopoulos, 1933a, pp. 385–386). In Weber, Kanellopoulos sees a tragic figure since he lived

---

[15] The Proceedings of the Conference of Social and Political Sciences on May 8, 1928, document a spirited discussion on the subject. One of the participants, Petros Zisis, a prominent lawyer, accuses Kanellopoulos of equating sociology's subject-matter with the sociological method per se. He proposes instead as the basis of sociological knowledge, 'the causal relation between social milieu and the products of human mental powers' (Kanellopoulos, 1928, p. 338). In the same exchange, Papanastasiou challenges the idea that Kanellopoulos' 'method' is unique to sociology. Natural sciences, he argues, are also driven by the idea of abstraction.

a life full of antinomies, pursuing scientific specialization and 'losing touch not only with life, but with the very idea of the spirit as the bond among different scientific specialisms' (1933d, pp. 367–368). Lamenting Weber's rejection of a promising political career, it is clear that Kanellopoulos, living in turbulent times himself, is haunted by the Weberian 'Gods and Demons' discussed in 'Science as a Vocation' and 'Politics as a Vocation', and by 1935 he had resigned his academic post after refusing to pledge allegiance to the king after the fall the Republic. Then, in December of the same year, he founded his own political party, and he became absorbed by the institution that as an academic, he was meant to oppose.

Reading Kanellopoulos, one cannot but appreciate him as a teacher and an intellectual force. He is remembered, as is documented in John Scott's work *Social Theory: Central Issues in Sociology*, for his 'commentaries for a Greek audience' (2006, p. 78) on a pleiad of sociologists such as Wiese (and Simmel's influence on him), Tönnies, Mannheim, Marx, Alfred Weber and Max Weber. He was thus responsible for exposing a generation of students to some of the key sociological theorists of his time. From the juxtaposition between individual and society, to the search for an epistemological basis for sociology, through the rejection of Marx's theory of history and its teleological overtones to the advocacy of the view of culture as a terrain of absolute values, he finally reaches his destination which coincides with an evocation of the past. His approach to sociology as a study of human interaction led him to the possibility of a fusion of concepts like Wiese's 'social distance' (*soziale distanz*), a necessary quality for the study of social forms (*Gebildelehre*) with Max Weber's emphasis on meanings that Kanellopoulos situates on (a) traditions emanating from blood bonds, (b) rational calculation and (c) emotions (Kanellopoulos, 1933c, pp. 287–288). Without distancing himself significantly from Wiese, he acknowledges the failing of Wiese's system to grasp the complexity of social life. Despite such imports that could have led to a rigorous research programme for sociology, there is something static, old fashioned and stale, Kanellopoulos' ideas already becoming outdated ideology in Mannheim's sense of the term. Whereas thinkers of his time recognize the necessity for social change and a drive towards a new modernity, Kanellopoulos rejects an explanatory (*erklärende*) sociology based on empirical reality and adopts instead a romantic stance that is better served through abstract generalizations. Although he acknowledges the culturally and historically contingent nature of social phenomena, he is reluctant to advocate the only method appropriate for studying them, that is, empirical analysis. The reader of protosociologists is left with the impression that 'all that is air has become solid' (Robin, 2020, p. 5). The political turmoil that followed Kanellopoulos' resignation (military coups, the Metaxas dictatorship in 1936, the Second World War and civil war, the ensuing violent regime and finally the Colonels' dictatorship in 1967) resulted in the exclusion of sociology from all academic curricula. The sociology Chair in Athens would be filled again in 1975 (Lambiri-Dimaki, 1987, p. 41). Despite their commitment to academic excellence, the protosociologists gradually distanced themselves from sociology as a specialized academic subject, while in the short lifetime of the two university posts, no research of any kind was produced (Koniordos, 2010, p. 232). In hindsight, we could claim that the inauguration of the Panteion School of Political Sciences in 1930 offered the only institutional opportunity for the future development of the social sciences and sociology in particular.

Lambiri-Dimaki explores the deeper causes of the 'underdevelopment' of sociology in Greece until the end of the interwar period. On the one hand, she attributes the unsatisfactory status of sociology to a turn to the study of folklore as a source of national identity. The poverty of the present turned Greeks to the discovery of a chosen past that functioned as a value principle, as a principle of organization of the present and as motivation for the future. Crucial to the development of folklore studies was according to John Peristiany, the publication of I. Fallmerayer's treatise in 1830 which argued that Slavic elements had eliminated claims to ancient Greek ancestry. Greek intellectuals, academics and even ordinary Greeks set a new task before them, to prove the Fallmerayer thesis wrong (Peristiany, 1968, p. 265). Unlike sociological studies, Greek folklore studies continued uninterruptedly from 1890 until today (pp. 265–272). Drawing on social anthropological work and especially Herzfeld's *Ours Once More: folklore, ideology and the making of modern Greece*, Kyrtsis questions Lambiri-Dimakis' assertion that folklore studies occupied the space of sociological studies. Michael Herzfeld documents the gradual decline of the role of folklore studies in the search for a uniquely Greek identity. According to him, after the Asia Minor catastrophe in 1922, research conducted by folklorists 'was now a matter of past history' and that 'the further development of that sense of identity passed mostly into other hands' (Herzfeld, 1986, p. 139). Further on, he gives us an indication of what this enigmatic comment points to, by stating that 'the Politis framework of folklore gave way to the German *Kulturkreis* theories' (140), that is, theories that emphasized cultural change through the cultural diffusion of ideas within a single culture or from one culture to another. It is entirely plausible that the forging of the Greek national identity was now in the hands of the people who framed the new political culture among them, the 'Sociologists' (Kyrtsis, 1996a, pp. 172–173). Apart from folklore, the second cause for sociology's underdevelopment is defined by Lambiri-Dimaki as 'the problematic of escape' from Greek reality (1987, pp. 33–34). This tendency is most pronounced in the arts and especially in literature and poetry. Theotokas' 'Argo' and Karyotakis' poetry are cases in point here. From messianic Marxists, who were shunned as a viable alternative at the time, to mystical poets, no social or political group was trusted to address the chronic social problems of Greek society (1987, p. 33). Finally, in analysing the possible 'causes' of the failure of sociology to create a distinct identity from other social sciences in the early twentieth-century Greece, one should always keep in mind the German influence and the fact that, as Moebius remarks, 'the beginning of sociology in Germany, with Simmel and Weber, was "anti-sociological" because it was closely linked with Nietzsche's and Dilthey's criticisms of French and English sociology' (2021, p. 15). Caught between 'explaining' and 'understanding', the Heidelberg circle members not only negated the dialectic itself (Kyrtsis, 2018, p. 96) but rather built its identity around theoretical discourses on value relations that remained abstract and divorced from any actual historical circumstances (105). In this way, they also took rather scant notice of the ramifications of Max Weber's 'conciliatory' position on sociology as 'a science concerning itself with the interpretative understanding of social action and thereby with a causal explanation of its course and consequences' (Weber, 1978, p. 4). Moreover, the 'philosophical worldview orientation' (Kyrtsis, 2018) kept sociology captive while providing legitimacy to an elite of experts who later set the terms of the political debate. Sociology could have aligned with more radical liberal groups, but its peculiarities ranging from individualism and aestheticism to romanticism and a metaphysical flight from reality put paid to its original aspiration to become the vehicle of social reform. Apart from this undermining of sociology from within, the Metaxas dictatorship in 1936 came to suspend all quasi-institutional endeavours to establish sociology as an academic discipline with the cancellation of the two academic chairs. Yet, the *Archive*'s work continued unabated until World War II, and the Occupation in 1940 since as Kanellopoulos notes, the Metaxas dictatorship did not encroach into all aspects of intellectual life as was the case with Mussolini in Italy or Hitler in Germany (Meletopoulos, 2021, p. 84).

Evangelos Lembesis: Sociologist of 'Ressentiment'

Unlike the thinkers examined so far, Evangelos Lembesis (1904–1968) defined himself as a sociologist from the very beginning of his career, but ironically, during his lifetime, he was able to teach sociology at Panteion University only during the academic year 1931–1932. As a student of Franz Oppenheimer (1864–1943), he was influenced not only by his teacher but also by Ludwig Gumplowicz (1838–1909) who is regarded as one of 'the earliest exponents of the sociological approach' in Austria (Torrance, 1976, p. 186). Oppenheimer's idea of the genesis and evolution of the modern state as 'a social institution, forced by a victorious group of men on a defeated group, with the sole purpose of regulating the dominion of the victorious group over the vanquished' (Oppenheimer, 1975, p. 8) plays a paramount role in Lembesis' understanding of the concept of *ressentiment*. The emergence of *ressentiment* is predicated upon the distinction between two types of 'revolutionary activity'; the first depicts the activity of a strong, ascending formation whose revolutionary activity is thwarted by the established regime, the latter being unable to stop such activity whose ultimate purpose is the seizure of state power. This social formation is labelled by Lembesis as 'the group', and its power is illustrated in the victorious battles of the bourgeoisie during the French Revolution or the organized proletariat during the Russian Revolution. The second social formation is witnessed in a type of a revolutionary activity that is 'negative'. Its victory would mean the end of the state. Examples of this are the sans-culottes (or mob) or the immiserated proletariat of the Bolshevik revolution. This is labelled as 'the mass', a crucially functional element in the fighting of the battles of the elites but one that is always excluded from power. Like Oppenheimer, he sees a teleology in the social positioning of the mass in the process of social differentiation (Lembesis, 1994 [1950], p. 38). The failure of the mass to become socially dominant, breeds *ressentiment* which is defined as the 'sum total of negative emotions (passions) of the mass *vis-à-vis* the regime' (39). Scheler's idea of the bearers of *ressentiment* as 'those who serve and are dominated, who fruitlessly resent the sting of authority' (Scheler, 2003 [1913], pp. 59–68), resonates here. At the heart of *ressentiment* lies the destruction of all values (Lembesis, 1994 [1950], p. 40) and the 'objectification' of man, its transformation into a machine (80). Both have unconsciously become the main 'projects' of the disenfranchised of the world. Indeed, Lembesis is probably the first sociologist in Greece who has uniquely attributed an explanatory value to moral sentiments. *Ressentiment* for Lembesis has a deeply anthropological character since it cuts across social classes and spans over all epochs in human history. It becomes a Simmelian form[16] whose content changes according to the historical moment. One may use this form to make historical and cultural comparisons, and yet, one always returns to the core of the human condition that is dominated by negative sentiments such as rancor, hate, frustration, envy and the 'thirst for revenge'. Lembesis' *The revolutionary mass: A contribution to the sociology of social revolutions* captures class conflict from the perspective of the 'will to domination', and as such, his agenda purports to be more extensive than Marx's own which was based solely on assigning an economic role to social classes (100–103). Unable to capture the significance of mechanisms uniquely possessed by the mass, Marxists have difficulty in explaining phenomena such as the rise of national socialism that appealed to the same mass 'the naked force' that the Communist party targeted (100–101). Suggesting that the sites of domination are more varied than Marx allows, he turns to ideas that are considered marginal today but undoubtedly had an enormous appeal at the start of the twentieth century. Although he does not use the term 'crowd' or 'mob', Lembesis discovers in the primitiveness, irrationality, emotionality and suggestibility of Le Bon's concept all those elements that can convert the revolutionary mass into a passive and easily manipulated mass (pp. 106–109). On the question of the responsibility of individual members of the mass, he turns to Sighele and Tarde but also to Gardikas, a professor of criminology in the University of Athens, all of whom concur, to greater or lesser extent, on the massified individual's legal responsibility in the case of crimes committed. On the other hand, ethical or social responsibility is indeed restricted (110–115).

It is interesting that in his exegesis, Lembesis does not include Ortega's *The Revolt of the Masses*, a work which made its appearance more than ten years before Lembesis' influential work in 1950. Yet, Lembesis, echoing Ortega, transforms the mass into a qualitative category: '[...] what was mere quantity—the multitude—is converted into qualitative determination, it becomes the common social quality, man as undifferentiated from other men, but as repeating in himself a generic type' (Ortega, 1964 [1930], pp. 13–14). These ideas find their application in social forms such

---

[16] There is more than a mere 'affinity' between Lembesis and Simmel's interest in mass phenomena. This is demonstrated in Lembesis' adoption of Simmel's terminology (social differentiation, sociation, sociality) to analyse functional aspects of the masses.

as 'the idiot' or 'public opinion'. In his essay, *The extraordinary importance of idiots in contemporary life*,[17] he elaborates with wit and insightfulness on a type that constitutes the embodiment of immorality (pp. 137–138), while in the *Critique of Public Opinion* (1929), he announces some of the ideas, for example, public opinion as the 'monster' akin to the mass (Lembesis, 1929, p. 420), that were later refined in the *Revolutionary Mass* and *The Sociology of the Press* (1992 [1951]). In this essay too (1929), published in Kalitsounakis' *Archive of Economic and Social Sciences*, he lays out a critique of bourgeois types, phenomena and mentalities that obstruct social change. His *Sociology of the Press* (1992 [1951]) is a prophetic reading (one would argue an obligatory reading for journalists)[18] whose breadth ranges from the qualifications of the journalist and a sociological analysis of public opinion and the subject of journalism to an analysis of the various dimensions of the press corporation and finally to the proletarianization of the journalist's profession with some extrapolations for the future of journalism. Like in all previous works, *ressentiment* is at the heart of *Myth and Reality of the Bourgeois Society* (2019 [1963], p. 115). It permeates all stages of the bourgeois revolution until it creates its end product, that is, 'the average man' (or woman) distanced from both empirical facts and reason (88). He/she harbours a vital lie, or a vital myth according to Sorel,[19] without which their universe would tumble down (88). The chapter titled 'Ideologies and Utopias' (69–113), discusses Gumplowicz's causal correspondence between natural and social laws, Sorel's mobilizing myths, Pareto's 'residues and derivations' and Michels'

---

[17] In this work, Lembesis makes extensive use of Simmel who states that 'inside a physically proximal crowd there are countless suggestions and nervous influences going back and forth, robbing individuals of thought and actions, so that the most fleeting stimulations often rise up in the crowd, avalanche-like, to the most excessive impulses, and the higher discriminating critical functions are as good as turned off' (Simmel, 2009 [1908], p. 166). The question of idiocy or stupidity can also be traced in Simmel. As he writes, 'thus the rapid essentially quite unfathomable changes in the mood in a mass; thus, the countless observations over the 'stupidity' of collectives' (p. 167). Moreover, Lembesis' connection between 'idiots' and the rise of quasi-fascist regimes like Ioannis Metaxas' 4th August dictatorship (Lembesis, 1994 [1941], p. 125) resonates Musil's term 'functional stupidity', that is, 'the politicization and ideologization of the mind and its subordination to masses and programs' (Isenberg, 2018, p. 62).

[18] See Meletopoulos (1999, p. 33).

[19] For Sorel an example of a powerful mobilizing myth is the general strike, a violent phenomenon in the nineteenth century that has now become incorporated into the arsenal of democratic tactics (1999 [1908], pp. 109–173).

'iron law of oligarchy' against the theoretical background of Freud, Nietzsche and Bergson and serves the author's purpose of establishing the dogmatic character of value judgements (85) as emanating from impressions, affects and emotions rather than reason. Echoing Simmel's 'tragedy of culture', Lembesis' work intends to demystify the Janus-faced bourgeois society representing itself as a rational system while, at the same time, being haunted by the irrational myths of technology, productivity, growth and progress (124–170).[20] The study of man and his culture should be approached as an artistic creation whose highly symbolic nature defies logical analysis. Certain Spenglerian themes can be discerned here such as the distinction between culture and civilization, the latter representing the technological turn-away from philosophy or art and therefore an inevitable decline. One might challenge the 'sociologist' label in the case of Lembesis. His analyses point to a philosophical anthropology that methodologically aims at transcending the limits of subjectivism (Lembesis defines subjectivism as the 'equation' of the researcher with its subject) and rejecting any outside influences for the sake of objectivity (1994 [1950], p. 142). Erudite, and piercing, witty and cynical, Lembesis remained a caustic observer of society and Greek society in particular. Attempting to find explanations of social phenomena in moral sentiments, Lembesis' work is characterized by the pessimistic orientation of the 'decline of Western civilization' tradition that Nietzsche, Scheler, Ortega and Spengler first introduced, and he thus joins the anti-modernist chorus of his time, a choice that once more has critical consequences for the scientific status of sociology in Greece.

---

[20] The book has many communitarian allusions deploring the technical essence of modern civilization. Communitarianism is another theme commonly encountered in the period under study. Its most renowned exponent was K. D. Karavidas whose book *Agrotika: Research on the Economic and Social Morphology in Greece and in the Neighbouring Slav Countries. A Comparative Study* (1931) (in Greek) analyses the major units of the Greek agricultural life. As Mouzelis writes, the interest in Karavidas' analysis rests on his use of what could be construed as a comparative Marxist methodology 'investigating relations and forces of production in their specific social setting' (1978, p. 28). Vergopoulos sees in Karavidas the virtues of communitarianism such as the 'autonomous, if not dominant social and economic organization as effected by social groups' (2010, p. 38). Recently Karavidas' work has been re-assessed in a negative light (Komninou, 1990, pp.13–28), and his version of communitarianism has been presented as an aspiring but ultimately failed authoritarian if not outright fascist 'third way' (e.g. control over the rural clan's members necessitated harsh sanctions such as public shaming) (Kyrtsis, 1990, pp. 99–115; Dragoumis, 2020, p. 9).

References

Anastasiadis, G. (Ed.). (2008). Το δημοκρατικό μανιφέστο και ο τύπος της εποχής [The democratic manifesto and the press of the interwar period]. In Αλέξανδρος Παπαναστασίου: Η σημαντική συμβολή του στη δημοκρατία και στον συνταγματικό λόγο: Μελέτες και τεκμήρια [Alexandros Papanastasiou: His outstanding contribution to democracy and constitutional discourse: Studies and documents] (pp. 265–288). The Greek Parliament Foundation for Parliamentarianism and Democracy.

Beaton, R. (2020). *Greece: Biography of a nation*. Penguin Books.

Bournazos, S. (1999). Αλληλογραφία της Π. Σ. Δέλτα, 1906-1940, (Ed). Χ. Lefkoparidis, Μνήμων, 21, 275–280 (Correspondence of P.S. Delta: 1906-1940). https://doi.org/10.12681/mnimon.801

Dertilis, G. B. (2016). *Επτά πόλεμοι, τέσσερις εμφύλιοι, επτά πτωχεύσεις: 1821-2016* [Seven wars, four civil wars and seven bankruptcies: 1821-2016]. Polis.

Dragoumis, M. N. (2020). Ελληνισμός και φιλελευθερισμός: είναι οι έννοιες ασύμβατες [Hellenism and liberalism: Are the concepts irreconcilable?] Retrieved June 8, 2020, from http://www.politeiako.gr/

Eleftheropoulos, A. (1921). Κοινωνικές τάξεις και κοινωνικά κόμματα [Social classes and social parties]. Αρχείον Οικονομικών και Κοινωνικών Επιστημών *[Archive of Economic and Social Sciences]*, 1(1), 3–19.

Eleftheropoulos, A. (1924). Ο θετικισμός εν τη φιλοσοφία: η κοινωνιολογία και η κοινωνία [Positivism in philosophy: Sociology and society]. Αρχείον Οικονομικών και Κοινωνικών Επιστημών *[Archive of Economic and Social Sciences]*, 2(4), 145–157.

Eleftheropoulos, A. (1926). Ο ατομικός άνθρωπος και η κοινωνία: Αρχικαί διευκρινίσεις [Atomized Man and Society: preliminary clarifications]. Αρχείον Οικονομικών και Κοινωνικών Επιστημών *[Archive of Economic and Social Sciences]*, 2(6), 97–110.

Eleftheropoulos, A. (1939). Ο κατ' ιδίαν άνθρωπος και η κοινωνία [Man in himself and Society]. Αρχείον οικονομικών και κοινωνικών επιστημών *[Archive of Economic and Social Sciences]*, 1(19), 45–86.

Gerolymatos, A. (2021). The Greek army in politics: 1909-1967. In O. Anastasakis & K. Lagos (Eds.), *The Greek military dictatorship: Revisiting a troubled past, 1967–1974* (pp. 15–33). Berghahn Books.

Habermas, J. (1988). *On the logic of the social sciences* (S. W. Nicholsen & J. A. Stark, Trans.). Polity (Original work published 1970).

Heberle, R. (1937). The sociology of Ferdinand Tönnies. *American Sociological Review*, 2(1), 9–25.

Herzfeld, M. (1986). *Ours once more: Folklore, ideology, and the making of modern Greece*. Pella.

Isenberg, B. (2018). A modern calamity: Robert Musil on stupidity. *Journal of Classical Sociology*, 18(1), 55–75.

Kanellopoulos, P. K. (1926). Ferdinand Tönnies and sociology. Αρχείον Οικονομικών και Κοινωνικών Επιστημών [Archive of Economic and Social Sciences], 4(6), 315-322.

Kanellopoulos, P. K. (1928). Μέθοδος και σύστημα της Κοινωνιολογίας: πρακτικά Εταιρείας των κοινωνικών και πολιτικών επιστημών [Method and system in sociology: Proceedings of the Society for social and political sciences]. Αρχείον Οικονομικών και Κοινωνικών Επιστημών [Archive of Economic and Social Sciences], 3(8), 332-342.

Kanellopoulos, P. K. (1929). Ο Γερμανικός ιδεαλισμός και αι ιστορικαί επιστήμαι [German idealism and the historical sciences]. Αρχείον Φιλοσοφίας και Θεωρίας των Επιστημών [Archive of Philosophy and Theory of Science], 1(3), 183-201.

Kanellopoulos, P. K. (1930). Ο Alfred Weber και η ιδέα της προόδου [Alfred Weber and the idea of progress]. Αρχείον Οικονομικών και Κοινωνικών Επιστημών [Archive of Economic and Social Sciences], 1(10), 91-98.

Kanellopoulos, P. K. (1931). Ο Ελευθερόπουλος και η Κοινωνιολογία του ["Eleftheropoulos and his sociology"]. Αρχείον Φιλοσοφίας και Θεωρίας των Επιστημών [Archive of Philosophy and Theory of Science], 2(4), 480-520.

Kanellopoulos, P. K. (1933a). Η κοινωνιολογία και οι επί την γένεσην και διαμόρφωσιν της επιδράσαντες πολιτκοί παράγοντες: Εναρκτήριον Μάθημα [Sociology and the political factors contributing to its genesis and development: Inaugural lecture]. Αρχείον Φιλοσοφίας και Θεωρίας των επιστημών [Archive for Philosophy and Theory of Science], 4(4), 371-386.

Kanellopoulos, P. K. (1933b). Το γλωσσικόν ζήτημα και αι εν Ελλάδι πνευματικαί κατευθύνσεις [The Language question and the Greek intellectual currents]. Αρχείον Φιλοσοφίας και Θεωρίας των Επιστημών [Archive of Philosophy and Theory of Science], 4(3), 265-276.

Kanellopoulos, P. K. (1933c). Το 'Σύστημα της Κοινωνιολογίας' του Leopold von Wiese ['The Sociological System' of Leopold von Wiese]. Φιλοσοφίας και Θεωρίας των Επιστημών [Archive of Philosophy and Theory of Science], 4(3), 277-288.

Kanellopoulos, P. K. (1933d). Max Weber και Heinrich Rickert: Μια σελίς της Ιστορίας του πνεύματος [Max Weber and Heinrich Rickert: A page in the history of the Spirit]. Αρχείον Φιλοσοφίας και Θεωρίας των Επιστημών [Archive of Philosophy and Theory of Science], 4(4), 362-370.

Komninou, M. (1990). Η σκέψη του Καραβίδα και η προβληματική των κοινωνικών επιστημών (Karavidas' thought and the problematic of the social sciences). In M. Komninou & E. Papataxiarchis (Eds.) Κοινότητα, κοινωνία και ιδεολογία: Ο Κωνσταντίνος Καραβίδας και η προβληματική των κοινωνικών επιστημών [Community, society and ideology: Konstantinos Karavidas and the problematic of social sciences], (pp.13-28). Papazisis.

Koniordos, S. (2010). Η συζήτηση για τη δημόσια κοινωνιολογία και η κοινωνιολογία στην Ελλάδα [The discussion of public sociology and sociology in Greece]. In M. Kousis, M. Samatas, & S. Koniordos (Eds.), Εξουσία και κοινωνία: Δωρήματα

στον Κωνσταντίνο Τσουκαλά [Power and society: Offerings to Constantine Tsoukalas] (pp. 227–50). Kastaniotis.
Kourahanis, N. (2014). Κοινωνικές επιστήμες, δημόσια πολιτική και ιστορία στην Ελλάδα του μεσοπολέμου και της πρώτης μεταπολεμικής περιόδου [Social sciences, social policy and history in the Inter-War and the first Post-War period in Greece]. In *Η Ελληνική ιστοριογραφία στον 20ό Αιώνα. Προβληματισμοί για την εθνική ταυτότητα και τον εκμοντερνισμό* [Greek Historiography in the twentieth century: Reflections on National Identity and Modernization] (pp. 1–61). University of the Peloponnese.
Kourvetaris, G. A., & Dobratz, B. A. (1971). Contemporary sociology in Greece. *International Journal of Contemporary Sociology*, 8(3–4), 46–58.
Kyrtsis, A. A. (1990). Το μεσοπολεμικό στίγμα του κοινοτιστή Κ.Δ.Καραβίδα [The interwar imprint of the communitarian K.D. Karavidas]. In Komninou & M. E. Papataxiarchis (Eds.), *Κοινότητα, κοινωνία και ιδεολογία: Ο Κωνσταντίνος Καραβίδας και η προβληματική των κοινωνικών επιστημών* [Community, society, and ideology: Konstantinos Karavidas and the problematic of the social sciences] (pp. 99–119). Papazisis.
Kyrtsis, A. A. (1996a). Κοινωνιολογική σκέψη και εκσυγχρονιστικές ιδεολογίες στον Ελληνικό μεσοπόλεμο [Sociological thought and Greek interbellum modernizing ideologies]. Nisos.
Kyrtsis, A. A. (1996b). Greek sociology: Does it really exist? *European Sociologist*, 4, 10–11.
Kyrtsis, A. A. (1998). Greek Interbellum Modernizers and the 'Sociological Idea'. *International Sociology*, 13(3), 311–324.
Kyrtsis, A. A. (2018). Die griechische Soziologie in deutscher weltanschauungsphilosophischer Gefangenschaft. In J. Pissis & D. Karydas (Eds.), *Deutschland und Griechenland im Spiegel der Philosophiegeschichte:Transfers im 20. Jahrhundert* (pp. 93–119). Romiosini.
Lambiri-Dimaki, J. (1987). *Η κοινωνιολογία στην Ελλάδα Σήμερα*, Τόμος Α' [Sociology in Greece Today Vol. I]. Papazizis.
Lembesis, E. (1929). Κριτική της Κοινής Γνώμης [Critique of Public Opinion]. Αρχείον Οικονομικών και Κοινωνικών Επιστημών *[Archive of Economic and Social Sciences]*, 3(9), 373–420.
Lembesis, E. (1992). Κοινωνιολογία του Τύπου [Sociology of the Press]. Arsenidis (Original work published 1951).
Lembesis, E. (1994). Η Επαναστατική Μάζα και η τεράστια σημασία των βλακών εν τω συγχρόνω βίω [The revolutionary mass and the extraordinary importance of idiots in modern life]. Friends' Publications (Original works published 1950 and 1941).
Lembesis, E. (2019). Μύθος και πραγματικότης της αστικής κοινωνίας [Myth and reality of bourgeois society]. Ekdoseis ton filon. (Original work published 1963).
Mackridge, P. (2009). *Language and national identity in Greece: 1766–1976*. Oxford University Press.

Marketos, S. (2000). Ο Αλέξανδρος Παπαναστασίου και η εποχή του: Αντινομίες του μεταρρυθμιστικού σοσιαλισμού [Alexandros Papanastasiou and his era: Antinomies of reformist socialism] [Doctoral dissertation ΕΚΠΑ -National and Kapodistrian University of Athens]. National Archive of Doctoral dissertations. https://thesis.ekt.gr/thesisBookReader/id/26542?lang=el#page/1/mode/2up

Marketos, S. (2007, June 7–8). Η ίδρυση του Πανεπιστημίου Θεσσαλονίκης: Μια πολιτική επιλογή [The founding of the University of Thessaloniki: A political choice] [Paper presentation]. The Historical Archives of the University of Athens.

Maroniti, N. (1997, December 4–5). Στον απόηχο του Ελληνοτουρκικού πολέμου: Παράλληλες αφηγήσεις [In the aftermath of the Greco-Turkish war: Parallel narratives]. In (no editor) Ο πόλεμος του 1897 [The war of 1897] (pp. 115–230). Moraitis School: Society for the Study of Modern Greek Culture and General Education.

Maus, H. (1962). *A short history of sociology*. Routledge & Kegan Paul (Original work published 1956).

Mavrogordatos, G. (1983). *Stillborn republic: Social coalitions and party strategies in Greece 1922–1936*. University of California Press.

Meletopoulos, M. (1999). Αφιέρωμα στον κοινωνιολόγο Ευάγγελο Λεμπέση [Special feature: Evangelos Lembesis]. *Nea Koinoniologia*, 28, 9–44.

Meletopoulos, M. (2021). Παναγιώτης Κανελλόπουλος: Ο πολιτικός, ο διανοούμενος και η εποχή του [Panagiotis Kanellopoulos: Politician, intellectual and his era] (2nd ed.) Kapon.

Moebius, S. (2021). *Sociology in Germany: A history*. Palgrave, Springer.

Mouzelis, N. (1978). Agrotika: A comparative study of rural social structures in the Balkans. *Greek Review of Social Research*, 32, 25–32. https://doi.org/10.12681/grsr.441

Nikolaou, L. (1974). *The growth and development of sociology in Greece*. Mass (Unknown publisher).

Offer, A. (1984). Using the past in Britain: Retrospect and prospect. *The Public Historian*, 6(4), 17–36.

Oppenheimer, F. (1975). *The state*. Free life (Original work published 1908).

Ortega y Gasset, J. (1964). *The revolt of the masses*. W. W. Norton & Co. (Original book published 1930).

Papadopoulos, P. (2006, September 3). 3 Σεπτεμβρίου: Η διακήρυξη του ΠΑΣΟΚ και ο 'Όμιλος Παπαναστασίου' [3 September: The declaration of PASOK and the 'Papanastasiou Society']. Konstantinos Simitis Foundation Archive (A1S6_PolSxoPar_F1T91) Athens.

Peristiany, J. G. (1968). "Sociology in Greece". In *Contemporary sociology in Western Europe and in America*. The Luigi Sturzo Institute of Rome (pp. 264–307).

Robin, C. (2020, November 12). The professor and the politician. *The New Yorker*. https://www.newyorker.com/books/under-review/max-weber-the-professor-and-the-politician.
Scheler, M. (2003). *Ressentiment*. Marquette University Press. (Original work published 1913).
Scott, J. (2006). *Social theory: Central issues in sociology*. Sage.
Sikoutris, I. (1933). Η επιστήμη ως επάγγελμα [Science as a vocation]. Αρχείον Οικονομικών και Κοινωνικών Επιστημών *[Archive of Economic and Social Sciences]*, 1(13), 205–286.
Simmel, G. (2009). *Sociology: Inquiries into the construction of social forms*, Vol. I (A. J. Blasi, A. K. Jacobs, & M. J. Kanijrathinkal, Trans.). Brill (Original work published 1908).
Sorel, G. (1999). *Reflections on violence*. Cambridge University Press. (Original work published 1908).
Stavridi- Patrikiou, R. (1988). Η σύνδεση των κοινωνιολόγων με το κίνημα του δημοτικισμού [The sociologists' connections with the demoticist movement]. *Ta Istorika*, 9, 353–370.
Torrance, J. (1976). The emergence of sociology in Austria: 1885–1035. *European Journal of Sociology / Archives Européennes de Sociologie / Europäisches Archiv für Soziologie*, 17(2), 185–219.
Three years of the archive. (1993). Αρχείον φιλοσοφίας και θεωρίας των επιστημών *[Archive of Philosophy and Theory of Science]*, i–vi.
Vergopoulos, K. (2010, November 7). Η χώρα μας είναι πρότυπο ομαδοποιήσεων [Our country is a poster child of group formations]. *Makedonia*. Retrieved June 6 from https://www.makthes.gr/filestore/docs/Afieromata/%2D%2DK OINOTIOSMOSlow.pdf]
Vezanis, D. S. (1927). Ελευθερόπουλου: Ο ατομικός άνθρωπος και η κοινωνία αρχικαί διευκρινίσεις: μια αντίκρουσις [Eleftheropoulos: Man in himself and society: preliminary clarifications: A reply]. Αρχείον Οικονομικών και Κοινωνικών Επιστημών *[Archive of Economic and Social Sciences]*, 1(7), 69–76.
Weber, M. (1958). Science as a vocation. *Daedalus*, 87(1), 111–134 (Original work published 1919).
Weber, M. (1978). Economy and society. In G. Roth & C. Wittich (Eds.) (Vol. I). University of California Press.

CHAPTER 2

From Academic Uncertainty to the Birth of Empirical Research: 1944–1974

Abstract The need for sociological analyses and programmes and of social research institutions became imperative in the wake of the post-war era. The depredation that Greece suffered because of the Occupation and the Civil War called for a full-scale reconstruction that depended on Western support and was reflected in definitions of sociology as social welfare. Sociology's hitherto oblique status changed radically when the *Athens Social Sciences Centre* was founded under the aegis of UNESCO in 1959. The strong ethnographic focus of the Centre did not head off the completion of an impressive corpus of empirical sociological studies related to the nature of modernization, the rural and urban communities, the Greek family and regional development, a precursor of future centre-periphery studies. Committed to the modernization paradigm, such works part with past traditions of scholasticism while breaking new ground through the introduction of empirical research, using sociological methodologies that inspired future generations of sociologists. The 1967 *coup d' état* marked the closing down of the Centre to be re-opened and renamed as *National Centre for Social Research*. In its renewed form, the various contributions to the *Greek Review of Social Research* are now influenced by the unsavoury political climate. Yet, the experience of the dictatorship inspired the turn to historical sociology and the dependency tradition in an effort to come to terms with the reasons that led to the downfall of parliamentary democracy.

© The Author(s), under exclusive license to Springer Nature Switzerland AG 2022
S. Gangas, G. Lagoumitzi, *Sociology in Greece*, Sociology Transformed, https://doi.org/10.1007/978-3-031-16190-2_2

Keywords Athens Social Sciences Centre • Human geography • Modernization • National Centre of Social Research • Social welfare

FROM SOCIAL WELFARE TO SOCIOLOGY: 1945–1962

The first post-war, post-civil war years in Greece have been variously characterized as the 'sociological Middle Ages' (Koniordos, 2010, p. 180), an 'infancy stage' for sociology (Nicolaou, 1974, p. 12) or 'a sorry tale' (Peristiany, 1968a, p. 283). A deeply divided society between 'victors' and 'losers' in the wake of the civil war and the radical authoritarianism of successive Greek governments established a nominal 'parliamentary democracy' under a monarchy, but actual power was rapidly passing in the hands of extra-parliamentary forces that undermined any semblance of political legitimacy (Svoronos, 1972, pp. 144–145). It is obvious that a country in which the Cold War mentality introduced the idea of a permanent 'internal enemy'[1] into its 1951 Constitution was less than ready to welcome 'vexing', if not outright 'dangerous' sociological analyses. As Tsoukalas recalls in his reminiscences of the *Athens Social Sciences Centre*, 'forty years after Alexandros Papanastasiou and more than twenty years since Metaxas exiled Kanellopoulos, "sociology" was still anathema for all those who, because of their ignorance or inherent suspicion, insisted on evoking its etymological, and other, affinities with "communitarianism", the better-sounding version of [...] communism or the marginally less unacceptable socialism' (Tsoukalas, 2003, p. 412). Kokosalakis too points out that 'sociology was considered an unnecessary and even illicit luxury by most politicians and academics' (1998, p. 326). For some time, sociology could only embrace conservative analyses that glorified the Greek spirit that was 'sadly' waning in the face of 'the lack of an organized, disciplined and spiritually driven society' (Tsakonas, 1974, p. 88). The antidote to the 'spiritual decay' would be certain attempts to ground a sociology on an

---

[1] Alivizatos quotes professor of administrative law Phaedon Vegleris to document the transformation of the 'the state of siege' clause of the Greek constitution into a permanent threat. The only time that the 'state of siege' clause was evoked was on the eve of the military dictatorship of 21 April 1967 (Alivizatos, 1983, pp. 181–190). The 'internal enemy' threat against public order was so broadly defined that it could refer arbitrarily to any action. Later, various 'emergency measures' were institutionalized. For a thorough analysis, see Alivizatos (2006 [1981], pp. 388–394). Anthropologists and sociologists that conducted fieldwork in the ravaged Greek villages in the 1960s often came up against the 'rule of the gendarme'.

ethical basis as the journal *Archive of Sociology and Ethics* edited by Avrotelis Eleftheropoulos and Dimitrios Tsakonas[2] demonstrates and where young Castoriadis contributed only to issue 2 (for Castoriadis see Chap. 4). Already in volume 1, Eleftheropoulos (under the alias Filolaos Eleftheros) attempts a demarcation of the boundaries of sociology not merely as a discipline addressing 'what is' but also 'what should be', thus incorporating the ethical dimension (1944, p. 4). In the same volume, Tsakonas refers to Georgios Skliros[3] as the first Greek 'applied sociologist' (1944, p. 37), while Skliros' death is described as marking the decay of Greek spirit which consisted of *leventia*[4] as well as mythical (the Grand Idea) and communitarian elements (Tsakonas, 1947, pp. 64–74). One should not forget that these ideas were formulated at the height of the Greek Civil War and served as indoctrination into an ethical vision of a society that had already lost its pre-industrial, communitarian underpinnings. The rootless, amorphous, alienated, atomized actor whose advent is generally abhorred in the subsequent volumes of the *Archive of Sociology and Ethics*[5] was in the making, and a moralistic sociology was being formulated as a warning against it. Given Greece's Ottoman past which prevented her from following a historical trajectory from enlightened despotism to parliamentary democracy, Tsakonas was convinced that Greece needed an authoritarian government based on strict state control, military intervention and a strong presence of the Greek Orthodox Church. He thus paved the way to the military regime and became its theoretical supporter (Dimirouli, 2021, p. 185).

When the traumas of the Occupation and the ensuing civil war were finally addressed, mainly through a modernization and industrialization

---

[2] Dimitrios Tsakonas (1921–2004) became the professor of sociology in Panteion School of Social and Political Sciences in 1968. He became an ideological supporter of and served the military regime from 1969 to 1974 through various ministerial positions and in 1974; he was fired as the collaborator of the dictators.

[3] Georgios Skliros (1878–1919) was the first Marxist who addressed the 'class problem' as related to the 'language question' in Greece in 'Our Social Question' (1907) (see Chap. 1).

[4] Untranslatable word that relates to a certain kind of heroic ethos.

[5] Such ideas appear above all in the volume titled 'Introduction to Sociology' which is effectively a textbook written by D. Tsakonas and used in his lectures (1968–1969 and 1969–1970) at Panteion School (1970, pp. 220–221). In his inimitable style, John Campbell writes: 'There was a professor of sociology at the Panteion School who lectured mainly on the German masters. I was invited to attend one of his lectures on Max Weber, delivered, I remember, in a high rhetorical style. This kind of teaching had little to do with the systematic and empirical study of social behavior […]' (Campbell, 2003, p. 433).

programme that needed data produced by social sciences and sociology, one stumbled against the poverty of social research. Sociology was 'an undeveloped and undernourished discipline in Greece' (Kourvetaris & Dobratz, 1971, p. 48). Protosociologists had failed to establish 'a broader sociological base which the younger generations of Greek scholars could use as a frame of reference and anchorage to further the institutionalization and legitimation of sociology in modern Greece' (p. 48). In his *Short History of Sociology*, Maus states that 'in Greece, sociology was at first regarded as social welfare' (1962/1956, p. 175), a remark that clearly points to the founding of the first Social Welfare School by the American College of Greece (Pierce) as early as 1945. Being originally part of 'the American Board of Commissioners for foreign Missions while still in Asia Minor, it was transferred to Greece in 1922 and reopened as a non-sectarian institution' (Kourvetaris & Moskos, 1968, p. 243), and in collaboration with Greek ecclesiastical and local authorities, it attempted 'to bring back to life' villages such as Neohoraki or St. George on mountain Velouchi (Tymfristos) as well as communities in Northern Greece with the help of Anatolia College students (Brochure 1958–1959, Athens). Based on the moto 'rehabilitation through social service', the idea of a social work curriculum was born with an emphasis on community organization and social work practicum modules.[6] The school operated until 1975 and served as a blueprint for other welfare schools in Greece either organized by the Greek branch of Young Women's Christian Association (YWCA) in 1947 or the Church of Greece ten years later. Moreover, it staffed public and private social service sectors at a time when modernizing initiatives were proliferating (Exarchou, 1996). Originally attracting Athenian elite women with a good knowledge of English, it quickly expanded to recruit students from rural areas in 1965, while the first male student was accepted in 1968 (Exarchou, 1996). The combination of practicum (at the Korydallos juvenile prison), social science courses and an international body of professors gave students a unique vantage point. However, as the Greek government withdrew its recognition in 1971, and funding became more difficult to secure, the social welfare programme was discontinued in 1975 and was eventually integrated into the liberal arts programme (Vrettos, 1975). With the abandonment of the social welfare/social

---

[6] However, one must notice that the differences between social welfare and social work never became explicit.

work programme, the American College of Greece took a more academic and less applied turn, and this was manifested in the establishment of the first sociology department in Greece in the academic year 1962–1963 under the directorship of renowned sociologist of law and criminologist Calliope Spinelli (Vrettos, 1975). References to it are made in many historical accounts of the status of sociology in Greece,[7] while Lambiri-Dimaki describes the department as pioneering (2000, p. 130). Moreover, in her 1974 uniquely detailed account of *The Growth and Development of Sociology in Greece* Nicolaou notes that:

> There is no distinct Department of sociology in any one of the Greek institutions of Higher Learning, outside the one operating within the American Deree College (which forms part of the Deree-Pierce College in Athens), providing instruction in English, leading to a BA. Greek universities do not train sociologists and do not grant degrees in sociology. Instruction of sociology at the Universities and the other Schools, where it is taught, does not move beyond the general introductory undergraduate level and is purely theoretical. Yet, some of the Higher Institutions provide doctorates in the social sciences based on a dissertation with a sociological topic. (1974, p. 10)

Over the years, the sociology curriculum at the American College of Greece which had originally embraced a sociology of deviance and criminological direction was enriched through the introduction of courses on modern Greece as well as on culture and personality by J. Koty.[8] Koty who had studied in Berlin is one of the earliest contributors to the second volume of *Sociological Research*, the first sociological journal in Greece. In his 'Introduction to the problem of national character', he alerts his audience to the detrimental consequences of stereotypes and stereotypical thought (1957, pp. 187–240). In the late 1960s, new subjects were introduced such as rural and urban communities, social policy, population and the sociology of modern Greece by D.G. Tsaoussis. 'Culture and personality' was taught by T. Gioka-Katsarou, who, as we will see below, was one of

---

[7] Apart from Peristiany (1968a, p. 283) and Lambiri-Dimaki, see Kokosalakis (1998, p. 331), Koniordos (2010, p. 181), Kourvetaris and Dobratz (1971, p. 50), Kourvetaris & Moskos (1968, p. 243) and Safilios-Rothchild (1968, p. 281).

[8] Koty highlighted in his works the myriads of problems that Greece faced in the post-war years which he attributed to the lack of education, poverty of the soil, a 'looting economy' of foreigners and natives and the general mismanagement of many governments (1958, p. 335).

the pioneering influences in the *Athens Social Sciences Centre*, and the sociology of the family was introduced by L. Moussourou and media and political communication courses by D.G. Carmocolias.[9] Finally, N. Tatsis' influence on the institution is still discernable through his instruction of several sociology courses in theory and other specialisms that form an essential part of the sociology curriculum until today. Indeed, one can argue that the teaching of sociology at Deree added more than 'lustre' (Peristiany, 1968a, p. 284) to the general picture. It contributed to sustaining the academic appeal of sociology over the next two decades during which there were no academic departments provided by the public sector,[10] but only isolated courses offered in some higher educational institutions. As Emmanouil argues, even when new sociology appointments were made in the public sector, professors were not necessarily selected from the field of sociology: 'The idea that lawyers, economists and folklorists are "to some extent" sociologists exercised once more its repressive influence' (Emmanouil, 1977, p. 44). As for those who were committed to a sociological training, there was one solution: expatriation (Peristiany, 1968a, p. 283).

THE EMERGENCE OF SOCIAL RESEARCH AND GREEK MODERNIZATION

The Athens Social Sciences Centre: 1959–1967[11]

The turning point for sociology in Greece came in 1959 when the Athens Social Research Centre (KKEA) was founded under the aegis of UNESCO, the supervision of the ministry of National Education and Religious Affairs and the directorship of Greek-Cypriot social anthropologist J.G. Peristiany (Argyriadou, 2003, p. 239). To this day, the Centre remains the only public institution in Greece dedicated to the social sciences. The original aims of the Centre included the collaboration between 'foreign' sociologists

[9] Carmocolias' study of the factors explaining the 'roots of the salient tendencies of newspaper politicization and bellicosity' and their 'implications and consequences upon Greek society and politics' is groundbreaking in political communication (1974, p. 109).

[10] It is the longest running department and programme of sociology in Greece.

[11] The *Athens Social Sciences Centre* (KKEA) is the forerunner of the National Centre of Social Research (EKKE) operating until today. The *Athens Social Sciences Centre* was closed down by the military junta, and in 1967 it re-opened under the name *National Centre of Social Research*. We will refer to it as 'Centre' throughout Chap. 2.

and anthropologists with their Greek counterparts as evidenced from the organization of Mediterranean conferences in sociology and anthropology in 1961, 1963 and 1966, the planning and carrying out of research, the provision of a library, encouraging an interest in the applied social sciences and finally the publication of sociological studies and especially of a sociological journal (Peristiany, 1968a, pp. 284–285). The creation of the Centre and its initial operation owes much to two academic figures, who served as UNESCO experts, namely, Clemens Heller (1959–1960), professor of sociology and later director of the *Aires Culturelles* of the VIe Section of the École Pratique des Hautes Études, and John Peristiany (1961–1967), lecturer in social anthropology at the University of Oxford. Heller brought to the Centre his interest in *Aires Culturelles*, which represented the French version of 'area studies' and which he was passionately pursuing in France in close collaboration with Fernand Braudel. Moreover, for a brief period of six months in 1962, John Campbell was asked by UNESCO to temporarily take on the position of Director of the Centre, while Peristiany had gone back to Oxford to explore the possibility of leaving Oxford permanently. Campbell's work embodying 'an emergent theory of practice' moved the Centre into the 'orbit of Mediterranean scholarship fostered by J.G. Peristiany' (Herzfeld, 2008, p. 154). Towards this direction, the Centre organized in Athens three 'Mediterranean Conferences in Social Anthropology and Sociology' in 1961, 1963 and 1966 (Argyriadou, 2003, p. 285). Such was the success of these conferences that during the last one, a decision was made to establish a Mediterranean Information Centre for Sociology and Social Anthropology which turned out to be yet another of the Centre's plan to be cut short by the colonels' *coup*. Throughout its operation, one should bear in mind that the main areas of interest of the Centre reflected the intersection of modernization as an objective for a developing Greek society and the intellectual/professional interests of those who served the Centre. Within this context, Peristiany's affiliation with the School of Social Anthropology in Oxford acted as a catalyst for the Centre's ethnographic turn as this is represented in pioneering studies of rural communities. This fieldwork can be found in the *Proceedings of the Mediterranean and sociological conference* of July 1963 (Peristiany, 1968b) and includes, among others, Damianakos and Fountoukou's demographic analysis of the age structure of the population in Greveniti (conducted during 1961 in East Zagori, Ioannina) or Moustaka's exploration of the 'attitudes towards migration' in 43 villages in Zagori and 8 villages on the island of Paros. Later, the results of Moustaka's study appeared in *The Internal Migrant: A comparative study in urbanization* (1964). The investigation of the respondents' attitudes towards the village and the town were soon transformed into an all too well-known story of the various socioeconomic and cultural reasons for urbanization tendencies (1964, pp. 69–95). Poverty, destitution, lack of property or status, large families, unemployment, low wages, the low cultural level in the village and finally a sense of liberation from parental authority were named as the main reasons behind urbanization pressures (70–73). The reasons mentioned here did not preclude the presence of opposite forces such as 'the spontaneous desire for the unsophisticated and emotionally satisfying life of a peasant society' (73). Moreover, modernization raised questions about the level of industrialization and the position of women between tradition and modernity. Between 1958 and 1960, Lambiri-Dimaki conducted a study of women being exposed for the first time to the influences of industrialization (1983a, pp. 143–156). The textile factory of Piraiki-Patraiki in the wider Megara area exposed women workers and especially girls to 'non-traditional values' and the possibility of 'emancipation' (146–147) from the shackles of traditional feminine roles. Yet, the pace of modernization remained slow, and, in the end, 'the effects of industrialization during the decade 1950–1960 on the disadvantaged position of the Greek woman and the traditional micro-society of Megara manifested themselves much more at the level of ideas (ways of thinking) rather than at that of actual social behavior' (154). After all, any monetary benefits for women were channelled into their dowry, an institution that increased their eligibility status towards marriage. In the follow-up study undertaken by Nikolaidou (1975, pp. 470–506), the composition of the factory population was different. Whereas in Lambiri-Dimaki's research the factory workers were primarily local recruits (from Megara and Elefsis), by 1974, internal migration triggered by industrialization meant that Epirot workers, among them women, had arrived and were living on their own, thus acquiring a measure of independence. Morally derogatory epithets like 'Katsambissa'[12] did not exist any longer, and women were more conscious about their economic role in the family. Yet, the institution of the dowry, a remnant of traditional Greek society, remained the main motivation for 'getting out of the house' to work in the factory. A further remnant of traditional gender roles was the lack of

[12] A woman who works for Katsambas, a Greek industrialist and owner of Piraiki-Patraiki textile industry.

any political consciousness which is assigned to traditional values rather than to the seven-year dictatorial rule (Nikolaidou, 1975, p. 490). Pioneering studies like Moustaka's and Lambiri-Dimaki's and later Nikolaidou's were instrumental in establishing the rural-urban/traditional-modern divide as an analytical tool for 'measuring' modernization and became therefore part and parcel of the modernization paradigm that defines the period in question. Modernization as industrialization and urbanization became the focus of interest of other researchers at the Centre. For example, challenging the idea of a sharp rural-urban divide, T. Gioka applied the technique of the rural-urban continuum to Greek data in her attempt to place the various communities under study along the continuum. She concluded that demographic differences such as population size were instrumental in establishing consistent variations in patterns of behaviour. Apart from valuable sociodemographic data produced, her study sensitized us to the administrative, historical and socioeconomic biases that influence the construction of similar tools (Gioka, 1966, pp. 41–70). Stratis Andreadis specifically questions the continuum given the level of transportation and communication systems in Greece (1966, p. 30) but recognizes that the study of internal migratory tendencies will be crucial in the future evolution of the differentiation between countryside and city seen from the perspective of two radically different value systems (30–31). Such analyses were intended to have practical consequences for policy makers and often furnished them with specific proposals towards a viable economic development in a modernizing country (p. 40). Similarly, Guy Burgel's holistic exploration of the inter-relationships of people, mentalities and space in Pobia, a Cretan village (1965), documents in detail the precarious position of the village amidst the growth of the commercialization of agricultural economy, owing mainly to the cultivation of vines (sultanas), of the croppers who struggle under quasi-colonial market relations or of the loss of habitat vis-à-vis the ever-growing arable land. Such changes lead to the rapid consolidation of social and economic inequalities (1981, p. 16). His pessimistic conclusions relating to the survival probability of Pobia can only be addressed through a 'restructuring of agricultural conditions' via technology and a reversal of population trends that lead to the greying of the village and the wider Messara area (pp. 16–17). Similar conclusions were reached by Pechoux studying another area of the island of Crete, namely, the Lasithi basin (1969a, pp. 40–50). Another landmark study of a rural community is

Bertrand Vernier's study of Pomaks[13] in Thrace conducted between 1966 and 1967. This is a study of the division of labour particularly in its relation to the mythical-ritual system, the kinship system and to inheritance patterns (1981, pp. 122–142). Moreover, John Campbell's study of transhumant Sarakatsani shepherds provided continuing inspiration for his students Juliet Du Boulay and Renée Hirschon. Outside the Centre and yet in direct connection to the paradigm established by Peristiany and Campbell, their respective studies of the Greek mountain village of Ambéli on the island of Evia[14] (1974) and the Asia Minor refugees in Pireaus (1989) are considered ethnographic classics. For Du Boulay who conducted her study in the mid-1960s, the viability of the idea of the village as a single community was challenged by the introduction of new values such as individual achievement (1974, p. 252) that were 'alien' to the community (7) on the one hand and on the other by phenomena such as emigration to the big city (261–264) that ultimately render Ambéli a 'dying village community' (3). Thus, modernization continues to be defined through changes in the traditional village value system. Binary assumptions such as 'traditional-modern', rural-urban and folk-urban form the basis of analysis of social phenomena and geographical space. Hirschon interrogates such binary interpretations of social and cultural change by positing a 'cyclical' rather than 'linear' pattern of change (Hirschon, 1989 p. 233). This enables her to discover traditional features such as the division and yet complementarity of gender roles or the centrality of family reputation and prestige in the urban *milieu* of Kokkinia, one of the refugee settlements of Piraeus (234). A further challenge to the rural-urban 'ideal-type' construct concerns the existence of a 'cultural lag' with respect to modernization, that is, the relatively independent movement between 'cultural values and ways of thinking' and 'patterns of conduct' (235). Hirschon seems to be pointing to the distinction between urbanization and urbanism as a social conduct. It is obvious that one is not a good predictor of the other. Finally, other ethnographic studies include Friedl's on the family as 'the most significant social unit' in the village of

---

[13] A Muslim minority of 20,000 to 30,000 people at the time of the study living mostly in the mountain villages of Rhodope along the Greek-Bulgarian frontier.

[14] Du Boulay uses the form Euboea. Here, we use the form Evia that is closer to the Greek pronunciation. Ambéli is a fictitious name.

Vasilika in Evia (1962, p. 18), Kenna's research on the island of Anafi (2001) and Lineton's in Mani (1971).[15]

Other significant areas that were launched by the Centre were human geography led by Bernard Kayser, G. Burgel, P.Y. Péchoux and M. Sivignon (1971), culminating in the publication of the *Economic and Social Atlas of Greece* (1964) in collaboration with geographer Kenneth Thompson of UC Davis[16] and Roger Vaternelle[17] who was the project's cartographer. Within a developmental context, external (geography and politics) as well as internal (administrative centralization, illiteracy, demographic factors such as population growth channelled into in- and out-migration) overdeterminations were found to weigh heavily on the geographic space ultimately contributing to its fragmentation, a condition that precluded the development that Greece needed (Kayser, 1966, pp. 100–111). Kayser, Péchoux and Sivignon continued their studies of population movements and specifically emigration and urbanization (1971). They even formulated what would be referred to today as a geopolitical conception of Greek space, not very far from the current idea of Greece as a bridgehead, the difference being that in the 1960s, this would be between Western Europe and an unstable East or Eastern bloc countries (Kayser, 1966, p. 105). External and internal constraints on Greece might have had a potentially disintegrating effect, but the agricultural and industrial capitalizations especially of Northern Greek areas were promising a different future for Greece (111). The impact of the French human geography school on the development of sociology could not be overstated. It defined the very mission of an ascending social science. The studies presented here are an intrinsic part of a geographical census of the Greek space: 'The exact knowledge of different areas of Greece is desirable not only because it fulfills scientific aspirations, but mainly because of its potential use as the cornerstone of regional development' (Sivignon, 1969, p. 4). Moreover, behind the division of Greece into regions lies more than physical causality. The economic dependence of Greece on mature industrial countries coupled with the country's history is for the first time in any analysis deemed responsible for underdevelopment or the late development of Greece. Secondly, the emphasis on demographic processes such as

---

[15] For a comprehensive summary of ethnographic work in Greece, see L. Sotiropoulos (1994).

[16] Kenneth Thompson launched a geography department at UC Davis in 1955 (University of California Digital Archives).

[17] *Institut Géographique National de Paris*.

urbanization renders 'the urban network as the basis of spatial organization' (6). The city dominates a certain region through its administrative, commercial, banking or health services. Consequently, the boundaries of urban influence must coincide with the boundaries of a geographical region (6). Finally, human geographers bring with them the French tradition of sociology as social engineering (programming) based on dynamic data collection. Their studies are not treated as destinations but rather as the origin for more in-depth research into ongoing social processes (6).[18] Some examples of this valuable tradition are Pechoux's study of the industrial city of Kavala in Northern Greece (Pechoux, 1969b, pp. 8–21), Sivignon's 'demographic evolution of Greece: 1961–1971' (1972, pp. 72–75)[19] or Burgel's account of the evolution of Athens as a Mediterranean capital that after 1974 finds itself at the crossroads between 'myth and gigantism, patrimony and modernity, the local and the global' (2004, p. 63). Only recently is Greece supposed to have overcome the stage of Balkanization implying an introverted preoccupation with the local and the national and to have been thrust into the whirlwind of the global polyphony.

Apart for internal migration manifested in studies of urbanization, the Centre continued to emphasize a need for a Greek migration policy (Goutos, 1966, p. 112). Already in the early days of the Centre, Michalis Goutos, who occupied the post of the General Secretary of the Centre from its inception to the imposition of military rule, stressed this need. Unlike earlier migratory waves, emigration to Europe and especially to West Germany after 1955 was highly organized. The structures of underdevelopment, that is, economic hardship, a decaying countryside and the 'overpopulation' evident in many areas of Greece (114), could never change unless the focus becomes not only economic but also social progress which, under the current circumstances of social marginalization and isolation of the Greek immigrant in host countries, is not a realistic prospect. The need for a bilateral 'cooperation on migration policy' (116)

---

[18] One should not omit a special reference to ACE (Athens Center of Ekistics) established in 1963 by Constantinos A. Doxiadis, urban planner, engineer, visionary, researcher, 'worldwide activist' and more. The target according to Doxiadis was 'to build the city of optimum size, that is, a city which respects human dimensions' (1970, p. 393). The journal *Ekistics* ran from 1957 to 2007.

[19] In this source which was originally published in the *Revue de Geographie de Lyon* (1972) 1, the translators of Sivignon's article appear as co-authors. E. Dimitras was appointed director of the renamed *National Center of Social Research* (EKKE) during the military regime.

between Greece and host countries becomes imperative. The migratory wave to Western Europe was indeed one of the socioeconomic problems that defined the 1950s and 1960s. In only three years from 1960 to 1963, the number of migrants to Germany only (23,354) had increased a little over seven times (167,436), yet the study emphasizes the temporary character of Greek migration to Europe, while at the same time, return migration is interpreted as an aversion on the migrants' part to go back to agricultural work. Unless they are offered economic and social rights that will satisfy them, return migrants might become fermentation loci of a new, radicalized politics (Filias, 1966, pp. 123–124). Finally, the Centre conducted a study (Vlachos, 1966, pp. 125–126) which documented the growing trend for return migration on the condition that the state fulfils demands such as social security and housing (p. 126). The many contributions of Lambiri-Dimaki[20] to the sociology of education reflect her incessant drive towards pioneering sociological research. Following Bourdieu and Passeron in *Les Heritiers*, published in 1964, she tries to correlate the students' socioeconomic 'origins' and their educational 'destinations', that is, choices of specific cognitive fields (Lambiri-Dimaki & Kelperis, 1983, p. 67). It is important to note that this study measures the impact of socioeconomic inequality on education before Georgios Papandreou's educational reform of 1964 which established a tuition-free education. Regardless of the reform, a social and economic system with 'limited occupational openings in industry and technology used university degrees and the positions they opened as a safety valve to the pressures of the masses for social movement into a more rewarding state of life' (Lambiri-Dimaki, 1983b, p. 107). Not only are the rewards of education limited, but the essence of education itself is circumvented through the emphasis on what Mouzelis has labelled 'cultural formalism' (1978, pp. 136–137), that is, sterile, unproductive learning rather than the development of critical skills (Lambiri-Dimaki, 1983b, p. 107). Lambiri-Dimaki contended that such studies in the social stratification and the sociology of education exposed the major contradiction of Greek education in the 1960s and early 1970s, namely, that 'it opens wide the gates of the universities to the members of its less privileged strata, only to close later on for them the gates to the upper layers of prestige, wealth, and power structure' (1983c, p. 119), a finding that departed from deeply embedded assumptions about

---

[20] Here also in collaboration with C. Kelperis who developed the statistical models of that study.

the role of Greek education as the vehicle of social mobility. One should note that Bourdieu's links to the Centre go beyond his sociology of education. He was instrumental in establishing cultural sociology as a distinct field within the Centre through his 1965–1966 comparative research about the impact of class factors on cultural consumption by focusing on the publics of Greek museums (Bourdieu & Darbel, 1991, pp. 153–159). Today, Demertzis and others continue the rich tradition of cultural sociology, as is evident in his bibliographical essay (Demertzis et al., 2017). Other studies under the auspices of the Centre include Maria Iliou's on the socioeconomic conditions to which the school dropout rate is attributable (2003). Moustaka and Kassimati's attempt to establish the perceptions and attitudes towards fatherland and other nations among students between the ages 9 and 11 started at the Centre in 1964. The study was repeated in 1977 and was ultimately published in the *Greek Review of Social Research* (1978, pp. 166–189).[21] Sufficient mention of the pioneering periodicals of the Centre, namely, *Sociological Research* (1957, biannual) and *Sociological Thought* (1966, biannual), has been made already. Through their pages, one acquires a vivid image of the research and researchers of the Centre. Evangelos Katsaros who acted as legal advisor to the Centre was the director of both periodicals. However, his greatest contribution was the *Dictionary of Social Sciences* in six volumes (1958), whose social function is directly stated in the 'Prologue' and points to 'popular enlightenment, the diffusion of scientific achievements to social groups and therefore a means for social advancement' (1958, Prologue). Eleftheropoulos,[22] in his introduction, praises the dictionary for the positive synthesis of the various 'Sciences of Man'. It seems that sociology in Greece never lost sight of the connection between in-depth knowledge of society and social change.

In conclusion, ideas about the 'suspect' and potentially 'subversive' status of sociology were fully incorporated into the official ideology of the military regime that followed these extraordinary decades. Making use of the 'state of emergency' measures[23] that were in place ever since the interwar years but were intensified during the civil war, the colonels closed

---

[21] The study would be the precursor to Frangoudaki and Dragona's *What is our Fatherland? Ethnocentrism in education* (1997).

[22] See Chap. 1 for his contribution to sociology in Greece.

[23] For an analysis of the evolution of the 'state of emergency', see Alivizatos (2006, pp. 383–398).

down the Centre, 'ousted' Peristiany and Goutos, imposed a new acting director, applied their infamous 'interrogation' techniques on some of the Centre's members and imprisoned members like Vassilis Filias, Gerasimos Notaras and Nikos Voulelis (Tsoukalas, 2003, p. 417). Peristiany left for Cyprus where he established a new Centre of Social Studies with the support of UNESCO and the President of the Republic, Archbishop Makarios. The new Centre continued to work from 1969 to the Turkish invasion in 1974. Far removed from the logic of an 'anthropological patriotism' (Kitromilides, 2003, p. 515), he offered opportunities for young social scientists to grow (Peristiany, 1976, pp. 345–354). In the absence of higher education institutions in Cyprus until 1989, mainly due to the peculiarities of the Cypriot social structure and education[24] (Peristiany, 1983, pp. 15–45), a research centre became instrumental for an analysis of Cypriot society on the path to modernization.[25] The Turkish invasion of Cyprus in 1974 was not only a tragedy for the people on the island and Hellenism in general but also for the social sciences that were just beginning to flourish. As Kitromilides notes, 'most social scientists turned to the study of the Cyprus Question abandoning scientific fields that Peristiany and his collaborators had inaugurated' (Kitromilides, 2003, p. 517). 1959–1967 and 1969–1974 were decades ripe with social research and left the indelible mark of interdisciplinarity on the intellectual history of sociology in Greece and Cyprus. As Guy Burgel writes, 'the legacy of the *Athens Social Sciences Centre* is in no need of a hagiography, but simply of recognition' (2003, p. 457).

The National Centre of Social Research: 1968–1974

The military coup saw the end of the 'sociological spring' (Iliou, 2003, p. 344), the closing down of the Centre, and its re-opening one year later under its current name, that is, the *National Centre for Social Research* (EKKE). Important collaborators of the *Athens Social Sciences Center* like

---

[24] Cypriot elites were educated in British universities, whereas the lower classes often turned to a vocational/technical education. Moreover, questions about the character, nationalist or cosmopolitan, of a university of Cyprus divided the community. For example, certain politicians suggested the adoption of English as the language for instruction to ensure a more cosmopolitan outlook for a new university of Cyprus. However, more nationalistic concerns prevailed.

[25] See Markides et al. (1978) *Lysi: Social change in a Cypriot village*.

Constantine Tsoukalas were now abroad and engaged in alerting European intellectuals and politicians to *The Greek Tragedy* (1969), an exploration into the socio-historical reasons that led to the dictatorship. Sociology was experiencing another backlash. The *Greek Review of Social Research* was now publishing material relating to the role of the military in Greek history or the ideological legitimation of the regime. The 1971 volume of the periodical is dedicated to military sociology through articles by Greek American contributors such as Moskos (1971, pp. 3–15) and Kourvetaris (1971, pp. 16–28), while Jean Siotis' account of the changes in the class structure of the Greek military provides an opportunity for ridiculing the regime (1971, pp. 29–38). At the time when 'social opinions certificates'[26] were imposed on university faculty, we encounter a debate about Greek universities under dictatorial rule in the periodical *Minerva*,[27] which demonstrates the ideological chasm among intellectuals abroad. The 'foreign factor' that was instrumental for the survival of the junta was not only about brutal repression but also about ideological legitimacy which was expressed through the various grants offered by the Ford Foundation[28] to intellectuals, artists and men and women of letters across the board. The traumatic experiences of this period, as Lambiri-Dimaki observes, inspired a whole generation[29] of sociologists such as Tsoukalas, Mouzelis and Poulantzas, to mention just a few, to turn to historical sociology attempting an explanation of the period that led to the junta. Therefore, the sociologists of the time developed a professional *habitus* influenced by the Enlightenment values of rationality and an ethic of responsibility that 'reflected the ideal of a Humboltian higher education' (Lambiri-Dimaki, 2002, pp. 72–73). Above all, the intellectuals of the period until the restoration of democracy in 1974 were driven by an optimism and regarded sociology as a science whose methods provided the tools to fulfil the desire

---

[26] Social opinion certificates were originally introduced in 1936 to ensure the absence of 'Csommunist sympathies' among Greek people. They were obligatory for employment in any position in the public or even private sector. Their use was generalized under the colonels' regime (Alivizatos, 1983, pp. 420–422, 591–600).

[27] See Haniotis (1968) and Siotis (1969).

[28] Ford Foundation in Greece Records. American School of Classical Studies at Athens https://www.ascsa.edu.gr/index.php/archives/ford-foundation-records.

[29] Lambiri-Dimaki (2002, pp. 68–73) uses Mannheim's concept of generation defined in terms of distinct collective experiences of given age groups, which stamp those age groups with a permanent separate identity. These experiences, in turn, give a new meaning to both individual (subjective) and historical (objective) time.

for policy making especially in relation to the ascending welfare state (72). The future was predicated on the study of the past which would now take a different turn.

REFERENCES

Alivizatos, N. (1983). Οι Πολιτικοί θεσμοί σε κρίση: 1922-1974 Όψεις της Ελληνικής εμπειρίας [The political institutions in crisis: 1922-1974 Aspects of the Greek experience]. Themelio.
Alivizatos, N. (2006). Καθεστώς «έκτακτης ανάγκης» και πολιτικές ελευθερίες: 1946-1949 [State of emergency and political freedoms: 1946-1949] In J. O. Iatrides (Ed.), Η Ελλάδα στη δεκαετία 1940-1950:Ένα έθνος σε κρίση [Greece in the 1940s: A nation in crisis] (pp. 383–398). Themelio (Original work published 1981).
Andreadis, S. (1966). Κοινωνική ασυνέχεια και προβλήματα οικονομικής αναπτύξεως στην Ελλάδα [Social discontinuity and problems of economic development in Greece]. Κοινωνιολογική Σκέψη [Sociological Thought], 1(1), 27–40.
Argyriadou, E. (2003). Ερευνητές, έρευνες και οργάνωση στο Κέντρο Κοινωνικών Επιστημών Αθηνών [Researchers, Research and Organization in the Athens social Sciences Center: 1959-1967]. In I. Lambiri-Dimaki (Ed.) Κοινωνικές επιστήμες και πρωτοπορία στην Ελλάδα: 1950–1967 [Social Sciences and Innovation in Greece: 1950–1967] (pp. 239–304). National Center of Social Research/Gutenberg.
Brochure, (1958–1959). "The hope of Greece", Academic brochures, ACG/IA PM003 (ACG Archives).
Bourdieu. P & Darbel, A, (1991). *The love of art: European art museums and their public*. Polity Press. (Original work published 1969)
Burgel, G. (1965). *Pobia: Ètude gèographique d'un village crètois*. Centre de Sciences Sociales d' Athènes.
Burgel, G. (1981). La Grèce rurale revisitée. Επιθεώρηση Κοινωνικών Ερευνών *[The Greek Review of Social Research]*, numéro speciale, 11–17. https://doi.org/10.12681/grsr.544
Burgel, G. (2003). Le Centre des Sciences Sociales d'Athénes: Une école humaine et scientifique In I. Lambiri-Dimaki (Ed.), Κοινωνικές επιστήμες και πρωτοπορία στην Ελλάδα: 1950-1967 [Social Sciences and Innovation in Greece: 1950-1967] (pp. 443–457) National Center of Social Research/ Gutenberg.
Burgel, G. (2004). Athènes, de la balkanisation à la mondialisation. *Méditerranée, 103*(3), 59–63. https://doi.org/10.3406/medit.2004.3368
Campbell, J. (2003). The Social Sciences Centre, Athens, 1962. In Κοινωνικές επιστήμες και πρωτοπορία στην Ελλάδα: 1950-1967 [Social Sciences and Innovation in Greece: 1950–1967] (pp. 431–435). National Center of Social Research/Gutenberg.

Carmocolias, D. G. (1974). *Political communication in Greece, 1965-1967: The last two years of a parliamentary democracy*. National Center of Social Research.
Demertzis, N., Souliotis, N., & Markatas, G. (2017). Πολιτισμική ανάλυση και κοινωνιολογία του πολιτισμού στην Ελλάδα, 1980-2014: Επισκόπηση βιβλιογραφίας και σχεδίασμα κοινωνιολογικής ερμηνείας [Cultural analysis and sociology of culture in Greece: Review of literature and a proposal for a sociological interpretation]. *Επιθεώρηση Κοινωνικών Ερευνών [The Greek Review of Social Research]*, 147, 143–170. https://doi.org/10.12681/grsr.14368
Dimirouli, F. (2021). Can dead poets speakbBack? C.P. Cavafy, Cold War propaganda and the Greek dictatorship. In O. Anastastakis & K. Lagos (Eds.), *The Greek military dictatorship: Revisiting a troubled past, 1967–1974* (pp. 164–197). Berghahn Books.
Doxiadis, C. A. (1970). Ekistics, the science of human settlements. *Science*, 170(3956), 393–404. https://doi.org/10.1126/SCIENCE.170.3956.393
Du Boulay, J. (1974). *Portrait of a Greek mountain village*. Clarendon Press.
Eleftheropoulos, A. (alias Filolaos Eleftheros). (1944). Κοινωνιολογία και ηθική [Sociology and Ethics]. *Αρχείον Κοινωνιολογίας και Ηθικής [Archive of Sociology and Ethics]*, 1, 3–11.
Emmanouil, A. (1977). *Κοινωνιολογία: Βασικά προβλήματα* [Sociology: Basic problems]. Karamperopoulos Publishers.
Exarchou, E. (1996). School of social welfare, the American College for Girls 1945–1975, Eklogi, School of social welfare. ACG/IA AR1230, Box 1/F5 (ACG Archives).
Frangoudaki, A., & Dragona, T. (Eds.). (1997). *Τι είν' η πατρίδα μας; Εθνοκεντρισμός στην εκπαίδευση* [What is our country? Ethnocentrism in education]. Alexandria.
Friedl, E. (1962). *Vasilika: A village in Modern Greece*. Holt, Rinehart & Winston.
Gioka, T. (1966). Το αγροτο-αστικό «συνεχές» και Ελληνικά κοινωνικοδημογραφικά μεγέθη [The rural-urban 'continuum' and sociodemographic data]. *Κοινωνιολογική Σκέψη [Sociological Thought]*, I(1), 41–70.
Goutos, M. (1966). Η ανάγκη μιας 'κοινωνικής πολιτικής' της μεταναστεύσεως' [The need for a social policy of immigration]. *Κοινωνιολογική Σκέψη [Sociological Thought]*, I(1), 112–116.
Haniotis, G. (1968). The situation of universities in Greece. *Minerva*, 6(2), 163–184.
Herzfeld, M. (2008). The Ethnographer as theorist: John Campbell and the power of detail. In M. Mazower (Ed.), *Networks of power in modern Greece: Essays in honour of John Campbell* (pp. 147–165). Hurst & Company.
Hirschon, R. (1989). *Heirs of the Greek catastrophe: The social life of Asia Minor refugees in Pireaus*. Clarendon Press.
Iliou, M. (2003). Η σύντομη άνοιξη της Ελληνικής κοινωνιολογίας: Αναφορά στο Κέντρο Κοινωνικών Επιστημών Αθηνών [The short-lived spring of Greek sociology: Report on the Athens Social Sciences Centre]. In J. Lambiri-Dimaki

(Ed.). *Κοινωνικές επιστήμες και πρωτοπορία στην Ελλάδα 1950–1967* [Social sciences and innovation in Greece 1950-1967] (pp. 329-344). Social Sciences Centre/Gutenberg.
Kayser, B. (1966). Για μια γεωγραφική απογραφή του Ελληνικού χώρου [For a geographical inventory of Greek space]. *Κοινωνιολογική Σκέψη [Sociological Thought]*, *1*, 100–111.
Kayser, B., et al. (1964). *Οικονομικός και κοινωνικός Άτλας της Ελλάδος* [Economic and social atlas of Greece]. National Statistical Service of Greece, Center of Economic research, Athens social Sciences Center.
Kayser, B., Pèchoux, P.-Y., & Sivignon, M. (1971). *Exode rural et attraction urbaine en Grèce* [Rural exodus and urban attraction in Greece]. Centre National de Recherches Sociales [National Centre for Social Research].
Kenna, M. E. (2001). *Greek island life: Fieldwork on Anafi*. Harwood Academic Publishers.
Kitromilides, P. (2003). Η παρουσία της Κύπρου στον χάρτη των κοινωνικών επιστημών: Η συμβολή του Ιωάννη Περιστιάνη [The presence of Cyrpus in the social sciences map: the contribution of John Peristiany]. In J. Lambiri-Dimaki (Ed.). *Κοινωνικές επιστήμες και πρωτοπορία στην Ελλάδα 1950–1967* [Social sciences and innovation in Greece 1950-1967] [pp. 511–517]. Social Sciences Centre/Gutenberg.
Kokosalakis, N. (1998). Politics and sociology in Greece: 1950-98. *International Sociology*, *13*(3), 325–343.
Koniordos, S. (2010). Η συζήτηση για τη δημόσια κοινωνιολογία και η κοινωνιολογία στην Ελλάδα [The discussion of public sociology and sociology in Greece]. In M. Kousis, M. Samatas & S. Koniordos (Eds.). *Εξουσία και Κοινωνία: Δωρήματα στον Κωνσταντίνο Τσουκαλά* [Power and society: Offerings to Constantine Tsoukalas] [pp. 174–195]. Kastaniotis.
Koty, J. (1957). Εισαγωγή στο πρόβλημα του εθνικού χαρακτήρα [Introduction to the problem of national character]. *Κοινωνιολογική Έρευνα [Sociological Research]*, *2*, 187–240.
Koty, J. (1958). Greece. In A. M. Rose (Ed.), *The institutions of advanced societies* (pp. 330–383). University of Minnesota Press.
Kourvetaris, G. A., & Dobratz, B. A. (1971). Contemporary sociology in Greece. *International Journal of Contemporary Sociology*, *8*(3–4), 46–58.
Kourvetaris, G. A., & Moskos, C. C. (1968). A report on sociology in Greece. *The American Sociologist*, *3*(3), 243–245.
Kourvetraris, G. A. (1971). Professional self-images and political perspectives in the Greek military. *Επιθεώρηση Κοινωνικών Ερευνών [Greek Review of Social Research]*, *7*, 16–28. https://doi.org/10.12681/grsr.539
Lambiri-Dimaki, J. (1983a). The impact of industrial employment on the position of women in a Greek country town (1960s) and a follow-up study (1970s) In

J. Lambiri-Dimaki (Ed.), *Social stratification in Greece: 1962-1982, eleven essays* (pp. 143–156). Ant. N. Sakkoulas.

Lambiri-Dimaki, J. (1983b). Democratization of education in (1960s-1970s). In J. Lambiri-Dimaki (Ed.), *Social stratification in Greece: 1962–1982, eleven essays* (pp. 80–117). Ant. N. Sakkoulas.

Lambiri-Dimaki, J. (1983c). Contradiction between the structure of educational opportunities in Greece: Two sociological hypotheses. In J. Lambiri-Dimaki (Ed.), *Social stratification in Greece: 1962–1982, eleven essays* (pp. 118–122). Ant. N. Sakkoulas.

Lambiri-Dimaki, J. (2000). Για την κοινωνιολογία [For sociology]. Sakkoulas.

Lambiri-Dimaki, J. (2002). Η κοινωνιολογία στην Ελλάδα σήμερα: Η ολοκλήρωση της τριλογίας 1959–2000 [Sociology in Greece today: The completion of the trilogy 1959-2000]. Papazisis.

Lambiri-Dimaki, J., & Kelperis, C. (1983). Differential trends in faculty enrolment according to sex and social class in Greece: 1962-1964. In J. Lambiri-Dimaki (Ed.), *Social stratification in Greece: 1962–1982, eleven essays* (pp. 61–79). Ant. N. Sakkoulas.

Lineton, M. J. (1971). *Mina, present and past. Depopulation in a Village in Mani, Southern Greece* [Unpublished doctoral dissertation]. University of Kent.

Markides, K. C., Nikita, E. S., & Rangou, E. N. (1978). *Lysi: Social change in a Cypriot village*. Publications of the Social Research Center.

Moskos, C. C. (1971). The breakdown of parliamentary democracy in Greece, 1965-67. Επιθεώρηση Κοινωνικών Ερευνών *[Greek Review of Social Research]*, 7, 3–15. https://doi.org/10.12681/grsr.538

Moustaka, C. (1964). *The internal migrant: A comparative study in urbanization*. Social Sciences Center Athens.

Moustaka K., & Kassimati K. (1978). Αντιλήψεις και διαθέσεις για την πατρίδα και άλλα έθνη [Perceptions and attitudes about the homeland and other nations] Επιθεώρηση Κοινωνικών Ερευνών *[Greek Review of Social Research]*, 33, 166–189. https://doi.org/10.12681/grsr.310

Nicolaou, L. (1974). *The growth and development of sociology in Greece*. (Unknown publisher).

Nikolaidou, M., & Lambiri-Dimaki, J. (1975). Η εργαζόμενη γυναίκα στην Ελλάδα: Μια δειγματολογική μελέτη [The working woman in Greece: A sample survey]. Επιθεώρηση Κοινωνικών Ερευνών *[Greek Review of Social Research]*, 25, 470–506. https://doi.org/10.12681/grsr.392

Pechoux, P.-Y. (1969a). Η πόλγη του Λασιθίου: Αγροτική κοινότης εις Μεσογειακήν ορεινήν λεκάνην [The Lasithi polje: An agricultural community in a Mediterranean mountain basin]. Επιθεώρηση Κοινωνικών Ερευνών *[Greek Review of Social Research]*, 1, 40–50. https://doi.org/10.12681/grsr.522

Pechoux, P.-Y. (1969b). Μια βιομηχανική πόλις της βορείου Ελλάδος: Η Καβάλα [An industrial city in northern Greece: Kavala]. *Επιθεώρηση Κοινωνικών Ερευνών [Greek Review of Social Research] 1*, 8–21. https://doi.org/10.12681/grsr.520

Peristiany, J.G. (1976). Anthropological, sociological and geographical fieldwork in Cyprus. In M. Dimen & E. Friedl (Eds.). *Regional variation in modern Greece and Cyprus: Toward a perspective on ethnography of Greece* (pp. 345–354). Annals of the New York Academy of Sciences, 268.

Peristiany, J. G. (1968a). Sociology in Greece. In *Contemporary sociology in Western Europe and in America* (pp. 264–307). The Luigi Sturzo Institute of Rome.

Peristiany, J. G. (Ed.). (1968b). *Contributions to Mediterranean sociology: Mediterranean rural communities and social change.* Athens Social Sciences Centre.

Peristiany, J. G. (1983). Η κοινωνική δομή και η ανώτερη εκπαίδευση στην Κύπρο [Social structure and higher education in Cyprus]. In *Proceedings of Conference titled: The new Universities and their social milieu* [Τα νέα πανεπιστήμια και ο κοινωνικός τους χώρος] (pp. 15–45). Science and Society Group and Naumann Foundation.

Safilios-Rothchild, C. (1968). The present status of sociology in Greece. *The American Sociologist, 3*(4), 280–284.

Siotis, J. (1969). The situation of universities in Greece. *Minerva, 7*(3), 490–493.

Siotis, J. (1971). Some notes on the military in Greek politics. *Επιθεώρηση Κοινωνικών Ερευνών [Greek Review of Social Research], 7*, 29–38. https://doi.org/10.12681/grsr.540

Sivignon, M. (1969). Από το περιεχόμενον και τας μεθόδους της ανθρωπογεωγραφίας [Of the content and methods of human geography]. *Επιθεώρηση Κοινωνικών Ερευνών [Greek Review of Social Research], 1*, 3–7. https://doi.org/10.12681/grsr.519

Sivignon, M., Dimitras, E., & Zombanakis, G. L. (1972). Η δημογραφική εξέλιξις της Ελλάδος, 1961-1971 [The demographic development of Greece: 1961–1971]. *Επιθεώρηση Κοινωνικών Ερευνών [Greek Review of Social Research], 13*, 72–75. https://doi.org/10.12681/grsr.492

Sotiropoulos, L. (1994). *Towards an anthropology of European Union* [Unpublished manuscript]. Cellule de prospective, European Commission.

Svoronos, N.G. (1972). *Επισκόπηση της Ελληνικής Ιστορίας* [A review of Greek History]. Themelio.

Tsakonas, D. (1944). Γεώργιος Σκληρός (Κωνσταντινίδης) [George Skliros-Konstantinidis]. *Αρχείον Κοινωνιολογίας και Ηθικής [Archive of Sociology and Ethics], 1*, 37–39.

Tsakonas, D. (1947). Εισαγωγή εις τον Νέον Ελληνισμόν [Introduction into the New Hellenism] *Αρχείον Κοινωνιολογίας και Ηθικής*, Τόμος Ι' [Archive of Sociology and Ethics, 10].

Tsakonas, D. (1970). Εισαγωγή εις την Κοινωνιολογία [Introduction to Sociology]. *Αρχείον Κοινωνιολογίας και Ηθικής*, Τόμος ΙΒ' [Archive of Sociology and Ethics], 12.

Tsakonas, D. (1974). *Κοινωνιολογική ερμηνεία του νεοελληνικού βίου: εισαγωγή εις την νεοελληνικήν κοινωνίαν*) [Sociological interpretation of modern Greek life: Introduction into modern Greek life]. Athens (unknown publisher).

Tsoukalas, C. (1969). *The Greek tragedy*. Penguin Books.

Tsoukalas, C. (2003). Η κοινωνική έρευνα πριν σαράντα χρόνια [Social research forty years ago]. In Lambiri-Dimaki J. *Κοινωνικές επιστήμες και πρωτοπορία στην Ελλάδα: 1950-1967* [Social sciences and innovation in Greece: 1950-1967] (pp. 411–420). Social Sciences Center/Gutenberg.

Vernier, B. (1981). Representation mythique du monde et domination masculine chez les Pomaques Grecs. *Επιθεώρηση Κοινωνικών Ερευνών* [Greek Review of Social Research], numéro speciale, 122–142. https://doi.org/10.12681/grsr.571

Vlachos, E. C. (1966). Εργάτες μετανάστες που επιστρέφουν από τη δυτική Ευρώπη στην Ελλάδα [Migrant workers returning from Western Europe to Greece]. *Κοινωνιολογική Σκέψη [Sociological Thought]*, *I*(1), 125–126.

Vrettos, L. (1975). Louis Vrettos papers, ACG/IA AR 5300, Box 3 SSW (ACG Archives).

CHAPTER 3

Institutionalization and Re-politicization Amid Modernization and Dependency: 1974–1990

Abstract The ending of the military dictatorship marked a paradigm shift in Greek sociology. Against the background of Greece's accession to the EC in 1981, a wider culture of challenging old orthodoxies emerged, and it became apparent to a new generation of sociologists that the modernization paradigm had run its course. Sociological analyses of Greece's failure to escape the vicious cycle of underdevelopment would have to embrace alternative explanatory models. A sociology of development focusing on dependency models (Frank, Amin) and Wallerstein's Systems Theory provided the theoretical background against which the Greek 'social asynchronisms' were investigated. The works of Filias, Tsoukalas and Mouzelis, Vergopoulos and Poulantzas are of central importance here. The present chapter records the progress made towards the institutionalization of Greek sociology following the fall of the junta and the restoration of democracy in July 1974. The year marks the re-appearance of social sciences, and a decade later, the first sociology departments are inaugurated. Greek sociology begins to be firmly established, while its Greek centeredness further contributes to a more complete understanding of contemporary Greek social reality.

Keywords Dependency • Institutionalization • *Metapolitefsi* • Underdevelopment

The Debate on the Greek Social Formation After 1974: The Turn to Dependency and Underdevelopment

The 1974 *Metapolitefsi*[1] signalled a new phase for the development of sociology in Greece. It became apparent that new conceptual tools were necessary to explain Greece's failure to avert what Tsoukalas has called 'the Greek tragedy' on the one hand and the inability of the Greek social formation to escape the fate of underdevelopment and dependence on the other. The collective trauma of the dictatorship and the subsequent transition to democracy against the background of the dramatic events in Cyprus became the basis from which novel, neo-Marxist analyses were 'launched'. Theorists like Tsoukalas and Mouzelis broke with the tradition of explanatory frameworks, mainly emanating from the Orthodox Greek Left that attributed the 1967 *coup d'état* to the intervention of the 'foreign factor' and turned to interpretations that attempted to be holistic while avoiding the 'sin of essentialism' (Mouzelis, 2010, p. 81) and which brought to the forefront issues such as class relations, the role of ideology and the breakdown of political institutions, the latter being totally unprepared to face such contingency (Manesis, 1999, pp. 37–38). Tsoukalas, for example, offers a class analysis to elucidate the advent of authoritarianism culminating in the establishment of the military junta in 1967. The pressures exerted from the lower classes on an illiberal political system kept rising after 1964. The democratization efforts of the Centre Union under Georgios Papandreou had unleashed a web of popular demands that would soon be translated into a seriously radicalized politics.

---

[1] The term has been variously translated as 'political changeover' or 'political transition' or 'polity change' and signals the period after the fall of the junta, the restoration of democracy in Greece and the foundation of the Third Republic. The efforts towards the democratization of Greek society, that is, the passage from authoritarianism to democracy, have been approached through sociology, history and political science (indicatively, see Diamantouros, 1983, pp. 52–87; Lyrintzis et al., 1996). Others (Avgeridis et al., 2015 pp. 17–18), using Bakhtin's term, view *Metapolitefsi* as a 'chronotope' denoting the inseparability of time and space, a 'starting point that allows us to reflect on the plural character of the term, that is, *Metapolitefsi* as an era, a historical period, a work in progress, a transition period defined on the basis of the expectations and planning of different subjects' (17). In creating narratives regarding an era that extends over more than forty years of Greek history, the temptation towards periodization is impossible to resist, and one of the latest ones positions the start of the period in question in the 1974 referendum about the future of monarchy in Greece and the end in another referendum that about austerity measures in 2015 (16).

It was this possibility that frightened the traditional conservative political actors, that is, the palace, the army and the conservative right, a coalition representing a bourgeoisie that clung to its 'medieval privileges' (Tsoukalas, 2020 [1969], p. 283) and which paved the road to authoritarianism (247–261). Tsoukalas' class analysis is sufficiently nuanced to include a voluntaristic element distanced from economistic and structuralist (Althusserian) views and, as Mouzelis says, to weave a totality out of the study of the specificities of the modern Greek historical formation (Mouzelis, 2010, pp. 80–81). Mouzelis, on the other hand, situates the collapse of parliamentary democracy in the 'incongruence' between the conditions that the Greek model of capital accumulation had created by the mid-1960s with the 'existing political superstructure' (Mouzelis, 1978a, p. 126). The rising social unrest especially after 1964 was an immediate effect of the 'uneven development of the forces and relations of production' (124). As he argues:

> By favoring big capital (indigenous, foreign and mixed) at the expense of the rural population, workers and also important sections of the old and new middle classes, it [the Greek model of capital accumulation] had created a level of discontent which could no longer be contained within the prevailing system of repressive parliamentarism. This system had to be either abolished or reinforced by the total removal of parliamentary rule. (126)

The system opted for the latter. On the ideological level, the fierce anticommunism already present during the interwar era was transformed into a principle on which an offensive strategy of social mobilization and social control was designed to shelter and reinforce a closed political system (Diamantouros, 1983, p. 62). For Diamantouros, the ultimate blow to the colonels came when the regime proved unable to make good on its 'promises' for liberalization. On the other hand, the pre-1967 political forces which had been silenced but apparently were undergoing a process of fermentation continued to mount the pressure under which the regime's illusive cohesion collapsed, while the regime itself retreated into the 'safe space' of repression, only to fall a few months later under the pressures of the *Polytechneion*[2] student uprising and the Cyprus crisis which the regime

---

[2] The *Polytechneion* or Polytechnic student uprising against the colonels' regime took place between 14 November and the early hours of 17 November 1973, when it ended up in bloodshed. It is one of the events that led to the fall of the regime in 1974. The other was the Cyprus crisis caused by the colonels that led to the Turkish invasion of the island.

itself had caused (85). Finally, the time factor is deemed crucial, as the relatively short duration of the regime ruled out any possibility for institutionalization and 'legitimation' of authoritarianism in Greece (86–87). The restoration of democracy brought changes that were seen by many only as an ostensible return to normalcy. Criticisms ranging from the return to power of political figures like Karamanlis who had dominated the post-war scene until 1964 to the continuing intervention of the 'foreign factor' were harnessed to prove that little, if anything, had change. Yet, long-term changes such as the rise of PA.SO.K. (Panhellenic Socialist Movement) under Andreas Papandreou into the major Opposition party, the collapse of the Centre, the abolition of monarchy and the recognition of KKE (Greek Communist Party) as a parliamentary force point to the fact that Greece had entered a new, and the most unequivocally democratic era in its history (56–57). Change during the first years of the democratization period targeted an antiquated political system, while after 1980, it was society that was perceived as antiquated and having to undergo foundational reconstruction (Mouzelis, 1986a, p. 149).

In what amounts to an epistemological break with old orthodoxies, Greek sociologists analysing the Greek social formation moved beyond the 'modernizing moment' in the development of Greek society and state. The result was a wide-angle view coupled with a historically nuanced perspective on the development of Greek capitalism, social classes and political organization. Given that 'catching up' with the West was ruled out except by way of superficial mimicry (Mouzelis, 1978a, p. 152), from the mid-1970s onwards, the discussion was embracing neo-Marxist terms such as dependency and peripheral/semi-peripherical/metropolitan distinctions. Within such framework, two approaches about Greece's path to capitalist modernity are discernible, namely, an analysis of the exploitative, neo-colonial, imperialist division of labour imposed by global capitalism and secondly the theorization of the character of the class structure within the Greek social formation. Issues of interest in the latter case involve questions about the cohesion of the dominant class in Greek society, and in case such cohesion is questioned, discussion turns to its hegemonic fractions during the different stages of Greek development or underdevelopment. Moreover, the discourse engages the degree of economic or political domination that characterizes each fraction of the dominant social class vis-à-vis the role of the state in facilitating its hegemony, thus re-politicizing the terms of the debate. Despite their differences, both approaches advocate the abandonment of the idea of a singular modernity unfolding through 'neo-evolutionist myths' (153) and the adoption of multicentred modernities.

International Capitalism as the Decisive Element in Underdevelopment: Vergopoulos and Poulantzas

In the *Agrarian Question in Greece*, Vergopoulos tries to shatter traditional illusions of modern agriculture as an 'archaic' sector (1975, p. 202) responsible for the backwardness of society as a whole and especially of the various bourgeois sectors. Such a perspective rests on the belief that the agricultural sector is unable to survive on its own; hence, the continuing demands made upon the state for substantial subsidies at the expense of the urban population. It follows that the only chance for lifting the backwardness imposed by this conjuncture is the replacement of small family landownership with a capitalist agriculture driven by profit and predicated on the liberalization of market competition (202). Such perspectives suffer from an ill-conceived role of the capitalist system. Vergopoulos turns this argumentation on its head by contending that small agricultural production, far from being a pre-capitalist remnant, is 'a form reproduced by modern capitalism and incorporated into it in an exemplary way' (207). Modern family-based agriculture does not belong to the sphere of non-capitalist activities; instead, it reveals the paradoxical face of 'a capitalism without capitalists' (207). For him, 'the greater the retreat of agrarian capitalism, the greater the incorporation of agriculture into capitalism in general' (209). Following Samir Amin but also Baran and Sweezy, Vergopoulos poses the capitalist core and periphery as forming a single space (387), while his analysis is a case in point that demonstrates the full incorporation of what we often label a pre-capitalist or semi-feudal agricultural sector into capitalism as a world system, that is, a system thriving on deformities, distortions, peculiarities and unevenness (289). One such distortion that became more apparent during the 1980s is what Vergopoulos labels as 'enrichment without modernization' (1986, p. 70), a process that thrust Greek society into consumerism at the expense of much-needed economic and political reconstruction. Another distortion relates to a form of 'state totalitarianism', a term that Vergopoulos uses to castigate the hyper-growth of the Greek state which in turn expresses the internalization of the conditions of international dependence. The major class conflict arises between those strata related directly or indirectly to the bureaucratic machinery of the state and the private, entrepreneurial sector allied with petty bourgeois and commercial strata (1978, pp. 20–25). This class schema has received various criticisms. In an important contribution to the sociology of underdevelopment, Petmesidou-Tsoulouvi (1987) argues that the real class antagonism in Greece is between those who have access in one way or another to state mechanisms, and, as a result, they are able to extract not only an income from them but also acquire significant and sudden wealth and those who are excluded from such mechanisms. Finally, the efficient operation of the Greek state in the framework of global capitalism is interrogated (Petmezidou-Tsoulouvi, 1984, pp. 24–25). Apart from the theoretical debts to Amin, Vergopoulos' analysis also draws upon Wallerstein's World Systems Theory, as he seems to adopt the perspective of global capitalism as a system of commodity chains binding all nations through a nexus of domination-exploitation relations, thus focusing less on the internal workings of capitalism within a particular society.

Poulantzas' attempt to outline the conditions of 'dependent industrialization' has defined the discussion of Greece's underdevelopment or uneven development from the start (see also Chap. 4). Such conditions include the capital's continuing relegation of lower-level functions to peripheral countries or the flight of profits from the country, the export of migrant labour and finally the low levels of technology and productivity, thus perpetuating underdevelopment (1975, pp. 13–18). The Greek dictatorship favoured the path of dependent development mainly because of the major force it represented, that is, a dominant comprador capital (12 and 19–20). In the end, dependent industrialization, in which the role of the state as constitutive of the relations of production,[3] produced a 'disequilibrium in the power bloc', led to the birth of a domestic bourgeoisie whose frustrated demands for liberalization ultimately rendered the regime vulnerable to the point of its own ruin (41–45). Here too, the role of a global capitalist system haunts the analysis throughout.

Vassilis Filias: Social Classes in Underdevelopment

Among the first to contribute to the debate within Greece was Vassilis Filias whose commitment to a Weberian interpretive schema leads him to the conclusion that underdevelopment owes to the absence of an

[3] This theme is discussed at length in Poulantzas' last work, *State, Power, Socialism* (1978).

'authentic' bourgeoisie (Filias, 1974). He thus attributes Greece's persistent uneven development to an oligarchy of plutocrats (landowners and diaspora bourgeoisie) motivated by capital accumulation and conspicuous consumption mentalities and practices which gradually are projected to the rest of the population. Such pre-bourgeois groups are responsible for the chronic inequality in income distribution, the low growth and competitiveness rates.

Constantinos Tsoukalas: Periphery and Underdevelopment—From Class Structure to Class Relations

Tsoukalas' early work on *Dependence and reproduction* has become an obligatory reference point for all subsequent theorizing on the making of the Greek class structure and the relations that characterize the various social classes. His theorization of the antinomies of the Greek class structure in the decades (1830–1922) that shaped the Greek social formation is of utmost theoretical and political importance for three reasons: first, as a Marxist approach that transcends the economism/essentialism[4] of previous Marxist theorizations that adopted a form/content distinction[5] and its implications about systems as 'totalities', thus failing to appreciate the complexity of other elements and the way these elements interact to produce a concrete social structure. Secondly, as a successful attempt to 'bring the state back in' through a position of 'relative autonomy' reminiscent of Poulantzas' (Tsoukalas, 1983, pp. 332–335) but also of Marx's earlier notion of the 'parasite state' run by a hierarchy of unproductive bureaucracy. As Tsoukalas states, 'the volume of state bureaucracy was decisive if compared to the evolution of other fractions of the domestic bourgeois class, not only from the perspective of the quantitative composition of the active population but also of its ideological impact' (2006 [1975], p. 215). This superstructure is analogous exclusively to a 'political society' rather than to a 'civil society' (215). Finally, Tsoukalas' work is groundbreaking in that it interrogates the function of the ideological state apparatuses (ISA) within a dependency framework, a function that produces distortions and asymmetries in the

---

[4] See Marcuse (1968, pp. 43–87). Lukács also adopts this view in his *History and class consciousness*.

[5] For a discussion of the concepts in relation to Marxist theories of the state, see Lagoumitzi (1985).

making of the Greek social class structure. Therefore, the hypertrophy of the state apparatus leads to 'backwardness' and capital accumulation of proportions that attribute to the state a 'broker' role. Once again, those who have access to the state and those who do not are sharply distinguished into two different social strata (Tsoukalas, 1983, p. 252–253, p. 323). Beyond this initial observation, one should be mindful about how relations between them are theorized. A common approach is through 'reciprocal' and 'mutually beneficial' clientelist relationships. In a very instructive conclusive section, Tsoukalas demonstrates the superficiality of the client-patron discourses that have dominated numerous debates (1983, pp. 322–343). Prophetically, he concludes that 'even today, the commitment to education,[6] the rather quick decision to turn to migration, the intense tendency towards nonproductive activities and a fanatical worship for antiquity constitute an inextricable part of the Greek collective consciousness' (1976, p. 576).

Nicos Mouzelis and the Capitalist Mode of Production as an Enclave Form

Mouzelis opens a new seam of concepts and ideas that challenge discourses that attribute Greece's uneven capitalist development to the simple existence or absence of particular social classes and practices. His analysis will not be inflected by functionalist or neo-Marxist reductionisms. On the one hand, functionalist approaches are rejected because they substitute class analysis with an analysis of social stratification 'measuring various distributions (income, mobility) or the attitudes of entrepreneurs, workers, peasants etc., in order to assess their degree of modernity' (1978b, p. 473). On the other, neo-Marxist approaches stressing the 'relative autonomy' of the state avoid economistic reductionisms, but they succumb to a different type of reductionism by refusing to acknowledge to political and economic phenomena the same ontological status and therefore 'according the 'materiality' of the economic sphere a superior explanatory status' (Mouzelis, 1986b, p. 201). After more than a century-old attempt to develop, Greece, as a late modernizer, was still portraying the classical features of an 'underdeveloped' economy, that is, '(a) a more disarticulated capitalist economy, (b) a more authoritarian polity, (c) and a more formalistic/disorientating culture' (Mouzelis, 1996, p. 220):

---

[6] Elsewhere, Tsoukalas uses the term 'over-education' (Tsoukalas, 1976, p. 422).

A look at the growth of the Greek economy, for instance, will show that, despite the serious development of the industrial sector during the 1960s, large sectors have remained both in industry and agriculture where small-commodity production still prevails, and where the links with the 'modern industrial' sector are clearly negative—meaning that these sectors, without being destroyed, are permanently kept in a depressed, vegetative state while their resources, through a variety of mechanisms, are systematically transferred to the technologically advanced sector and abroad. It is precisely in this sense that, in Greece and in other underdeveloped countries, the articulation between capitalist and non-capitalist modes of production is negative. (Mouzelis, 1978b, p. 478)

Thus, 'in social formations where the capitalist mode of production is peripheral, its dominance takes an enclave form' (65) and co-exists along pre-capitalist modes of production such as small landowning interests and which in the case of Greece have demonstrated an admirable persistence. This explains to some degree why the passage from patronage to class politics has never been completed. Finally, under such circumstances, the precarity of capital more often than not resorts to '*dependent integration and dictatorial exclusion*' (480 [original emphasis]) of the masses as the only paths to political incorporation/exclusion. Mouzelis' work, through its new, dynamic theorization of the relationship between class structure and collective action was already reorienting comparative historical sociology in Greece.

INSTITUTIONAL DEVELOPMENTS: 1974–1990

With the fall of the colonels' regime, the chair of sociology in the University of Athens was occupied after remaining vacant for forty years. Sociology was only a subject taught at the university level by G. Kavvadias whose study on the *Sarakatsani, a Greek pastoral community* (1991) is considered a classic text in sociology and ethnography. Another influential figure who was appointed at the University of Athens to teach civil law was G. Michailidis-Nouaros. Yet, his study of the survival of matriarchal institutions in his native Karpathos linked him to folklore and ethnography. One could claim that the 'take-off' for sociology in Greece arrived with the sociology departments in two major universities. The first public university department of sociology was established at Panteion University in 1984 (then named Panteion Higher School of Political Sciences) and was followed by a new department, in Crete (Rethymno) in 1987/1988. Against a background of growing politicization of debates relating to the nature and the role of the public university during the years of the socialist government's hegemony, it seems that the intellectual forces at universities acquired a certain 'relative autonomy'. For example, the 'moving forces' behind the effort towards the institutionalization of sociology at Panteion were V. Filias and D.G. Tsaoussis who had in mind 'the free and detached quest for truth and the nature of things and relations between them' under the prospect of European integration (Tsaoussis, 1993, p. 62). Related to the scientific (empirical research) profile of sociology was Tsaoussis' belief, expressed in an interview by *Diavazo* magazine, in the creation of 'a body of new sociologists to be recruited by the public sector as head analysts of the social dimensions of various social practices and political decisions' (1985, p. 69).

The early days of the department at Panteion were marked by the urgent need for textbooks in Greek. Sociology professors like D.G. Tsaoussis and N. Tatsis were pioneers in this gigantic effort. D.G. Tsaoussis' translations of T.B. Bottomore's *Sociology*, Lienhardt's *Social Anthropology* as well as works that he authored such as *A user's dictionary of sociology* (1984) and *The society of humans: Introduction to sociology* (1985b) were instrumental at a time when even basic textbooks were absent. N. Tatsis' *The instruction of sociological theory* (1986) was intended to have not only an educational but also a pedagogic function. As such, it aimed at grounding thinking about society and its problems on a solid rationalist basis (1986, pp. 9–10). Moreover, in the field of the sociology of the family, L. Moussourou, apart from her own numerous works on women and the family, translated A. Michel's *Sociology of family and marriage* (1985). In May of the same year, *Diavazo* magazine published a special issue on *Sociology* including an interview with D.G. Tsaoussis which addressed the major issues related to the study of sociology in Greece in secondary and higher educational institutions (Tsaoussis, 1985a, pp. 66–71). At the end of the decade, the publication of the *Sociology Almanac* in the same year (1989) under the editorship of Milios and Stamatis could be seen as the first effort towards a public sociology aiming at forging links between social scientists and a wider audience.

The National Centre of Social Research continued its empirical and theoretical work. One of the monographs it published was by Terlexis (1975) on a structural-functional understanding of the political system. According to Gabriel Almond, then fellow at the University of Cambridge and distinguished political scientist who prefaced Terlexis' book, the work is praised for its synthetic value along with the nearly impossible task of effectively 'transferring these concepts in any foreign language for the first time' (Almond in Terlexis, 1975, p. xv). Terlexis' contribution to sociology continued through the founding of the journal *To Vima ton Koinonikon Epistimon* (Social Science Tribune) in 1989 as well as the Social Science and Opinion Poll Workshop at the University of Thessaly where sociology has been introduced as a subject since 1992. In the desert-like environment of Greek publications in sociology written either by Greek sociologists or available in translation, the urgent matter to make the discipline known and available to the Greek public was also covered by Filias (1977). With a two-volume work on social systems, he made valuable contributions with a discussion of social thought prior to sociology (from Locke and Rousseau to utopian socialists and Marx) before explaining further (Filias, 1978) the Asiatic mode of production, the Greek city-state, feudalism and the transition to capitalism. Such works served as textbooks in the newly founded sociology department at Panteion University.

Theoretical investigations examined the scope and boundaries of sociology, often providing astute theoretical reconstructions. Illustrative here are the 1970s contributions of Yiorgos Veltsos. Even as Veltsos himself was shaping the sociological discourse in the mid-1970s, it became apparent that no robust features were aimed to be assigned to sociology. Before entering post-modernism, Veltsos' keen sense for the factors of indeterminacy in sociology made a sustained attempt to defend sociology by rethinking ways to absorb indeterminacy's multiple blows to claims of logical and empirical certainty. Thus, if the focus on language and society (Veltsos, 1976a) leans prima facie towards language rather than society, while it nonetheless contains a sympathetic parallelism between Poulantzas' state as structure (see also Veltsos, 1976b, pp. 70–78, for a review of Poulantzas' *Political power and social classes*) and language as a structure, as well as nuanced (and groundbreaking for the then Greek public) reconstructions of Marx's categories through language, it is the book on indeterminacy (Veltsos, 1981) that pushes indeterminacy towards sociology's terrain rather than the reverse. Being among the first to theorize Marx in terms of *Darstellung* within the Althusserian model (rather than the Hegelian exposition of concepts that would mark Psychopedis' approach), Veltsos displays in pictorially evocative language its relation to sociology:

When we say that the relation of social psychology with sociology is *structural*, we mean that the social element, namely the "subject-matter" of sociology, exists and acts as *cause* and within socio-psychological phenomena. It acts, therefore, like their "concept" (*Darstellung*) or as an immanent in them structure. This means that it does not absorb these phenomena, nor subsumes them under its all-powerfulness in some imperialist sociologism, but, rather, "baptizes" them in "light", determining their specific weight, like the way Marx wrote about economic phenomena. (1981, p. 76 [original emphasis])

In this sense, social psychology becomes a special branch of sociology and its homology with Marxism. To substantiate further this claim, he draws on what is still, one should note, an insufficiently appreciated sociological thought of Georges Gurvitch. Veltsos (following Tsaoussis, 1976) retrieves Gurvitch's visionary 'sociology in depth' (*sociologie en profondeur*) (Gurvitch, 1950, pp. 49–97). Interestingly enough, Tsaoussis' focus on Gurvitch may have to do with the latter's systematic layering of sociology's interest in social reality and its dissection into levels of social morphology, social organizations, social roles, values and beliefs, among others. The profundity in question reflects the levels' recalcitrance to sociological research and conceptualization. Despite this accommodation to indeterminacy, Gurvitch's architectonic of sociality's classification retains as foci the collective and individual sources of freedom (1976, p. 61). It is an impressive system, for Tsaoussis, built around an intentionally indeterminate core. Through this lens, Veltsos attempts to consider sociology (and retain its validity) along two different levels of explanatory abstraction: one that renders sociology tuned to the search for a theory of society capable of generalizations based on cause-effect determinism and a latent one that subjects causality to interpretive schemes conscious of probabilistically wrought social relations (p. 178). (We may suggest that this is a reconfiguration of the *Methodenstreit* between nomothetic and ideographic sciences.) It is the last claim to hermeneutic openness that Veltsos' non-sociology will later radicalize (see Chap. 5).

The two-volume treatise on the sociology of institutions (Veltsos, 1977, 1979) comprises textbook material but tinged with Veltsos' admitted paradox: a didactic sociology book that begins with the renunciation of sociology (1977, p. 9). Nonetheless, Veltsos (168–173) discusses Castoriadis' idea of the 'imaginary institution of society' (for the great relevance and contribution of Castoriadis to Greek sociology, see Chap. 4).

One last institutional development characteristic of the period we are examining was the *Association of Greek Sociologists* which was formed in 1983. This was soon incorporated into the ISA (*International Sociological Association*) and started publishing *Sociogram*, its main journal. With time, the association became less academically oriented, turning to the protection of the rights of sociologists in secondary education and social service positions. It asserted nevertheless the growing interest in sociology as a discipline that was gaining status and power in the Greek academic world.

References

Avgeridis, M., Gazi, E., & Kornetis, K. (2015). Introduction. In M.E. Avgeridis, E. Gazi & K. Kornetis (Eds.), Μεταπολίτευση: Η Ελλάδα στο μεταίχμιο δύο αιώνων [Metapolitefsi: Greece at the threshold of two centuries] (pp. 11–26). Themelio.

Diamantouros, N. (1983). Η μετάβαση από το αυταρχικό στο δημοκρατικό καθεστώς στην Ελλάδα [The transition from an authoritarian to a democratic regime in Greece]. Επιθεώρηση Κοινωνικών Ερευνών [Greek Review of Social Research], 49, 52–87. https://doi.org/10.12681/grsr.181

Filias, V. (1974). Κοινωνία και εξουσία στην Ελλάδα, Η νόθα αστικοποίηση: 1800-1864 [Society and domination in Greece: The fake embourgeoisement]. Synchrona Keimena.

Filias, V. (1977). Κοινωνικά συστήματα [Social Systems]. Livanis and Nea Synora editions.

Filias, V. (1978). Κοινωνικά συστήματα [Social Systems]. Livanis and Nea Synora editions.

Gurvitch, G. (1950). *La vocation actuelle de la sociologue. Vers une sociologie différentielle*. Presses Universitaires de France.

Kavvadias, G. (1991). Σαρακατσάνοι, μια Ελληνική ποιμενική κοινωνία [Sarakatsani, A Greek pastoral society]. Bratzioti.

Lagoumitzi, G. (1985). Formalism and economism: Modern theories of the state. *Syntagma*, *1*, 13–41.

Lyrintzis, C., Nikolakopoulos, I. & Sotiropoulos, D. (Eds.) (1996). Κοινωνία και πολιτική: Όψεις της Γ΄ Ελληνικής δημοκρατίας [Society and politics: Facets of the Third Hellenic Republic]. Themelio.

Manesis, A. (1999). Ο εύκολος βιασμός της νομιμότητας και η δύσκολη νομιμοποίηση της βίας [The effortless rape of legality and the difficult legitimation of violence]. In G. Athanasatou, A. Rigos, & S. Seferiadis (Eds.), Η δικτατορία 1967-1973: Πολιτικές πρακτικές-ιδεολογικός λόγος-αντίσταση [The dictatorship 1967-1974: Political practice-ideological discourse-resistance] (pp. 37–52). Kastaniotis.

Marcuse, H. (1968). The concept of essence. In *Negations: Essays in critical theory* (pp. 43–87). Penguin Press.
Milios, J., & Stamatis, G. (Eds.). (1989). *Sociology almanac*. Exantas.
Mouzelis, N. P. (1978a). *Modern Greece: Facets of underdevelopment*. Macmillan.
Mouzelis, N. (1978b). Class and clientelistic politics: The case of Greece. *The Sociological Review, 26*(3), 471–497.
Mouzelis, N. (1986a). Παράδοση και αλλαγή στην ελληνική πολιτική: Από τον Ελευθέριο Βενιζέλο στον Ανδρέα Παπανδρέου [Tradition and change in Greek politics: From Eleftherios Venizelos to Andreas Papandreou]. In (unknown editor), Η Ελλάδα σε εξέλιξη [La Grèce en Movement], [Special issue] *Les Temps Modernes*, 473 (pp. 149–162). Exantas.
Mouzelis, N. P. (1986b). *Politics in the semi-periphery: Early parliamentarism and late industrialization in the Balkans and Latin America*. Macmillan.
Mouzelis, N. (1996). The concept of modernization: Its relevance for Greece. *Journal of Modern Greek Studies, 14*(2), 215–227. https://doi.org/10.1353/mgs.1996.0028
Mouzelis, N. (2010). Παγκοσμιοποίηση, μύθοι και πραγματικότητες [Globalization, myths and realities]. In M. Kousis, M. Samatas & S. Koniordos (Eds.). *Εξουσία και κοινωνία: Δωρήματα στον Κωνσταντίνο Τσουκαλά* [Power and society: Offerings to Constantine Tsoukalas], (pp. 80–84). Kastaniotis.
Petmesidou-Tsoulouvi, M. (1987). *Κοινωνικές τάξεις και μηχανισμοί κοινωνικής αναπαραγωγής* [Social classes and mechanisms of social reproduction]. Exantas.
Petmezidou-Tsoulouvi, M. (1984). Προσεγγίσεις στο θέμα της υπανάπτυξης του Ελληνικού κοινωνικού σχηματισμού: Μια κριτική θεώρηση [Approaches to the subject of underdevelopment of the Greek social formation: A critical perspective]. *Σύγχρονα Θέματα [Contemporary Issues], 22*, 12–29.
Poulantzas, N. (1975). *The crisis of the dictatorships: Portugal, Spain*. New Left Books.
Tatsis, N. (1986). *Η διδασκαλία της κοινωνιολογικής θεωρίας* [The instruction of sociological theory]. Gutenberg.
Terlexis, P. (1975). *Το πολιτικό σύστημα. Κοινωνιολογική θεώρηση της πολιτικής ζωής* [The political system. Sociological theorization of political life] (with preface by Gabriel A. Almond). National Centre of Social Research.
Tsaoussis, D. (1976). Ο Ζ. Γκυρβίτς και η κοινωνονιολογία του (G. Gurvitch and his sociology). In G. Gurvitch, *Μελέτες για τις κοινωνικές τάξεις* [Studies on social classes]. D. Tsaousis (Ed.) (pp. 11–66) (M. Lykoudi, Trans.). Gutenberg. (Original work published 1963).
Tsaoussis, D. G. (1984). *Χρηστικό λεξικό κοινωνιολογίας* [A user's dictionary of sociology]. Gutenberg.
Tsaoussis, D. G. (1985a). Interview. *Diavazo, 119*, 66–71.
Tsaoussis, D. G. (1985b). *Κοινωνία του ανθρώπου: Εισαγωγή στη κοινωνιολογία* [The society of humans: Introduction to sociology]. Gutenberg.

Tsaoussis, D. G. (1993). *Το Ελληνικό πανεπιστήμιο στο κατώφλι του 21ου αιώνα: Ζητήματα εκπαιδευτικής πολιτικής* [The Greek university at the threshold of the 21st century: Issues of educational policy]. Gutenberg.

Tsoukalas, C. (1976). Some aspects of "over-education" in modern Greece. *Annals of the New York Academy of Sciences, 268,* 418–428.

Tsoukalas, C. (1983). *Κοινωνική ανάπτυξη και κράτος: Η συγκρότηση του δημόσιου χώρου στην Ελλάδα* [Social development and state: The making of the public sphere in Greece]. Themelio.

Tsoukalas, C. (2006). *Εξάρτηση και αναπαραγωγή: Ο κοινωνικός ρόλος των εκπαιδευτικών μηχανισμών στην Ελλάδα, 1830-1922* [Dependence and Reproduction: The social role of educational institutions in Greece, 1830-1922] (6th ed.) Themelio. (Original work published 1975).

Tsoukalas, C. (2020). *Η ελληνική τραγωδία* [The Greek tragedy]. Patakis (Original work published 1969).

Veltsos, G. (1976a). *Κοινωνία και γλώσσα (για την αμίλητη και τη μιλημένη γλώσσα)* [Society and language on the unspoken and spoken language]. Papazisis.

Veltsos, G. (1976b). *Κείμενα πολιτικής (και) κοινωνιολογίας* [Essays in politics (and) sociology]. Papazisis.

Veltsos, G. (1977). *Κοινωνιολογία των θεσμών Ι. Ο θεσμικός λόγος και η εξουσία* [Sociology of institutions, I. Institutional reason and authority]. Papazisis.

Veltsos, G. (1979). *Κοινωνιολογία των θεσμών II. Οικογένεια και φαντασιακές σχέσεις* [Sociology of institutions, I. The family and imaginary relations]. Papazisis.

Veltsos, G. (1981). *Οι απροσδιόριστοι παράγοντες. Δοκίμιο δομικής κοινωνικής ψυχολογίας* [The indeterminate factors. Essay on structural social psychology]. Papazisis.

Vergopoulos, K. (1975). *Το αγροτικό ζήτημα στην Ελλάδα: Το πρόβλημα της κοινωνικής ενσωμάτωσης της γεωργίας* [The agrarian question in Greece: The problem of the social incorporation of agriculture]. Exantas.

Vergopoulos, K. (1978). *Κράτος και οικονομική πολιτική στον 19ο αιώνα* [State and social policy in the 19th century]. Exantas.

Vergopoulos, K. (1986). Οικονομική κρίση και εκσυγχρονισμός στην Ελλάδα και στον ευρωπαϊκό νότο [Economic crisis and modernization in Greece and the European south]. In *Η Ελλάδα σε εξέλιξη* [La Grece en movement] [Special issue] *Les Temps Modernes* (473, pp. 61–105). Exantas.

CHAPTER 4

Boundary Challenges from Abroad and from Neighbouring Disciplines

Abstract Accounts of sociology in Greece (regardless of scope) give little attention to Cornelius Castoriadis and Nicos Poulantzas. Usually, the argument invoked is that the bulk of their intellectual life and contributions is of French origin. Particularly for Castoriadis, the unmistakable sociological aspects of his thought recede before philosophy and political theory. This chapter rectifies this appraisal and shows that in the case of Castoriadis the sociological current of his thought is at least as prominent as the aforementioned two and along with Poulantzas' political sociology their interventions, lectures and impact in Greece provide sufficient and valid ground for a relevant re-classification. Moreover, the chapter makes a strong case for the consideration of Panagiotis Kondylis' *magnum opus*, *The Political and Man*, which is, essentially, a powerful engagement with classical and contemporary sociological theory that enables Kondylis to appreciate sociology's validity but also to build a conceptual tier underneath it, namely, social ontology. The chapter concludes with Psychopedis' normative interdisciplinary research programme that accommodated sociological theory to epistemology.

Keywords Castoriadis • Disciplinary boundaries • Kondylis • Poulantzas • Psychopedis

'Sociology in Greece': Prolegomena on Re-classification Issues

Symptomatic of classification challenges in accounts of Greek sociology are the cases of Cornelius Castoriadis (1922–1997), Nicos Poulantzas (1936–1979) and Nicos Mouzelis. Illustrative here is Kyrtsis' remark: 'Important Greek social scientists such as Castoriadis and Poulantzas, and Mouzelis, were born and brought up in Greece but made their careers abroad' (1998, p. 322 n1).[1] To complicate matters further, the canonical three-volume work by Lambiri-Dimaki on *Sociology in Greece Today* (see Chap. 6) which includes samples of work from 113 sociologists from 1959 to 2000 has no reference to Castoriadis and Poulantzas but includes Mouzelis, featuring as representative of his sociology work published when he was part of the British academia. Such asymptotic accounts are not altogether unwarranted given the global networking of sociological labour and the tendency of Greek sociologists to pursue career opportunities abroad. What emerges, however, is a paradoxical omission caught between career trajectories and formal education criteria in sociology. Helpful in this direction is Kokosalakis' claim:

> Some [Greek sociologists] stayed abroad and became distinguished international names in sociology such as C.Castoriadis, N. Poulantzas, N.Mouzelis and many others. It is no accident, of course, that almost invariably they were Marxists and it is not accident that their ideas and writings influenced significantly Marxist sociological thought and sociology generally in Greece from 1974 onwards. (1998, p. 330)

As we shall see later, Mouzelis became quickly housed under Greek sociology's umbrella, mainly due to his later writings in Greek (see Chaps. 5 and 6) and the work on populism which was directly relevant to a sociology of Greece (as seen in Chap. 3), while Castoriadis' and Poulantzas' affiliation to Greek sociology remains blurred and contested. Issues of

---

[1] In another apostrophe, Kyrtsis writes: 'French intellectuals of Greek origin, like Nicos Poulantzas and Cornelius Castoriadis, who gained contact with the Greek public after the abolition of the dictatorship, and Nicos Mouzelis' role as a distinguished scholar at the London School of Economics where many Greek social scientists studied, have both exercised a visible impact on the younger generation' (1996, p. 11). We shall see later in this chapter that for scholars in Greece and abroad, Poulantzas and Castoriadis are also considered Greek intellectuals.

influence in Greece seem to be elided from accounts of the formative decades of sociology in Greece. These treat Castoriadis' and Poulantzas' impacts in Greece as isolated episodes, leaving unaccounted the substantive sociological debates that inform their work as well as their own entanglement with Greece and its contemporary intellectual life. This lacuna in hitherto accounts of sociology in Greece risks becoming a stagnant handicap if not urgently reappraised.

Castoriadis and Poulantzas' writings in Greek, the continuing rehabilitation of their thought by Greek epigones (as well as their standing contact with Greece's intellectual niche), but more importantly the substantive sociological issues they grappled with, can reinstall their profiles into Greek sociology, thus enriching the discipline's intellectual capital in Greece. Thus, this chapter aims to persuade sceptics against the hesitation to include such important thinkers in accounts of sociology in Greece. The prime competitor for such appropriation of Castoriadis and Poulantzas in its own history and institutional development is France. Yet even recent accounts of French sociology (e.g. Masson & Schrecker, 2016) do not include reference to their work.[2] While both Castoriadis and Poulantzas built their careers in France (politically adverse reasons and ideological disillusionment with the Stalinist stamp of Communism in Greece led both thinkers to seek intellectual fruition in France), their intellectual ties with Greece and Greek sociology call for re-classification and sociological repatriation. Four reasons can be adduced to support this claim: (a) lectures and talks in Greek given in Greece, (b) writings in Greek, (c) influence on Greek sociology and (d) visibility on the Greek media.

This chapter also addresses the influence and relevance for sociology of two prolific Greek scholars whose thought flourished in Germany, but both constitute an important asset for Greek sociology. We concentrate on Panagiotis Kondylis' *The Political and Man*, a work of sustained and deep engagement with sociology, and we conclude with remarks on the contribution to the formation of normative issues in sociology by Kosmas

---

[2] Somewhat different is the case of Nicos Mouzelis who figures in accounts of British sociology (Scott, 2020). Yet as we shall address in the next chapters, Mouzelis' work is considered to represent Greek sociology too. In fact, Lambiri-Dimaki suggests that those considered to cultivate Greek sociology extend beyond those sociologists based at 'universities or colleges' in Greece but also those, like Mouzelis as she mentions, that 'work abroad, but are active in Greece as well and that in their studies they address issues about Greek society' (2000, p. 134). We find no reason why this category could not stretch to the past to include Castoriadis and Poulantzas.

Psychopedis and the *Axiologika* journal. The issue of interdisciplinary cross-fertilizing is by no means completed with the theorists addressed here. It will reemerge in the next chapters as an alignment of sociology in Greece with the burgeoning climate of border-crossing among disciplines but also as an index of a prematurely diluted sociological paradigm formation in Greece.

Cornelius Castoriadis: Sociological Contribution and Legacy in Greece

As these lines are written, Greece celebrates 100 years from Castoriadis' birth in 1922. An opportunity thus arises to rehabilitate part of Castoriadis' work in the history and development of sociology in Greece. To be sure, Castoriadis never considered himself a sociologist. His background and practice in psychoanalysis and his preoccupation with the ontological foundations of the social were formulated as part of a philosophical discourse with the project of autonomy as its guiding thread.[3] However, three reasons can be adduced for Castoriadis' relevance to sociology: (a) a genealogical approach that traces his first writings in Greece back to 1944 that are published in a sociology journal; (b) the substantive sociological dimension of his magnum opus, *The Imaginary Institution of Society* (1975); and (c) the influence that sociological aspects of his thought exerted on Greek academia during his lifetime and since his death.

Associated with the *Socialisme ou Barbarie* (1949–1966) socialist group in France, Castoriadis' thought impacted social theory in significant ways. He became an iconic thinker in radical social theory for the journal *Thesis Eleven* (see Arnason & Beilharz, 1997; Beilharz, 2020). Critical Theory's initial reception of Castoriadis' views on imaginary societal ontogenesis was voiced with criticism almost concurrently in Germany (Habermas, 1987b, pp. 327–335) and in Greece (the 1985 Castoriadis ERT filmed discussion to be addressed shortly). In philosophy too his work gained attention, albeit at different degrees of sympathetic criticism (see Rorty, 1991, pp. 177–192; Heller, 1989).

---

[3] Castoriadis' thought works like a labyrinth as his work resists classification in any single knowledge domain (Dosse, 2015, p. 10). Dosse (367–368) connects Castoriadis to the sociological and ethnographic circle in France around Olivier Fressard. In Germany too Castoriadis' work is taught in sociology modules (545, n.76).

The 1944 Writings

Young Castoriadis' 1944 writings reflect his involvement with the newly founded journal *Archive of Sociology and Ethics*.[4] Locating its genesis in the debris of the then ongoing warfare, Castoriadis all too quickly adheres to a cultural-lag enunciated notion of societal crisis the dynamo of which is a technological impetus inversely related to a 'theoretical and practical collapse of society' (2014a, p. 25). In his 1988 addition to this passage, Castoriadis slightly revises the source of social crisis, claiming now that it resides in the current imaginary signification that subsumes technology to the rational mastery of 'nature and humanity' (26). This admission brings him close to Weber's disenchantment thesis and to all subsequent narratives of instrumental rationality's grip over autonomy and authenticity (as in Heidegger).

Through this diagnostic and practical lens, Castoriadis summons to duty 'the responsible representatives of all intellectual cultivation' hoping to ensure a broad spectrum of mutual coordination of such intellectuals with 'politicians and sociologists' adding though that 'such distinctions are schematic' (27). Such hesitation to subscribe to clear-cut distinctions across disciplines may account for the fact that his later work can be accommodated under social theory, although it may just as easily qualify as philosophy, sociological theory and political science with strong bearing on psychoanalysis too.

For the mission of the journal, Castoriadis (27–28) sees the imperative to clarify the scope and nature of social science research and to develop it accordingly. These goals reflect the journal's contribution to the theoretical analysis of 'social life'. For the practical desideratum of specifying concrete paths of action, any such possibilities are identified in the economic sphere's material conditions, in civil society and in the active attainment of citizens' political power, while on the level of 'pure civilization' the aim at a general enhancement of intellectual capabilities. Key adjunct to this mission is the retrieval of the ontological foundation of social life, a project that, for Castoriadis, has been brushed aside by the quest for social scientific validity. Coupled to the deontological call for practical autonomy, the journal should cultivate the 'reunification of theory with action' (29). In

[4] All in-text citations from the 1944 original writings (Castoriadis, 1944a, 1944b, 1944c) reflect the respective English translations.

what is a Kantian-Marxian synthesis of theory and practice, Castoriadis sees theory's focus on action both as its subject-matter and as its Janus-faced other: after all, theory is a practical activity serving human agency. Practice, for its part, is conscious (hence theoretical) of its goals, and the correctness of its purposes presupposes 'the correct theory' (29). Finally, the journal should extend the wedlock of theory and practice to 'Greek reality' attentive to 'Greek social scientists' in light of what Castoriadis already discerns in 1944 as 'the global distribution of labor' (30). Such anchoring in modern Greece requires recourse to 'classical antiquity' and 'contemporary science' abroad (31) in what, according to Castoriadis' judgement, is an underdeveloped society.

The other key 1944 text is Castoriadis' commentary on his translation of Part I ('Methodological Foundations') of Max Weber's *Economy and Society*. Following a short introductory note, the translation is supplemented by dense notes that elaborate Weber's observations around a sociological and philosophical architectonic that bears largely on neo-Kantian philosophy of consciousness. In the section on the theory of the social sciences (2014b), Castoriadis digs deeper into the neo-Kantian epistemology[5] and its focus on the logic of the categories (e.g. Emil Lask) as well as its relations to types of judgements. Science (including social science) begins with the critical analysis of the problem of knowledge in a transcendental framework. For the young Castoriadis, 'Even skepticism is dogmatism, in the sense that skepticism does not acknowledge that the possibility of any cognitive problem presupposes the possibility of cognition, and that consequently the solution which it gives to the problem contradicts the conditions for the possibility of the problem' (2014b, p. 49). While placed within Lask's problem of knowledge and the construction of categories (rightly identified by Kranaki (1944) as the desideratum for a

---

[5] Meletopoulos (2008, pp. 54–57) confirms the neo-Kantian influence that emanated from young Castoriadis' participation in the K. Tsatsos university tutorials under the neo-Kantian mind-set that had also shaped Kanellopoulos' intellectual circles and the Heidelberg School (see Chap. 1). Meletopoulos rightly quotes the following passage: 'It suffices to observe here that this is the decisive point from which the internal coherence of Kantianism leads to Hegelianism; Kantianism remains incomplete without Hegelianism and Hegelianism without Kantianism remains unfounded' (Castoriadis, 2014b, p. 45). Yet in the 1988 annotations, Castoriadis writes that given the omission of the role of the imaginary in the early texts, his ideas 'on the complementarity of Kantianism (criticism) and Hegelianism (universalism) [...] do not coincide with the ideas I began articulating after 1965' (42).

deduction of sociology's categories), Castoriadis (53) repels obliquely, but bitingly, Durkheim's realism of social facts and the distinction between the normal and the pathological. In the generously provided notes to the Weber translation, Castoriadis makes sharp exegetical remarks on Weber's key concepts that could further reveal his own debt to neo-Kantianism and to the role of indeterminacy that a science of society should consider. Added annotations in 1988 reveal revisions mostly in the direction of viewing the socio-historical phenomena in terms of the 'world's imaginary significations'.

The Imaginary Institution of Society (1975)

Castoriadis' *magnum opus* exerts, as we have already intimated, a continuous impact in the formation of international debates in sociology and social theory. In Greece it has attained an iconic status. Appearing in Greek in 1978 (with the translation approved by Castoriadis himself, including a note by him at the end of the book about the glossary[6]), it quickly became a key reference point for Greek intellectuals in philosophy and social theory. Given the work's synthetic scope, originality and depth, this is hardly surprising. What concerns us here is not so much a synopsis of Castoriadis' multi-layered argument, but rather the sociological relevance of the book, which enables us to counter previous accounts of sociology in Greece and to consider Castoriadis' work to bear on sociology. Starting, therefore, from the last pages of *The Imaginary Institution of Society*, it is interesting to note that apart from revisiting Marx, Castoriadis concludes with explicit caveats on Max Weber and with a hardly difficult-to-miss consideration of Durkheim. Regarding Weber, Castoriadis places the methodology of the 'ideal type' at a level of abstraction that is premised on the primordiality of society's imaginary significations, which the ideal-type must for analytical purposes 'solidify' in mental abstractions. Yet in the sociological core in Castoriadis' ontology of the social imaginary, the impact and relevance of Durkheim are obliquely acknowledged despite the polemics:

---

[6]Castoriadis (1978, pp. 519–526) touches here on the poverty of demotic Greek and its defenders and proposes various models for enriching the conceptual accuracy of language in philosophy and in the social sciences. This is an issue that is pertinent to the 'language question' in Greece. For a sociological presentation of this debate, see Frangoudaki (1992).

[...] the terms 'collective representation' or 'social representation' by means of which certain sociologists have attempted, correctly although insufficiently, to sight an aspect of what we are attempting to reflect on in this way, are themselves unsuitable and are in danger of generating confusion. (Castoriadis, 1987, p. 366)

Indeed, the Durkheimian project of collective effervescence that gives rise to collective representations is the closest bridge between the creative instituting of society and the classical tradition of sociology. Castoriadis rebuts, of course, Durkheim's realism and its objectivist concomitance (this goes back to the 1944 writings) as well as the latter's insistence on an 'average' or 'typical' collective configuration that would function as a prerequisite for instituted significations. Following a critical revision of the Marxist revolutionary project, which for Castoriadis got totally derailed under Stalinist USSR, the imperative of autonomy becomes now the guiding axis for praxis. Abandoning conclusive and universally binding invocations of a rational philosophy of history, Castoriadis proceeds by summoning the 'collective dimension' (91) of doing. To this he adds what is a further shift towards indeterminacy. Drawing on psychoanalysis he adduces the unconscious as the chief element of indeterminacy in the psyche of the individuals who make up society. The unconscious testifies to the forever elusive quest for transparency of the self to itself and to others, stretched now by Castoriadis to society's immanent indeterminacy. This is tantamount to neither the pluralism of the countless human interactions nor to an intersubjective mutuality nor even to the crystallization of these in institutions. Rather, the 'social' is inherently tied to the 'unformed forming element' (112) that makes the social an ongoing (but forever incomplete) process of institutional approximation that conveys the semblance of 'order' until its next magmatic eruption. We insist that this is a reformulation of Emil Lask's epistemology (already, as we mentioned, an identified sociological area as early as 1944 in Greece). The distance, Castoriadis tells us, between 'society as instituting' and 'what is, at every moment, instituted' is not a negative retreat to agnosticism or to relativism, but the very condition of making 'society' contain '*more* than what it presents' (114 [original emphasis]).

It is the partially mediated reciprocity of *legein* (saying, the signitive relation) and *teukein* (social doing, finality and instrumentality) that constitutes the irreducible entity of the magma of social significations and of collective doing. Thus, society institutes itself⁷ as 'a common world–*kosmos koinos*' (370) that is made up of shared frames of reference that prescribe what is capable of acquiring meaningful representation and coordinated action. Thus, Castoriadis maintains that the:

> fabrication of individuals in society, the imposition on somato-psychic subjects in the course of their socialization not only of *legein* but also of all the codifiable attitudes, postures, gestures, practices, comportments and know-how is obviously *teukhein*, by means of which society makes these subjects exist as social individuals, starting from somato-psychic givens, in a manner appropriate to life, to their life in this society and in view of the place that they will have in it. In this way, social individuals are made, as standing for individuals and as serving for certain social 'roles', 'functions' and 'places' (261).

As Castoriadis notes, the substratum from which modes of *legein* and *teukhein* emerge is the mode of 'magma':

> A magma is that from which one can extract (or in which one can construct) an indefinite number of ensemblist organizations but which can never be reconstituted (ideally) by a (finite or infinite) ensemblist composition of these organizations (343).

It is not irrelevant to think of Castoriadis' 'magma' as a contemporary reconstruction of *Lebensphilosophie*,[8] stripped, however, of any reactionary connotations which had characterized its German fin-de-siècle and Weimar era inception and subsequent reception in *Kulturkritik* sociology. Castoriadis places his basic ontological thesis in direct dialogue but also in contradistinction to sociology. The abridged lengthy passage below from

---

[7] For all of Castoriadis' recourse to the political imaginary of autonomy in ancient Greece (see, e.g. 1983, 1997, pp. 84–107), the classical tradition he invokes fails to be linked up in his thought with sociology's founders (Marx, Durkheim Weber). Generally, however, Castoriadis revisits systematically the ancient Greek heritage (see Castoriadis in Marker, 2018 [1989]). See also Haritopoulos (2000).

[8] Axel Honneth (1995, pp. 180–181) discerns 'surprising coincidences' with Bergson's vitalism. And for this reason, even if formulated in more tactful language compared to Habermas' critique of Castoriadis, Honneth concludes that 'fleeing from its own radicalism, his [Castoriadis'] theory of society leads in the end into a metaphysical cosmology which today can scarcely be discussed with rational arguments' (183).

a short essay (in alignment with *The Imaginary Institution of Society*) demonstrates this clearly and unambiguously:

> Society is irreducible to "intersubjectivity"—or to any sort of common action by individuals. Society is not a huge accumulation of face-to-face interactions. Only already socialized individuals can enter face-to-face, or back-to-back situations. No conceivable "cooperation" or "communicative action" of individuals could ever create language [...] Society, as *always already instituted*, is self-creation and capacity for self-alteration. It is the work of the radical imaginary as instituting, which brings itself to being an instituted society and, as given, each time specified, social imaginary. [...] But society is not a property of composition; neither is it a whole containing something more than and different from its parts, if only because these "parts" are made to be, and to be thus and not otherwise, by this "whole", which nevertheless can only be in and through its "parts".[...] This state of affairs has nothing to do with "systems theory" or with "self-organization", "order from noise", or something else. And it would be erroneous to say, as some do, society produces individuals, which produce society. (Castoriadis, 1992a, pp. 270–271 [original emphasis])

In this dense passage, we discern many sociological paradigms that range from phenomenological sociology (Schütz), everyday-life interactionism (Goffman), communicative action (Habermas), Durkheimian holism, systems theory (Parsons, Luhmann) and even structuration theory (Giddens), which seem inadequate for theorizing society's imaginary self-institution. For all of Castoriadis' ballast against sociology, what is adumbrated immediately after is his own version of sociological dualism:

> Society is the work of the *instituting* imaginary. The individuals are made by the *instituted* society at the same time as they make it and remake it. The two mutually irreducible poles are the radical instituting imaginary—the field of social-historical creation on the one hand, and the singular psyche on the other. (271 [original emphasis])

And it is society that attempts to answer the fundamental questions, such as 'Who are we as a collectivity? What are we for one another? Where and in what we are? What do we want; what do we desire; what are we lacking?' (1987, pp. 146–147). (Questions that may reflect the collective twist that Durkheim gave to Kant's interests of reason in the first *Critique*.)

Epigones of Critical Theory and of contemporary sociological and social theory returned to Castoriadis' legacy and relevance in more sympathetic terms. For example, Joas and Knöbl (2009, pp. 401–417) in their successful textbook on social and sociological theory discuss Castoriadis' ontology of indeterminacy and the self-instituting of the social under French anti-structuralism. Joas himself has a direct interest in including Castoriadis in the textbook due to his own theoretical programme of the 'creativity of action' (Joas, 1996) in sociological theory, noting Castoriadis' impact on Alain Touraine. And prior to that book, in his rehabilitation of pragmatism in social theory, Joas (1993) devotes a book chapter to Castoriadis where he suggests that 'for sociological theory' Castoriadis' work draws on the 'theory of action' but eschews the 'rigid dichotomy' of rational action and its normative rehabilitation (158).

Influence and Presence in Greece

Castoriadis' work still exerts influence and fascination in contemporary Greek social theory (see Haritopoulos, 2004). The sociological aspects of his thought come across most forcefully in Leledakis (1995, 1999) who provides a nuanced and systematic attempt to rethink some of the basic building blocks of sociological theory through Castoriadis. Mouzakitis (2014a, 2014b) too provides solid expositions of Castoriadis' key configurations like 'creation' and the 'social historical' often in association with Peter Wagner's (1994) recourse to Castoriadis. Such reception of Castoriadis' multifaceted work was considered to be directly relevant to sociology.[9] For example, Yiorgos Veltsos in the *laudatio* to Castoriadis award of an honorary PhD in political science at Panteion University on 15 February 1989 states Castoriadis' programmatic question as follows: 'What is society? In particular, what is the unity and the identity of a society or what is society's integration?' (Veltsos, 1989, p. 13). Castoriadis' first lectures in Greece were delivered initially between 13 and 24 of February 1989 at the French Institute in Athens, at Panteion University,

---

[9] The Department of Sociology at the University of Crete had organized an international workshop on 'Social Theory and the Work of Cornelius Castoriadis' (28–30 September 2000). In commemorating the one hundredth-year anniversary from Castoriadis' birth, the Department of Political Science at the Aristotle University of Thessaloniki held the international conference titled 'Cornelius Castoriadis, 1922–2022: One hundred years since the birth of the philosopher of autonomy' (March 11–13, 2022). One of its broad areas of interest was sociology.

in Volos, Rethymnon and Irakleion as well as to a group of psychoanalysts in Athens and span topics like the 'end of philosophy', power and autonomy, psychoanalysis, democracy and revolution and 'technoscience', all discussed in the context of Castoriadis' idea of society's imaginary institution (see, e.g. Castoriadis, 2000b, pp. 43–44). He also gave lectures in Greece in February 1993 at the Aristotle University of Thessaloniki, the French Institute in Thessaloniki on topics ranging from anthropogony in Aeschylus and Sophocles, the importance of psychoanalysis for understanding the genesis of society, on ecology, on education and democracy, the latter on the occasion of the award of an honorary PhD at the Democritus University of Thrace (see Castoriadis, 2001).

Castoriadis (1984) appeared on Greek television in the *Paraskinio* show in an interview to Teta Papadopoulou, mentioning the crisis of Marxism, the Scylla of totalitarian distortions of it in the Eastern bloc and the Charybdis of contemporary liberal oligarchies, as he calls them, in the West. Addressing briefly the contemporary Greek search of identity, Castoriadis considers it to be antinomic because it invokes two mutually exclusive 'beginnings': the ancient Greek and the Byzantine-Christian traditions. He ends with a solemn mood about his attachment to archetypal elements of the Greek landscape and to social and cultural aspects of Greece even if these have been 'invaded' by Western consumer modernity, ending with the aporia that had he stayed in Greece he may have not had accomplished as much as since his emigration to France. Rarely commented upon, and in the context of Castoriadis' intellectual embeddedness in the Greek context, is a seventy-minute discussion filmed for the programme *Themata kai Vivlio* (Themes and Books) by the *Hellenic Broadcasting Corporation* (ERT) in 4 December 1985. The discussants are Cornelius Castoriadis, Kosmas Psychopedis (then Professor of Political Science, Panteion University), Dimitris Markis (then Dean of Philosophy, University of Crete) and Pantelis Bassakos (then Lecturer, Panteion University). Castoriadis is introduced by Psychopedis as a 'Greek theorist' whose thought has often been received with an emotional (and mythological) aura by Greek acolytes.[10]

The discussion focused on problems that stem from *The Imaginary Institution of Society* in light of its Greek translation and provides critical commentaries on Castoriadis' thesis about the primacy of the imaginary,

---

[10] For the reception of Castoriadis in Greece and the wide attention his work received from the Greek press and the media, see Bitsakis (2005, p. 167).

the magma and the spontaneous creativity of society that solidifies in institutions. How can spontaneity be approached outside the already established historical structures? Is Castoriadis eliciting an ontology of the primordial initiation of societies? Is this thematization a regress to historicism and, moreover, isn't his understanding of Marx(ism) a sort of 'patricide' as far as Castoriadis' initial commitment to Marx is concerned? To this first round of questions posed by Psychopedis, Castoriadis (1985) places Marx's commitment to the idea of the control of nature and of the development of productive forces within the 'capitalist imaginary' itself. In this sense, the idea of patricide (which goes back to Oedipus) is, for him, tantamount to philosophizing: being independent as it were of sacrosanct philosophical systems but always tied to a responsible shape of criticism that takes seriously such systems.

Dimitris Markis notes a similarity between Castoriadis and Adorno's negative dialectics, suggesting that Castoriadis' positing of the imaginary as primordial ignores the very historicity of the imaginary and initiates a new ontology. Interestingly enough, at this juncture, Markis makes the emphatic caveat that Castoriadis' *The Imaginary Institution of Society* should be considered primarily to be a work of philosophy rather than 'proto-sociology' (assuming tacitly that it is the latter standpoint that prevails). Retorting, Castoriadis installs briefly a sociological hook to the discussion. He suggests that he stretches Max Weber's principle of *Verstehen* to access the 'imaginary' of each society, mentioning Jacob Burckhardt as a telling case of someone who intuited this imaginary for ancient Greece with his concept of *agon* (contest).[11] It is this arbitrary 'other', as Castoriadis says, that elides the socio-historical field.

To Pantelis Bassakos' critical remarks that discern a 'glossomorphic' reduction of society to language, Castoriadis responds that words do not have fixed meanings; rather they are open (and *open us* as agents) to indeterminacy. Adducing language's function in primary socialization, he underlines the imaginary's presence in language through the tacit meanings commanded by a layperson versus the professional linguist. Concluding, Psychopedis wonders about the political consequences that flow from the primacy of the imaginary and the magma. To this Castoriadis responds that 'creation' has no axiological load whatsoever. He even lumps together the creation that led to the Parthenon, to Beethoven, to

---

[11] Castoriadis refers to Jacob Burckhardt's book *History of Greek Culture* that was published posthumously in two volumes (in 1898 and in 1902).

Auschwitz and to the Gulag[12] as outcomes of this value-neutral and primordial creativity, and, somewhat frustrated, he objects to Plato's error to equate 'Being' with the 'Good'. Ultimately, for Castoriadis (1985), there is no way to persuade a radical sceptic or to persuade Hitler, Stalin or Khomeini; what one can only hope for is to expect that some of their advocates will be 'logically inconsistent'[13] and be persuaded against serving such bestial shapes of the imaginary.[14]

[12] References to historical shapes of totalitarianism are a recurring motif in Castoriadis' dissociation of magmatic creativity from a teleological or axiological philosophy of history that discerns dignified shapes of creativity onto historically binding institutions (the paradigm that brings together Plato, Aristotle, Kant, Hegel, Marx, Durkheim and Parsons, among others). In his words, 'We do not approve of what contemporary history offers us, simply because it "is" or because it "tends to be". Should we arrive at the conclusion that the most probable, even certain, tendency of contemporary history is the universal establishment of concentration camps, we would not deduce from this that we have to support them' (Castoriadis, 1987, p. 100). And even in the 1989 lectures in Greece, Castoriadis adduces the value-neutral, as he claims, conception of the 'imaginary'. Under this rubric, 'Auschwitz is creation, requiring enormous imagination and plenty rationality' (Castoriadis, 2000b, p. 82). Such programmatic invocations of the ontology of the imaginary risk reduction to a nominal and empty of normative content rendition of creation, which in the cases of mass extermination translates, obviously, to its antithesis (creation = creation and/or destruction). This is indeed what Castoriadis affirms (Athenians' massacre of the Melians, the Inquisition, Auschwitz, the Gulag, the H-bomb) when he places such destructive eruptions under the rubric of the Greco-Western tradition which 'created massive monstrosity' (1983, p. 272).

[13] The political act of 'inconsistency' is adduced by Castoriadis for the cases of Havel and Solzhenitsyn as ethically defensible standpoints under totalitarianism (Castoriadis, 1997, p. 113).

[14] As these lines are written during the Russian invasion in Ukraine, it could be potentially interesting to ponder on the bestial shape of the imaginary and to seek the instituted probability modicum for such a violent imaginary's disruption. We suspect that Castoriadis would be appalled at the sight of massive suffering and destruction in Ukraine but would, perhaps, reiterate that society 'creates, each time, its proper or own world [...]. It defends itself by defending its being-thus, that is to say, its proper world. It has boundaries—not necessarily geographical boundaries, but imaginary ones that are even more important, for the latter ensure that ideas, representations, and behaviors coming from the outside will be either metabolized or rejected—or, in borderline cases, will ultimately prove fatal to the existing institution of society. And society therefore has pushes, the first of which is the push tending towards its self-preservation' (Castoriadis, 1992b, pp. 87–88). In a 1994 interview for the newspaper *Sunday Eleftherotypia*, Castoriadis offers alarmingly prescient insights on the still persistent attachment of 'Russia, Ukraine, the Balkans, including Greece' to a 'medieval political situation' and to Stalin's and Lenin's rehabilitation of a statist-'religious' dogma that draws on the Byzantine empire (see Castoriadis in Papadopoulou, 2000, pp. 22–23).

Castoriadis did not abstain from contributing his share of socio-political diagnostics[15] on contemporary Greek society and its discontents. For example, he engaged critically a number of the then current issues of political culture and society in interviews for Greek newspapers. These covered topics from the caricature of the *Socialisme ou Barbarie* project in Greece to his activist Trotskyist (and bitter) affinity to the then Prime Minister Andreas Papandreou. (For these and other Castoriadis interventions in the press, see Papadopoulou, 2000.) Yet despite this zest with Greece, much of his legacy is still set up in France (see Association Castoriadis, 1997).

NICOS POULANTZAS: SOCIOLOGICAL CONTRIBUTION AND LEGACY IN GREECE

Nicos Poulantzas is a major figure in twentieth century Marxist sociology. As Jessop suggests, 'Poulantzas was one of the leading theoreticians of left-wing Eurocommunism and the problems of a democratic transition to democratic socialism' (1985, p. 361). The classification of Poulantzas' work under the broad rubric of 'social science' is not inaccurate but obfuscates the sociological interests and paradigms that inform his system and Poulantzas himself incorporated systematically into his work. For Jessop, Poulantzas is 'a Greek sociologist' (3) whose early writings fell into philosophy and sociology; on the latter field 'Poulantzas developed an interesting account of the modern legal system and the modern state *qua Rechtsstaat*' (49). Prior to Jessop's masterly account, it was Simon Clarke (1977) who considered Poulantzas' theory of the state to be part of sociology. In fact, Clarke's multi-layered critique constantly emphasizes not only the direct placement of the theory of the state in sociology, but, ultimately, it considers its Althusserian load in Poulantzas' structuralism as a radical (but not Marxist!) reproduction of Parsonsian structural-functionalism. This model, for Clarke, is disappointing for Marxist theory because, essentially, it grasps classes as 'distributive' entities and theorizes production as 'a technical process'. In Poulantzas, the 'Marxist theory of the state thus becomes parasitic on debates in bourgeois sociology'

---

[15] Castoriadis is not alone among Greek intellectuals' penchant for social malaise diagnostics. Lambiri-Dimaki's empirical study about the Greek journal *To Dendro* and how Greek non-sociologists (but holders of social/cultural capital) address society adopts Bourdieu's term 'spontaneous sociology', 'quasi-scholarly sociology' and 'amateur sociology' (Lambiri-Dimaki, 2000, pp. 18–20).

(Clarke, 1977, pp. 29–30). In an important sociological theory textbook, Waters (1994) discusses Poulantzas' theory of power (and in what is for the author its tautological grounding) (1994, p. 228), the relative autonomy of the state (229–230) and his class theory (328–330).

Poulantzas' work matured in France and became known through structural Marxism. He dealt systematically with the class structure of capitalist societies (Poulantzas, 1975) but exclusively within the apparatus of the state, thus reconfiguring the idea of political power (1978, 1980). He also addressed the logical concomitants of the aberrations of fascism and dictatorship (1979). In 1975 Poulantzas wrote a short treatise on the crisis of dictatorships in Greece, Portugal and Spain. In that book (published in Greek in 2006), he considers the Greek dictatorship as a political phenomenon that drew support from comprador capital (banking, finance and commercial sector, shipping, shipyard construction, oil refineries) which, for reasons that had to do with Greece's economic underdevelopment, had prevailed since the early 1960s. This was due to Greece's dependence on the European Economic Market (EEC) and on the United States and to its dual position as a sphere of primitive accumulation of capital in a part of the Mediterranean region and as a failed economy in terms of a timely and domestic accumulation of capital (2006, p. 12). In this process of 'dependent' growth, the domestic bourgeoisie stands ipso facto as a force that can potentially contest dictatorships which draw, as in the case of Greece, on comprador capital and the latter's subjugation to the leverage of (US) imperialism and NATO. Opposed to this was the domestic bourgeoisie's alignment with the EEC. The organic ties between comprador capital and the US interests would discern in a burgeoning domestic bourgeoisie the risk of a partial dependence displacement: instead of a direct dependence on US interests, Greece (and other peripheral nation-states in Europe) would only be indirectly dependent due to the emergence of the EEC. Furthermore, Poulantzas refuses to subsume the Greek dictatorship under the umbrella of fascism. This is so because the Greek dictatorship did not gain leverage among the lower-middle classes (unlike Nazism) (he even mentions *rembetika* as songs of resistance) nor had built, prior to the coup, any fascist mechanisms of political control and ideological indoctrination. Lack of leverage on the colonels' part was also detected not only in the state mechanisms but also in the ideological state apparatus. For example, the lower clergy of the Greek Orthodox Church had close affinities with the people, continuing an alliance that spanned the resistance against fascism in World War II; internal splits surfaced also in how schools and universities faced the new regime with marked resistance particularly (but not exclusively) among the lower ranks of the academic hierarchy. Other duplications of such strains took place in the justice system, in trade unions, in the press, in state bureaucracy and even in the army (106–113).

In this sense, a latent convergence between the domestic bourgeoisie and the working class was effected that would render the Greek junta precarious at its very inception. For Poulantzas, the Karamanlis government after the restoration of democracy reflected this convergence (52), and, consequently, unlike the situation in Portugal where the exit from military dictatorships moved to the 'Left', in Greece it moved to the 'Right' (59). While massive resistance to the Greek junta did not occur, the November 1973 Polytechnic uprising could be considered as an event that may not have directly caused the demise of the colonels' regime, but nonetheless exacerbated the inherent contradictions of the Greek dictatorship (68–69).

The 'Miliband-Poulantzas' Debate[16]

In late 1969 Poulantzas engages with Ralph Miliband's book *The State in Capitalist Society*. From this first critical encounter with Miliband's (1969) view of the capitalist state, Poulantzas (1969) took issue with the sociological trope of the social actor and the grounding of structural patterns into the motivations of individual actors. This, he considered to be a typical pattern of thought stemming from Weber and from functionalism. He sought to reaffirm the Marxian approach that treats individuals as bearers of 'objective instances'. Having established this intransigence in sociological accounts, he takes Miliband's Marxism to be entangled with this problem of motivation; hence, he thinks, Miliband's explanation of the ruling class reproduces an individually founded explanation because it addresses managers in terms of profit-seeking motivation. Stemming from this, he adduces support from Marx, Engels and Lenin to remind Marxists that the state apparatus, as a par excellence social category, instantiates its position (and repression) across the social category of the 'bureaucracy' irrespective of the latter's diversification into the class origins of its members. For Poulantzas, therefore, 'the State forms an *objective system* of special "branches" whose relation presents a *specific internal unity* and obeys, to

---

[16] This debate along with an intemperate exchange on totalitarianism and class struggle between Nicos Poulantzas and Jean-Pierre Faye was published in Greek in a single volume with a short prologue by Poulantzas (Poulantzas et al., 1981).

a large extent, *its own logic*' (1969, p. 75 [original emphasis]). Althusser's distinction, energized by Poulantzas, between 'repressive apparatus of the State' (government, army, police, tribunals and administration) and the 'ideological apparatus of the State' (church, the family, schools, unions, the political parties, mass media) caps the state determinism of his scheme whereby the ideological apparatuses have only relative autonomy because they have as their 'condition of possibility' the repressive apparatus of the state.

Now this 'structural super-determinism' constitutes, for Miliband (1970), a dangerous deviation and, one may add, an illusion of homologies that fails to discern substantive differences between a state ruled by conservative or social democrat bourgeois constitutionalists, as opposed to one that is ruled by fascists. This point aims straight into the normative/ethical consequences of Poulantzas' theory of the state. Its logical entanglement with the ideology of the dominant classes is reiterated on the consequence of WWII's death toll as a result of the conflation between parliamentary legitimacy and a Caesarist legitimacy of the executive that was conspicuously missed, according to Miliband, by the German Comintern-Marxism. In continuing the debate, Miliband (1973) aims to reverse the 'state—political parties' hierarchy and to point, historically, to counter-cases from Great Britain, Italy and Germany that demonstrate organizational capacities of classes outside the exclusivity of the role that Poulantzas reserves for the state.

Shortly after the publication of the masterly *Classes in Contemporary Capitalism* (1975), Poulantzas rejoined the debate with Miliband. Countering methodically the charges of 'abstractionism' (a methodological orientation that excludes concrete facts), 'formalism' (this part of his reply addresses Ernesto Laclau's criticisms),[17] 'difficult language' and, ultimately, a capitulation to 'structuralism', Poulantzas (1976a) draws on sociology with eclectic erudition and strategic intent. For example, to eliminate the charge of 'abstractionism' Poulantzas adduces Durkheim's similar warnings against 'common sense' and the 'illusions of the evident'; he also considers his abstract method to be in line with late Marx's recourse to the 'order of exposition' (*Darstellung*) and the ensuing confusion

---

[17] Ernesto Laclau published a long and nuanced exposition (and critique) of Poulantzas (and Miliband) (Laclau, 1975, 1977). Mouzelis (1978) rejoined the debate with a critical perspective on Laclau's book.

between the order of theoretical exposition and the order of research.[18] The sociological relevance for Poulantzas' project is evinced from Poulantzas' reply which places Miliband in the antipodes of Marxist sociology, regarding it as symptomatic of 'bourgeois social science' of 'institutionalism-functionalism', which 'harks back to Max Weber' (and Hegel) whereby the 'structures/institutions' hold power and brandish it in the arena of 'relations of power between "social groups" flowing from this institutional power' (1976a, p. 73). Fields like the sociology of work or the sociology of organizations reflect this view and 'non-critically' enable 'this tendency to contaminate Marxism' (73). This type of 'modern sociology' discusses classes but not class struggle. He also rebuts the condensation of his debate with Miliband as one between the latter's instrumentalist approach to the state and Poulantzas' own structuralist approach.

The 1966 'Class and the State' Lectures/Seminars and the 1976–1977 Lectures at Panteion University

Now that the sociological base in Poulantzas' thought has been sketched, we must note two major contributions from his presence in Greece. Indicative of the strains that afflict the omission of Poulantzas from current accounts of Greek sociology is the fact that Poulantzas was never detached from the Greek intellectual life.[19] This is confirmed through his numerous interventions in the Greek press while in France.

Putting aside some early 1950 scattered interventions, Poulantzas, from the 1960s until 1979, contributed several articles, essays and interviews to Greek journals and newspapers like *Agonas, Anti, Avghe, Diavazo, Eleftheria, I Kathimerini, Kommounistiki Theoria kai Politiki, Ta Nea, O Politis, Poreia, Prooptiki, Thourios* and *To Vima* on topics like the state of Greek intellectuals, the military *coup* in Greece, the democratization of education in Greece, the Greek popular culture, the crisis of Marxism and the Left in Europe, among others (see Jessop, 1985, pp. 365–372). In

---

[18] This problem of *Darstellung* became the guiding thread for the research programme and journal *Open Marxism* which Kosmas Psychopedis promoted in Greece (and from which he launched his own qualified critique of Poulantzas' structuralism). See, indicatively, Psychopedis (1992, 2001).

[19] We take distance from other attempts that draw largely on personal life details to 'demonstrate' Poulantzas' attachment to Greece (see Meletopoulos (2000, pp. 37–38), despite the author's qualification (26) that Poulantzas can be considered equally a Greek, a French and an international intellectual).

1966 and during the 'Second Week of Contemporary Thought' 4–15 May lectures (at the 'Kentrikon' theatre) and seminars (at the *Centre of Marxist Studies and Research*) held in the heart of Athens, featuring, among others, Roger Garaudy, Poulantzas left his mark on the shift of Marxist studies in Greece away from doctrinaire and Soviet-Marxist interpretations that mostly aligned with the Greek Communist Party (KKE). In his first lecture, Poulantzas (1966a) explored the nuances of Marx's critique of Hegel's theory of the state. Interestingly enough Poulantzas repels the 'erroneous' (1966a, p. 290), as he calls it, iconic 'inversion' of Hegel's thesis, pointing also to the tensions that arise in Della Volpe's subsequent endeavours. Suggesting that young Marx is still caught in the idealist categorical scheme of Hegel since he had not developed the scientific outlook that would culminate in *Capital*, he considers that Marx's mature perspective transforms rather than merely inverts the notions of the state and of the bourgeois society. It is through this lens that Poulantzas rebuts the reference to Castoriadis and to the *Socialisme ou Barbarie* group by a member of the audience (321–322), suggesting that Castoriadis reads the state through young Marx's perspective that sees institutions to contain alienation, a notion which, as Poulantzas is quick to underline, lacks scientific validity. Now the level of economic relations is not limited to the humanist materiality invested to subjects in young Marx but, rather, to the objective structures (301) of the mode and the social relations of production. Yet the state is also being transformed. It is no longer seen as the phenomenal alienation of human subjects, but as an objective structural whole within which the special structures acquire their significance and dependence by performing their social role. In this sense, we reach, for Poulantzas, Marx's understanding of the class state. The discussion makes caveats to sociologists like C. Wright Mills but focuses on explaining Bonapartism and the idea that the ruling class is 'by nature unworthy' (είναι από τη φύση της ανάξια) (308), due to its immanent conflicting interests, to constitute itself as a political entity.

The seminar he delivered on 'Classes and the State' (Poulantzas, 1966b) is also interesting because it oscillates between a historical and a theoretical/logical interpretation of the concept of class. From the dense interventions that followed, Poulantzas takes issue with C. Wright Mills' zero-sum notion of power (1966b, pp. 357–358). With the rest of the discussion shifting to humanism and ideology, what must be noted is Titos

Patrikios' intervention (368–374; 376–377)[20] which attempts to salvage the descriptive (and ideological) humanist theories and invokes a scientific exposition of concepts that enables theory to revisit and reabsorb elements of the initially articulated descriptive humanism and its (repelled) content. Such a sublation and 'return' to humanism through a Marxist science expresses for Patrikios authentic, as opposed to alienated human relations. Philosopher Yannis Imvriotis caps this exchange between Poulantzas and Patrikios, suggesting that Marx's notion of alienation supersedes its objective properties and certainly points to an 'axiological concept' (379) the valence of which, we may say, survives the concept's descriptive or ideological underpinnings. Here, perhaps, lie the seeds of Psychopedis' (see end of this chapter) approach to Marx through axiology.

Invited by Yiorgos Veltsos and in his capacity as visiting professor, Poulantzas gave a series of lectures in Greek at Panteion University in Athens during the academic year 1976–1977. These lectures are important for a number of reasons: first, they display Poulantzas' charisma and loose style of exposition of what, admittedly, are demanding concepts of great sophistication; second, they demonstrate Poulantzas' concern for connecting his theory of the state in capitalism, social classes and imperialism with phenomena specific to the Greek context; third, they attest to the dialogue format of accommodating student questions and brief interventions by Kosmas Psychopedis, Kostas Vergopoulos and Yiorgos Veltsos. Eventually published in 2019 (with the support of the liberal-conservative *Konstantinos Mitsotakis Foundation*), the lectures reveal some interesting patterns:

(a) Poulantzas understands Marxism as a sociological theory (2019, p. 63). The neo-Weberian hegemony of social stratification theory on social class has no room for class struggle. He emphatically defends the idea of class struggle even if class (and revolutionary) consciousness is not in place, thus countering Lukács' seminal essays on reification and the consciousness of the proletariat. Drawing on the thought experiment of some absolute social mobility (viz. that the workers would occupy capitalist positions and that the capitalists would experience downward mobility towards the working-class strata), the capitalist order, according to Poulantzas,

[20] Titos Patrikios is a highly esteemed and awarded Greek poet and novelist who had studied sociology at the *École Pratique des Hautes Études* in Paris.

would not be in the least altered. Possibly the occupants' habitus would be altered, but the objective social positions associated with capital and labour would still prevail. On these grounds, Poulantzas exposes the ideological load of sociological theories of socialization in institutions (96). Some of the most exciting and pedagogical segments of the lectures pertain to the historical rupture of the labourers from the means of production (74–86).

(b) Moving to the explanation of the state from a 'sociological-Marxist sense' (90), Poulantzas counters Psychopedis' intervention that in Greece the state is the generator of the bourgeois class, rather than its epiphenomenal adjunct. In this sense, like in France and Greece, as Poulantzas suggests (101–102), the state mediates between the bourgeoisie and the working class (as well as the lower-middle class) in order to avoid breaching a logic of compromise. Its compromising intervention inhibits the creation of a bloc around the working class, the latter being a prospect that would threaten the capitalist state. He also repels a genealogical explanation (in the lectures this seems to have stemmed from Vergopoulos' remarks) suggesting with plenty of irony that the fact that the Greek state was created without being preceded by a capitalist class is a pseudo-problem (150). What matters instead is the logical and historical correspondence (rather than some dialectical relation which, as he admits, he finds a repugnant notion (151)) between the state and a class society. Ultimately, the theory of the state oscillates between a view that sees the state as an 'object', namely, an instrument that is subdued by ruling classes, and one that treats the state as a 'subject' and ascribes (after Hegel) to it a voluntarist (and normative) potential, keeping the ruling classes in check. However, the recurring crises of capitalism will inevitably be transferred to the crisis of the state (149).

(c) Poulantzas draws on facets of Greek society to illustrate the relevance of the theory of the state. In explaining the mechanisms by which the state adds institutional layers of control, he adduces the state's training of public officers for positions that are instrumental in consolidating a monopoly-politics. A typical case, as he mentions, is the establishment in 1963 of the Department of Public Administration at Panteion University (115). At the same time, such observations on the role of the state could not ignore issues of dependency. It is at this juncture that Poulantzas uses Greece as a case study of a country the industrialisation of which is dependent on foreign capital investment. Notwithstanding the Greek working class' creation of surplus value for foreign capital, the slow industrial development led also to the formation of a Greek capitalist class (a domestic bourgeoisie) that aimed to redistribute within the global capitalist division of labor the shares of surplus-value creation. The most representative case, for Poulantzas, is the tourist industry (it has become standard in common parlance—even now—to refer to it as Greece's 'single industry' or 'heavy industry') as one example of an endogenous bourgeois class, which unlike a comprador capitalist class (the Greek shipping magnates), at the time of these lectures, played up its dependence with the then European Economic Market (EEC) versus its dependence on US capital. In this sense, to nationalize corporations like the Olympic Airlines (144) merely transfers the profit dividends to the state, yet the exploitative relation of the company to the workers remains intact. Its gravity centre shifts towards diverting the working classes from the regrouping of capitalist power aided by the state. Thus, the new balance of power among Greek capitalists, for Poulantzas, demanded the confiscation of the Andreadis Group assets with the public opinion being directed to the group's founder and his collaboration with the colonels' junta. Such diversion, says Poulantzas (157–158), occludes other less subtle bridges between Greek capital and the junta regime. Employing what today David Harvey's geography of capitalist accumulation suggests, Poulantzas maps Athens and Thessaloniki as metropolitan 'poles of development' (187) and as nodes of capital's drive in locating optimal conditions for its reproduction. The last lecture on imperialism abandons references to Greece, focusing instead on the historical experience of fascism after capital's crises (an argument similar to Karl Polanyi's *The Great Transformation*). Interestingly, Poulantzas takes distance from USSR imperialism (he mentions the Soviet accumulation of capital in India) which, as he emphatically points out, is devoid of socialist internationalism. In fact, he calls the Soviet invasion in Czechoslovakia simply 'fascist' rather than 'social-fascist' (199). Such remarks flow from repeated audience questions on the issue of the Soviet state and its relation to classes and to capital.

Intellectual networks can be fascinating. For example, Psychopedis had met Poulantzas in 1966 as an undergraduate student in Constantinos Tsoukalas' house as part of a study group that focused on Marx's *The Jewish Question* (Psychopedis, 2003, p. 429). While Psychopedis' work is rooted in political and social theory, the critical confrontation with Poulantzas took recourse to Simon Clarke's approach. Clarke had already contributed to the short-lived but vanguard journal *Open Marxism* published by Pluto Press and edited by Werner Bonefeld, Richard Gunn (the Edinburgh School of Marxism) and Kosmas Psychopedis.[21] Its mission was to emancipate Marxian explanation from dogmatic Marxism(s), including the structural Marxism of Althusser and Poulantzas (see, indicatively, Psychopedis, 1992). Particularly, for Psychopedis (2001, pp. 148–149), the tensions that arose in Poulantzas' theory of the state stemmed (a) from the configuration of the state as a mechanism/guarantor of the interests of the dominant class, (b) from the constraint of practices that indicate each class' range of action versus structural barriers and (c) from the fact that Poulantzas' conception of structure seems to be theorized as a completed totality (hence the risk of Poulantzas' capitulation to functionalism), rather than as an inherently antinomic order under capitalism. *Contra* Clarke then, Poulantzas' 'functionalism' returns, for Psychopedis, as an abstract affirmation of society's integration in front of crises wrought by the antagonistic social relations under capitalism. This shift in the Marxian problematic towards the problem of values and of the value constitution of reality is not unnoticed elsewhere. Jessop attributes to Poulantzas' early works the pursuit of 'the chimera of establishing the dialectical unity of fact and value as a basis for an axiology of legal relations and institutions' (1985, p. 48). In an important collection of essays (Rigos & Tsoukalas, 2001), following a major international conference on Poulantzas' work and legacy,[22] Psychopedis treats Poulantzas' late work as anticipatory of the problematic of a neo-Marxist epistemological explanation that builds on society's 'materiality' (as distinct from orthodox definitions of materialism). This reconstruction of materiality includes now the

---

[21] Other notable collaborators of *Open Marxism* were the Frankfurt School and Adorno disciples Hans-Georg Backhaus and Helmut Reichelt who approached the logical exposition of categories in Marx's late work through concepts drawn from Hegel's Logic and from neo-Kantianism (Simmel; problem of validity [*geltung*]). It is under the rubric of the mediations between politics and problems of method that Psychopedis partially revises his agreement with Clarke and the latter's charge that Poulantzas' theory of the state regressed into functionalism.

[22] The Nicos Poulantzas Institute (1997) (see https://poulantzas.gr/en/the-institute/) is affiliated to the SY.RIZ.A party, but even as Poulantzas friends and colleagues admit (Elefantis, 2006, p. 125), it has not yet promoted the Greek sociologist's legacy to the degree his international reputation and relevance demand.

potency of values and organizational accomplishments that could constitute emancipatory praxis, releasing themselves from their alienated constitution under bourgeois society and its value form.

The 'Poulantzas-Castoriadis' Polemic

Although seen by many scholars in Greece and abroad to be 'expatriate' intellectuals whose trajectories never really intersected except through their common nourishment in Marxism, Castoriadis and Poulantzas found themselves entangled in an intemperate controversy that unfolded in the Greek newspaper *Avghe*. We can surmise though that since the appearance of *The Imaginary Institution of Society* in 1975, Poulantzas had already become disaffected with the book's central thesis. In his very short prologue to Veltsos' 1976 book about society and language, Poulantzas, despite praising Veltsos, makes an interesting but hardly enigmatic apostrophe: he notes that Veltsos is more vulnerable than he himself thinks to the influence of 'certain modernist trends of contemporary irrationalism' which as a result of the periodic ideological crises in Europe 'deal with "desire"' (Poulantzas, 1976b, pp. 8–9). This could be seen as a preamble to Poulantzas' subsequent attack on Castoriadis.

Indeed, in 1977 New Year's Day, Poulantzas extols rekindling Marxism in Greece among authors like Tsoukalas, Elefantis, Moskov, Veltsos, Iliou, Vergopoulos and Patrikios. In the antipodes, he reiterates what was stated in the 1976 prologue, namely, that 'in our country' (meaning, Greece), a sort of ersatz revolutionary counteroffensive has begun 'in the guise of an eclectic jumble of words and as a popularized by-product of European irrationalism, particularly in the writings of our compatriot Cornelius Castoriadis about which there has recently been much discussion and which so greatly seem to inspire the neo-Christian Orthodox philosopher Christos Giannaras' (Poulantzas in Psarras & Karidas, 2019). Beyond this elective affinity with an irrationalist thought style (and substance), Poulantzas extends an ad hominem critique against Castoriadis on the grounds that he served as a leading executive in OECD and has refused 'the slightest even symbolic participation (such as a signature of protest in 1967 or following the student Polytechnic uprising) in the opposition to the dictatorship' (ibid). Following an equally acerbic rebuttal by two Castoriadis defenders (see Psarras & Karidas, 2019) who accuse Poulantzas of lying, Poulantzas rejoins in 1977 and clarifies that for him revolutionary action cannot be entirely detached from the political practices of Castoriadis. He objects to Castoriadis' levelling of the 'progressive forces' in Greek politics as articulated in Castoriadis' book *The Revolutionary Question Today* (2000a, pp. 47–48).[23] He even proceeds in making a sociological remark on the style of the public sphere in Greece: 'Greece must finally cease to be regarded as a place where anyone can say anything in expectation of a profit, and where an elementary political morality must be established. Because every reason stands somewhere and comes from somewhere, unless we still believe in the *freischwebende Intelligenz* [the free-floating intellect, a concept introduced by Karl Mannheim]' (Poulantzas in Psarras & Karidas, 2019). Castoriadis never really responded, except one year later in an article titled 'Les crises d' Althusser' (The Crises of Althusser) published in the French journal *Libre* in 1978, and only with a brief derogatory nod (Castoriadis, 1986, pp. 220–221; Psarras & Karidas, 2019) in a scathing critique of Althusser titled 'From wooden to rubber language' (Castoriadis, 1986, pp. 217–231).

Sociological Theory Input from Neighbouring Disciplines and Scholars

Under the domains of social theory, philosophy, epistemology, criminology and social psychology, Greek scholars engaged with sociological theory and provided important contributions to interdisciplinary cross-pollination. Dialogue with sociology was seen to be enabling for such fields' relevancies to the historical shape of traditional, modern and contemporary societies and its impact on the self. The richness of sociology (and sociological theory) became a partner of philosophical discourses that sought to supplant sociology with hitherto unavailable categories that would either galvanize epistemological hiatuses (as is the case with Kondylis) or would contribute to wider social science problem-solving potential under an epistemological-normative programme (as is the case with Psychopedis).

---

[23] Poulantzas may have been irritated by Castoriadis' pejorative remark in that book about 'an industry of nylon thought' to which the French specialize and include structuralism, various pseudo-psychoanalytical strands, Althusser, semiotics, and so on. (2000a, p. 50).

Panagiotis Kondylis

For Kyrtsis, '[s]ociologically minded political scientists and social historians, social anthropologists, even some economists and representatives of literary criticism and educational science enlarge the circle of sociological literates' (1996, p. 10). This is an important acknowledgement endorsed by other accounts of Greek sociology, yet the community of Greek sociologists has been largely reticent about most of these contributions. Spectacular in this omission are Panagiotis Kondylis' (1943–1998) writings, which stem from philosophy and political science and embrace decisionism (Tepstra, 2008), the descriptive version of which Kondylis reached through multiple and sophisticated intellectual paths and trajectories. His intellectual edifice exhibits remarkable degrees of coherence and erudition, but also a tendency to closure with regard to inaugurating a self-contained social theory of the political grounded in what he calls 'social ontology'. His formative years of university education in Greece and later Germany (where he studied with Dieter Henrich and associated with notable historians Werner Conze and Reinhart Koselleck (see Koselleck, 2002)) equipped Kondylis with an intellectual impetus that was soon to give fruition in his seminal intellectual history of the Western Enlightenment (a work that is cited by the generally eclectic Habermas (1987a, p. 430 n.23)). Charles Taylor (1983) also wrote a book review of Kondylis work on German Idealism. Following numerous books in the history of philosophy and political theory (all published first in German and then translated by Kondylis himself in Greek), Kondylis became intensely involved with sociological theory in his effort to ground a 'social ontology'. It is to this work that we must now turn.

Kondylis' Sociologically Informed and Incomplete The Political and Man

Kondylis' unfinished *magnum opus The Political and Man* (Das Politische und der Mensch) was published posthumously in Germany in 1999 and then translated in Greek in 2007. It is not an exaggeration to say that this is one of the handful of landmark sociological theory works from Greek scholars whether these have been sociologists or not (for the sociological relevance and background of the book, see Harth, 2002, p. 87, 93, 99–102). It is Kondylis' most synthetic and systematic work, drawing on nearly all traditions of classical and contemporary sociological theory.

Greek sociology's regrettable lack of addressing it systematically must be noted, and it may have to do both with Kondylis untimely death at a time when the book had not been published in Greek, but it is hard to explain since its 2007 translation in Greek.[24]

Kondylis introduces the necessity of clarifying the layer of social ontology in early twentieth-century philosophy which was under the influence of sociology. As a result, sociology and social ontology became closely entangled, virtually indistinguishable at points, crystallizing in a hybridization that proved to be detrimental to both sociology and social ontology (2007, p. 150). Kondylis' quest for a socio-ontological realm, from which historical configurations are formed and sociological categories crystallize through various shapes (positivism, ideal-typical methodology, *Verstehen* hermeneutics, functionalism, conflict theory, formal sociology, symbolic interactionism, rational choice theory, systems theory, communicative action, among many other sociological paradigms), proceeds with a very systematic, albeit selective, interpretation of key sociology texts. Central to Kondylis' reconstruction of sociological theory in its entirety is his repulsion of rationalist and normative accounts of the social (Durkheim, Parsons, Habermas). For him these paradigms elevate the (communicative) rationality of the agent to being the sole criterion of the series of causally discernable phenomena in 'nature' and to thus subject the latter to deontological judgements. The 'is'-'ought' tension is irreconcilable for Kondylis, and normative paradigms that claim otherwise end up as an index of the impasses of sociological Enlightenment and its culmination in 'ethical nihilism' (at this point Kondylis complained that Habermas misunderstood his own book on Enlightenment, seeing it as a corroboration of the utopia of reason, while Kondylis is essentially upholding a

---

[24] In a conference on 'The continuing relevance of Panagiotis Kondylis' thought' held at the ancient site of Olympia between 26 and 28 of January 2018, none of the papers presented reflected the sociological crux of Kondylis' book. (The remaining two and unwritten volumes would have been on 'Society as a political collectivity' and on 'Identity, power, culture'.) Rather, most of the attention focused on the key text *Power and Decision* (1991) which proposes a descriptive (or value-free) theory of decisionist value relevancies and reflects a radicalized and non-normative neo-Kantian epistemology. Kondylis' last and laborious venture to sociology is a continuation of this fundamental idea of perspectivism and decisionism in face of reality's indeterminacy (see, e.g. Kondylis (1991, pp. 23–84)). On brief commentaries about Kondylis' social ontology, see Kavoulakos (1999) and Tsivakou (2021).

philosophical nihilism (75, n.111)).[25] The questions (249) that lead to a reconstruction of sociology through the lens of a now crystallized socio-ontological level pertain to the constitution of the social in such a way that any causal hierarchies and law-like regularities prove to be inherently unstable. This is because they are vulnerable to the fluid boundaries among sociology specialisms or to the multitude of factors and forces that stem from the socio-ontological realm (indeed, the 'social' is constituted by them); their indeterminate crisscrossing renders open and malleable the social's own becoming. According to the socio-ontological standpoint, the social being is beyond consolidation (in a historical or institutional teleology) and hierarchical ordering (in terms of functions or degrees of normative fulfilment). Arguing against sociological hypostizations or de-historicizations, Kondylis mobilizes social ontology on the side of historicism as opposed to what he calls a 'superficial sociologism' (256) that occludes this indeterminate and fundamental realm. Such socio-ontologically grounded historicism halts normatively configured sociological concepts and reveals their inadequacy when the latter claim trans-historical or universal validity. Symmetrically as it were, Kondylis rebuts what he calls 'relativist vulgar sociology' (494) that treats categories as mere projections on the part of the social scientist. Rather, it is the socio-ontological bedrock that is the condition for understanding diverse life-worlds. Drawing on Weber's perspectivism (a likely source of which is Emil Lask), Kondylis holds that any 'substantial axiological relativism (on the part of the researcher) accommodates not only the historical method but also the historical equibalance' (776). Such relativism is precisely the 'vehicle for the understanding that is grounded in social ontology' (815). Part of Kondylis' strategy is to retain the primordial realm outside any mediations by history and by society's institutional constitution and to ensure that all (historically specific in terms of genesis) institutional crystallizations that claim supra-historical adequacy collapse and are somehow 'renewed' by the primordial which in its indeterminacy may include even the vitality of what is archaic. The special sociological relevance of Kondylis' project is reflected in the following claim:

[25] In defining nihilism as the recognition that 'appearance' is the 'only Being', Kondylis adduces sociology once more. In the same passage, he writes 'Nihilists limit themselves, therefore, to a psychological and sociological genealogy of ethics [...]' as they describe the genesis of how 'in the context of social life, self-love, through institutions, is transformed to ethics [...]' (1981, p. 171).

Social ontology is the ontology of the social. The social is what specifically characterizes the being of society; in other words, society as a special socio-ontological concept and the social coincide. The being of society, as a primordial fact, consists as such the natural beginning of social ontology, exactly as the being of the world generally, a primordial fact too, was the intellectual conditio sine qua non of philosophical ontology (263).

Working with limiting concepts such as 'order' and 'disorder' at the extremes of the socio-ontological spectrum, Kondylis urges the historian and the sociologist to examine specific historically and sociologically valid shapes of 'order' and 'disorder' and to focus on the specific causes and reasons that shift the socio-historical pendulum in this or that direction within this spectrum.

The constitutive socio-ontological moments are 'the social relation', 'the political' and 'man'. Similar is the model of justification for the 'political'. The nuanced and elaborate exposition of these concepts transcends the scope of our brief sojourn to Kondylis' sociological uses. Like the 'social relation' spectrum with its 'friend' and 'enemy' extremes (or even with the movement between a 'convergence' and a containment of 'deviating' actors' interests (393)), so, for Kondylis, at this ontological layer, the political is the 'interaction of all interactions' (277) and accounts for the order and integration of the social. As for the anthropological dimension of the social ontology, this oscillates between an integrally induced sociality and an integrally induced human finitude. Such is the being of society that justifies the perspective and subject-matter of social ontology (287).

In fact, the decisionist spectrum of the 'friend-enemy' distinction (Kondylis himself recognizes it but takes distance from Carl Schmitt) resembles Castoriadis' ontology of the imaginary: 'Total order and total disorder are not the components of the real, but limiting concepts which we abstract from it, pure constructions which, taken in absolute terms, become illegitimate and incoherent' (Castoriadis, 1987, p. 72). If Kondylis had contained his quest for the socio-ontological in the heuristic value of concept formation, he would have escaped Castoriadis' objections to such limiting concepts. Because, however, Kondylis posits that the 'socio-ontological level is deeper than the ethical' in that it 'includes ethical as well as non-ethical standpoints' (2007, p. 533) as the real end of the broadest possible spectrum, he can be seen to regress to a decisionist foundationalism. It is on these grounds that Kondylis admits that Weber came closest to socio-ontology when he conceived the multitude of combinations between 'value-rational' and 'instrumental rational' actions but 'erred (as a sociologist)' on how he 'extended ideal-typical in their elaboration historical-sociological contents to the area of social ontology' (792), erroneously using the juxtaposition between 'value-rational' and 'instrumental-rational' actions as the criterion for understanding socio-ontological situations.[26]

It is to Kondylis' credit that he sets criteria of self-reference and self-refutation for his theory (and, incidentally, for him theories are manifestations of the will to power), but the criterion to which he seeks the role of the tribunal cannot be another contesting theory (since this is power-driven) but an 'empirical research' (292) that, interestingly, supersedes the conceptual toolkit of Kondylis' proposed theory. Now why such empirically adduced falsification cannot stem from a rival theory remains unaccounted for. We cannot enter the antinomies and paradoxes that stem from Kondylis' supremely ambitious work. It is the merit of his quest for a social ontology as sociology's condition of possibility that requires a sustained and nuanced response from Greek sociologists.

Kondylis' Sociological Diagnostics

A second relevance of Kondylis' work for sociology comes by way of *Kulturkritik*. The 1995 Greek translation of his 1991 book *Der Niedergang der bürgerlichen Denk- und Lebensform. Die liberale Moderne und die massendemokratische Postmoderne* (see also the review by Julien Freund (1992)) contains a long and dense introduction written specifically for the Greek readers. Its title is 'Introduction to the Greek edition: The sickliness of the bourgeois element in contemporary Greek society and ideology' (Kondylis, 1995, pp. 11–47).[27] In this polemical text, Kondylis explains the methodological presuppositions for the critique to be unfolded:

> Understanding goes into depth only if the historical and sociological categories, or types, are supplemented with intuitions and representations, capable

---

[26] For a critique of Kondylis' appropriation of Weberian sociology, see Faraklas (2018).

[27] Prior to this work, Kondylis had demonstrated his approach in the context of Greek Enlightenment that considers 'sociological analysis' to be an important extension of the philosophical arsenal in explaining the shaping of ideas (Kondylis, 1988, p. 13).

of enlivening, within their immediate existential and experienced references, those individual and collective human states, from the condensation of which in this or that level of abstraction, our concepts came to be. (1995, p. 11)

There is a *Lebensphilosophie* tone here when Kondylis refers to intuitions and lived experience and proceeds to provide a chronicle of Greek society's capitulation to mass democracy. Key structural and culturally specific causes include the pre-capitalist and pre-bourgeois mode of economic development in modern Greece, which lacked the Prometheanism of the entrepreneurial spirit that spurred industrialization in Europe and elsewhere. Thus, the modern Greek state emerged in the unhappy tango between the establishment of parliamentary processes, including universal suffrage, and a patriarchal society. Social mobility opportunities which inevitably flowed from the expansion of the state built on the occupation of social positions by public officers who held the status of party acolytes. Clientelism (along with nepotism and cronyism) implies, for Kondylis, the transference of familial patriarchy from society to the state. In this sense the divestiture of the state was effected by patriarchal modes of management, communication and petty exchanges with the citizens; as a result, such 'methods' solidified into collective mentalities and practices, constraining an entire people into a game that locked large petty middle-class clusters into a pendular movement between the 'liberal'/'right' and the 'left' of the political spectrum. This 'paradox' for Kondylis can be summarized in his own words: 'in order for the state to accommodate as much as possible the multitude of clientelist demands, it was forced to provide low wages; in other words, its misery was the inversely necessary dimension and precondition of its generosity' (25). Tethered to clientelist particularisms, the separation between state and church remains in limbo as well as the demarcation between state and civil society. Another deficiency discerned by Kondylis' *coup de grâce* diagnostics was the unwarranted extension of the idea of the nation beyond the boundaries of the state. This proved to be a historical and structural deficiency that mythologized the Greek nation, leading to 'hellenocentric' narratives and a concomitant hegemonic framework capable of cementing heterogeneous forces across, for example, the political spectrum of Greek society. 'Hellenocentric' morphologies include classicist humanism and Christianity which led to a Byzantine-centred rehabilitation of the historical role of the Greek Church, extended also to elevating the Greek language to a measuring rod of appraisals in policies and personalities (37). With even more value-laden terminology, Kondylis explains the 'monstrous modernization' (40) of the post-Civil War decades, noting the predominance of an 'artificial' middle-class and an 'impure' mass democracy still tied to traditional shackles of particularism-driven practices. Such frustrated rhetoric (even other sociologists and philosophers have not been immune to it in their numerous interventions and commentaries on Greek society's modernization)[28] reaches its apex when Kondylis adumbrates what he calls a 'collective schizophrenia' (44) that afflicts the majority of Greeks today who seem to be caught between the pincers of a 'parasitic consumerism' and a 'prickly nationalism' (44–45). Ultimately, for Kondylis, 'Greece figures in a very low position in the international system of material and intellectual labor' (p. 47). Kondylis' elective affinity with sociology did not go unnoticed in the admittedly scant sociological quarters in Greece. He gave an interview (Kondylis, 1998, pp. 16–36) to *Nea Koinoniologia* (New Sociology), a journal that reflected to a considerably degree Kondylis' *Kulturkritik* 'jargon of authenticity' versus what was seen by the journal's editors to be an 'inauthentic' in political, academic and cultural terms contemporary Greece (see Chap. 6 on the journal's 'end of an era' farewell announcement).

The Kosmas Psychopedis Axiologika *Interdisciplinary Group*

Neither Poulantzas' structural Marxism nor Castoriadis' ontology of the imaginary could accommodate issues of values and norms. Kondylis' work did, but, schematically put, he placed them in the epiphenomenal realm of perspectivism, descriptive theory and incessant power aggrandizement. In his sceptical thought experiment about Greek sociology and whether it really exists, Kyrtsis includes the journal *Axiologika* along with the closely related publisher *Sakis Karagiorgas Foundation* among those fora that specialized in 'social and political theory' (1996, p. 11). Kyrtsis' judgement is correct in including *Axiologika* among those outlets that drew on sociology's theoretical heritage to upgrade the epistemological and normative hooks of social and political theory. Indeed, in *Axiologika* many essays of sociological interest have appeared (see, indicatively only, Alexandropoulos, 2006, Halaris, 1994, Simopoulos, 1992, Tsinorema,

---

[28] In this sense, the penchant for polemics and intemperance that compromises descriptive, explanatory and prescriptive adequacy, even by Greece's foremost intellectuals, could be approached through a sociology of Greek intellectuals' public discourse.

1994), while the *Sakis Karagiorgas Foundation*[29] published some volumes of direct sociological relevance (see Gangas, 2009; Pantazis, 2005). The intellectual inspiration behind such efforts was Kosmas Psychopedis (1944–2004) whose education in Germany formed a particularly solid and principled 'alliance' between German Idealism (Kant, Hegel) and Marx, without occluding, however, challenges to normative rationalism launched from Weberian perspectivism. Through this lens Psychopedis (1993, 1994) grappled with Weber's critique of normativity considering with paramount sophistication his methodology in light of problems of indeterminacy and value polytheism. The necessity of exploring the epistemological substratum of the social sciences[30] in how logical concepts assume normative claims and entanglement with historical shapes of institutions was prompted by the idea that indeterminate are those social relations that sustain unfreedom, alienation and injustice. In fact, one of Psychopedis' latest texts [written in the early 2000s but published posthumously (see Psychopedis, 2008)] sought to discern this normative justification in Talcott Parsons' sociological understanding of the economy and its ethical-normative underpinnings.

Thus, it no coincidence that, for Psychopedis, sustained epistemological and axiological bridge-building between diverse normative paradigms in social theory would see in Castoriadis and Kondylis manifestations of irrationalist tendencies in Greek theoretical thought (Psychopedis, 2002)[31] not only at odds with rational projects of solidary political and economic emancipation but epistemologically vulnerable too due to their embrace of a primordially unmediated irrationality in social imaginaries and social ontology.

---

[29] Sakis Karagiorgas (1930–1985) was Rector at Panteion University and an active member of the resistance against the Greek junta. He has become an emblematic figure since his untimely death and the foundation under his name, established in 1989, addresses interdisciplinary issues on the social, economic and political aspects of the state. On Karagiorgas and his era, see Psalidopoulos (1999, pp. 265–271).

[30] Such interest in social and sociological theory led to the publication of a valuable reader (with texts from Marx, Menger, Durkheim, Weber to Althusser, Parsons, Giddens and Luhmann (Kouzelis & Psychopedis, 1994)) for Greek students given the then relative lack of available sources in translation.

[31] For a systematic critique of Kondylis relativist decisionism (as an amalgam of Weber's value-relativism, Nietzsche's will-to-power, Schmitt's 'friend-enemy' distinction and Menger's formal indeterminacy), see Psychopedis (1999).

Acknowledgements Raymond Petridis provided invaluable information about Kondylis' thought, and the conversations held with him illuminated grey areas. We are grateful to his insights and enthusiasm.

References

Alexandropoulos, S. (2006). Ο πραγματισμός και η κατασκευή της κοινωνικής πράξης. Μια κριτική προσέγγιση [Pragmatism and the construction of social praxis. A critical approach]. *Axiologika, 15*, 181–199.

Arnason, J. P., & Beilharz, P. (1997). Castoriadis and Thesis Eleven. *Thesis Eleven, 49*(1), vi–viii.

Association Castoriadis. (1997). Retrieved May 8, 2022, from https://www.castoriadis.org/fr/

Beilharz, P. (2020). Remembering Castoriadis. *Thesis Eleven, 161*(1), 5–13.

Bitsakis, E. (2005). Επιστήμες και φιλοσοφία. Η περίπτωση του Κορνήλιου Καστοριάδη [The sciences and philosophy. The case of Cornelius Castoriadis]. *Utopia, 67*, 155–168.

Castoriadis, C. (1944a). Κατευθύνσεις του περιοδικού [Directions of the Journal]. *Αρχείον Κοινωνιολογίας και Ηθικής [Archive of Sociology and Ethics], 2*, 89–93.

Castoriadis, C. (1944b). Σημειώσεις. Max Weber: Μεθοδικές βάσεις της κοινωνιολογίας [Notes on Max Weber's methodological foundations of sociology]. *Αρχείον Κοινωνιολογίας και Ηθικής [Archive of Sociology and Ethics], 2*, 112–140.

Castoriadis, C. (1944c). Εισαγωγή στη θεωρία των κοινωνικών επιστημών [Introduction to the theory of the social sciences]. *Αρχείον Κοινωνιολογίας και Ηθικής [Archive of Sociology and Ethics], 2*, 141–150.

Castoriadis, C. (1978). Εισαγωγικό σημείωμα για το γλωσσάρι της μετάφρασης [Introductory note about the translation's glossary]. In C. Castoriadis (Ed.), *Η φαντασιακή θέσμιση της κοινωνίας* [The imaginary institution of society) (pp. 519–526). (S. Chalikias, G. Spantidaki & K. Spantidakis, Trans.). Kedros. (Original work published in 1975).

Castoriadis, C. (1983). The Greek *Polis* and the creation of democracy. In D. A. Curtis (Ed.), *The Castoriadis Reader* (pp. 267–289). Blackwell.

Castoriadis, C. (1984). Εκπομπή Παρασκήνιο: Συνέντευξη στην Τέτα Παπαδοπούλου (*Paraskinio* show: Interview to Teta Papadopoulou). ERT (Ellinikí Radiofonía Tileórasi A.E (Hellenic Broadcast Corporation). ERT archive number: 0000068811.

Castoriadis, C. (1985). Εκπομπή Θέματα και βιβλίο. Η φαντασιακή θέσπιση της κοινωνίας. Συζήτηση με τον Κορνήλιο Καστοριάδη: Κοσμάς Ψυχοπαίδης, Δημήτρης Μαρκής, Παντελής Μπασάκος [*Themes and Books* show. The imaginary institution of society. Discussing with Cornelius Castoriadis: Kosmas Psychopedis, Dimitris Markis, Pantelis Bassakos]. ERT (Ellinikí Radiofonía

Tileórasi A.E (Hellenic Broadcast Corporation). ERT archive number: Undetected.

Castoriadis, C. (1986). Η Γαλλική κοινωνία [The French society]. Ypsilon.

Castoriadis, C. (1987). *The imaginary institution of society* (K. Blamey, Trans.). Polity. (Original work published 1975).

Castoriadis, C. (1992a). Power, politics, autonomy. In A. Honneth, T. McCarthy, C. Offe, & A. Wellmer (Eds.), *Cultural-political interventions in the unfinished project of Enlightenment* (pp. 269–297). The MIT Press.

Castoriadis, C. (1992b). On wars in Europe. In M. Gondicas & P. Vernay (Eds.), *Cornelius Castoriadis. A society adrift: Interviews and debates, 1974-1997* (pp. 83–99). Fordham University Press.

Castoriadis, C. (1997). *World in fragments: Writings on politics, society, psychoanalysis and the imagination* (D. A. Curtis, Trans.). Stanford University Press. (Original works published 1986–1993).

Castoriadis, C. (2000a [1975–1976]). Το επαναστατικό πρόβλημα σήμερα [The revolutionary problem today]. Ypsilon.

Castoriadis, C. (2000b). Οι ομιλίες στην Ελλάδα [The lectures in Greece]. Ypsilon.

Castoriadis, C. (2001). Ανθρωπολογία, πολιτική, φιλοσοφία. Πέντε διαλέξεις στη Βόρειο Ελλάδα [Anthropology, politics, philosophy. Five lectures in Northern Greece]. Ypsilon.

Castoriadis, C. (2014a). Directions of the Journal *Sociological and Ethical Archive* (V. Karalis & A. Stephens, Trans.). In V. Karalis (Ed.), *Cornelius Castoriadis and radical democracy* (pp. 25–31). Brill (Original work published 1944).

Castoriadis, C. (2014b). On the work of Max Weber (Introduction to the theory of the social sciences) (V. Karalis & A. Stephens, Trans.). In V. Karalis (Ed.), *Cornelius Castoriadis and radical democracy* (pp. 32–58). Brill (Original work published 1944).

Clarke, S. (1977). Marxism, sociology and Poulantzas's theory of the state. *Capital and Class, 2*, 1–31.

Dosse, F. (2015). Καστοριάδης. Μια ζωή [Castoriadis. A life] (A. Pappas, Trans.). Polis (Original work published 2014).

Elefantis, A. (2006). Επίμετρο (Postscript). In Poulantzas, N. (2006). Η κρίση των δικτατοριών. Πορτογαλία, Ελλάδα, Ισπανία [The crisis of the dictatorships: Portugal, Greece, Spain] (C. Agriantoni & A. Apostolopoulos, Trans.). (pp. 121–125). Themelio/Nicos Poulantzas Institute. (Original work published 1975).

Faraklas, G. (2018). Machanspruch und Relativismus. Zum weberianischen Philosophen Panajotis Kondylis. In J. Pissis & D. Karidas (Eds.), *Deutschland und Griechenland im Spiegel der Philosophiegeschichte* (pp. 203–212). Edition Romiosini.

Frangoudaki, A. (1992). Diglossia and the present language situation in Greece: A sociological approach to the interpretation of diglossia and some hypotheses on today's linguistic reality. *Language in Society, 21*(3), 365–381.

Freund, J. (1992). Revue: Panajotis Kondylis. Der Niedergang der bürgerlichen Denk- und Lebens formen. Weinheim, Acta humaniora, 1991, 301 p., *L'Année sociologique* (1940/1948). *Troisième série, 42*, 408–411.
Gangas, S. (2009). Κοινωνία και ηθική. Αξίες και νεωτερικότητα στην κοινωνιολογία και τη φιλοσοφία του *Émile Durkheim* [Society and ethics. Values and modernity in *Émile Durkheim's sociology and philosophy*]. Sakis Karagiorgas Foundation.
Habermas, J. (1987a). The theory of communicative action. Volume 2. Lifeworld and system: A critique of functionalist reason (T. McCarthy, Trans.). Polity Press. (Original work published 1981).
Habermas, J. (1987b). *The philosophical discourse on modernity* (F. Lawrence, Trans.). Polity Press. (Original work published 1985).
Halaris, Y. (1994). Η επιστροφή του υποκειμένου στη σύγχρονη κοινωνιολογική θεωρία [The return of the subject in contemporary sociological theory]. *Axiologika, 7*, 156–173.
Haritopoulos, A. (2000). Three works from Cornelius Castoriadis. *European Journal of Social Theory, 3*(2), 260–267.
Haritopoulos, G. (2004) Κορνήλιος Καστοριάδης. Κριτική επισκόπηση της σκέψης του [Cornelius Castoriadis: A critical survey of his thought]. Ypsilon.
Harth, D. (2002). Χαϊδελβέργη-Αθήνα μετ' επιστροφής. Οι φιλοσοφικές διαδρομές του Παναγιώτη Κονδύλη [Heidelberg-Athens, return ticket. The philosophical routes of Panagiotis Kondylis] (A. Daskaroli, Trans.), *Nea Estia* (1747), 84–103. (Original lecture given in 2000).
Heller, A. (1989). With Castoriadis to Aristotle: from Aristotle to Kant: from Kant to us. *Revue européenne des sciences sociales, 27*(86), 161–171.
Honneth, A. (1995). *The fragmented world of the social: Essays in social and political philosophy*. State University of New York Press.
Jessop, B. (1985). *Nicos Poulantzas: Marxist theory and political strategy*. Macmillan.
Joas, H. (1993). *Pragmatism and social theory*. The University of Chicago Press.
Joas, H. (1996). *The creativity of action* (J. Gaines & P. Keast, Trans.). Polity Press. (Original work published 1992).
Joas, H, & Knöbl, W. (2009). *Social theory: Twenty introductory lectures* (A. Skinner, Trans.). Cambridge University Press (Original work published 2004).
Kavoulakos, K. (1999). Κοινωνική οντολογία και κριτική θεωρία: Πρώτες σκέψεις για την κοινωνική θεωρία του Π.Κονδύλη [Social ontology and critical theory: first thoughts on P.Kondylis' social theory]. *Nea Estia, 1717*, 533–537.
Kokosalakis, N. (1998). Politics and sociology in Greece, 1950-1998. *International Sociology, 13*(3), 325–343.
Kondylis, P. ([1981] 2004). *Ο Ευρωπαϊκός Διαφωτισμός. Τόμος δεύτερος* [The European enlightenment. Volume two]. Themelio.
Kondylis, P. (1988). *Ο νεοελληνικός διαφωτισμός. Οι φιλοσοφικές ιδέες* [The modern Greek enlightenment. The philosophical ideas]. Themelio.

Kondylis, P. (1991). *Ισχύς και Απόφαση. Η διαμόρφωση των κοσμοεικόνων και το πρόβλημα των αξιών* [Power and decision. The formation of worldviews and the problem of values]. Stigmi. (Original work published 1984).
Kondylis, P. (1995). *Η Παρακμή του αστικού πολιτισμού: Από τη μοντέρνα στη μεταμοντέρνα εποχή και από το φιλελευθερισμό στη μαζική δημοκρατία* [The decline of bourgeois culture: From the modern to the postmodern era and from liberalism to mass democracy] (p. Kondylis, Trans). Themelio. (Original work published 1991).
Kondylis, P. (1998). Συνέντευξη: Συνομιλώντας με τον Παναγιώτη Κονδύλη [Interview: Conversing with Panajiotis Kondylis]. *Νέα Κοινωνιολογία [New Sociology]*, 25, 16–36.
Kondylis, P. (2007). *Το Πολιτικό και ο άνθρωπος. Βασικά στοιχεία της κοινωνικής οντολογίας (Δίτομο)* [Man and the Political: Basic elements of social ontology (Two Volumes)] (L. Anagnostou, Trans.). Themelio. (Original work published 1999).
Koselleck, R. (2002). Παναγιώτης Κονδύλης [Panajiotis Kondylis] (K. Koutsourelis, Trans.) *Nea Estia*, (1747), 67–83 (Original speech given in 2000).
Kouzelis, G & Psychopedis, K. (Eds.) (1994). *Επιστημολογία των κοινωνικών επιστημών. Κείμενα* [Epistemology of the social sciences. Texts]. Nisos.
Kranaki, M. (1944). Η λογική του Λασκ και η κοινωνιολογία [Lask's logic and sociology]. *Αρχείον Κοινωνιολογίας και Ηθικής [Archive of Sociology and Ethics]*, 2, 99–111.
Kyrtsis, A. A. (1996). Greek sociology: Does it really exist? *The European Sociologist*, 4, 10–11.
Kyrtsis, A. A. (1998). Greek interbellum modernizers and the 'sociological idea'. *International Sociology*, 13(3), 311–324.
Laclau, E. (1975). The specificity of the political: Around the Poulantzas-Miliband Debate. *Economy and Society*, 4(1), 87–110.
Laclau, E. (1977). *Politics and ideology in Marxist theory: capitalism – fascism – populism*. Verso.
Lambiri-Dimaki, I. (2000). *Για την κοινωνιολογία* [For sociology]. Sakkoulas.
Leledakis, K. (1995). *Society and psyche: Social theory and the unconscious dimension of the social*. Berg Publishers.
Leledakis, K. (1999). An appreciation of Cornelius Castoriadis (1922-1997): Theorist of autonomy and openness. *European Journal of Social Theory*, 2(1), 95–98.
Marker, C. (2018). *The owl's legacy*. Icarus films. (Originally filmed in 1989).
Masson, P., & Schrecker, C. (2016). *Sociology in France after 1945*. Palgrave Pivot.
Meletopoulos, M. (2000). *Νίκος Πουλαντζάς 1936-1979. Η ζωή και το έργο ενός κορυφαίου μαρξιστή – Κριτική προσέγγιση* [Nicos Poulantzas 1936–1979. The life and work of a major Marxist – A critical approach]. Ellinika Grammata.

Meletopoulos, M. (2008). Η άγνωστη νεότητα του Κορνήλιου Καστοριάδη [The unknown youth of Cornelius Castoriadis]. *New Sociology*, *44*, 51–80.
Miliband, R. (1969). *The state in capitalist society: The analysis of the Western system of power*. Quartet Books.
Miliband, R. (1970). The capitalist state – Reply to N. Poulantzas. *New Left Review*, *59*, 53–60.
Miliband, R. (1973). Poulantzas and the capitalist state. *New Left Review*, *82*, 83–92.
Mouzakitis, A. (2014a). Creation *ex nihilo*. In S. Adams (Ed.), *Cornelius Castoriadis. Key concepts* (pp. 53–64). Bloomsbury.
Mouzakitis, A. (2014b). Social-historical. In S. Adams (Ed.), *Cornelius Castoriadis. Key concepts* (pp. 89–100). Bloomsbury.
Mouzelis, N. (1978). Ideology and class politics: A critique of Ernesto Laclau. *New Left Review*, *112*, 45–61.
The Nicos Poulantzas Institute. (1997). Retrieved April 29, 2022, from https://poulantzas.gr/en/the-institute/
Pantazis, A. (2005). Η γένεση του μεθοδολογικού ατομισμού στις κοινωνικές επιστήμες. *Προβλήματα κατασκευής κοινωνιολογικών και οικονομικών εννοιών* [The genesis of methodological individualism in the social sciences: Problems in constructing sociological and economic concepts]. Sakis Karagiorgas Foundation.
Papadopoulou, T. (2000). (Ed.). *Του Κορνήλιου Καστοριάδη. Συνεντεύξεις, μεταφράσεις* [Of Cornelius Castoriadis. Interviews, translations]. Polis.
Poulantzas, N. (1966a). Θέματα περί της μαρξιστικής αντίληψης περί κράτους [Issues regarding the Marxist understanding of the state]. In F. Iliou, T. Patrikios, & D. Spathis (Eds.), *Μαρξισμός και επιστήμη. Β' εβδομάδα σύγχρονης σκέψης* [Marxism and science. 2nd week of contemporary thought] (pp. 283–326). Themelio.
Poulantzas, N. (1966b). Τάξεις και κράτος. Σεμινάριο [Classes and the State. A seminar]. In F. Iliou, T. Patrikios, & D. Spathis (Eds.), *Μαρξισμός και επιστήμη. Β' εβδομάδα σύγχρονης σκέψης* [Marxism and science. 2nd week of contemporary thought] (pp. 327–383). Themelio.
Poulantzas, N. (1969). The problem of the capitalist state. *New Left Review*, *58*(1), 67–78.
Poulantzas, N. (1975). *Classes in contemporary capitalism*. (D. Fernbach, Trans.). Verso. (Original work published 1974).
Poulantzas, N. (1976a). The capitalist state: A reply to Miliband and Laclau. *New Left Review*, *95*, 63–83.
Poulantzas, N. (1976b). Πρόλογος (Prologue). In G. Veltsos, *Κοινωνία και γλώσσα (για την αμίλητη και τη μιλημένη γλώσσα)* [Society and language (about the unspoken and the spoken language)]. Papazisis Publishers.
Poulantzas, N. (1978). *Political power and social classes* (T. O'Hagan, Trans.). Verso. (Original work published 1968).

Poulantzas, N. (1979). *Fascism and dictatorship: The Third International and the problem of fascism* (J. White, Trans.). Verso. (Original work published 1970).
Poulantzas, N. (1980). *State, power, socialism* (P. Camiller, Trans.). Verso. (Original work published 1978).
Poulantzas, N. (2006). *Η κρίση των δικτατοριών. Πορτογαλία, Ελλάδα, Ισπανία* [The crisis of the dictatorships: Portugal, Greece, Spain] (C. Agriantoni, A. Apostolopoulos, Trans.). Themelio/Nicos Poulantzas Institute. (Original work published 1975).
Poulantzas, N. (2019). *Κράτος, κοινωνικές τάξεις, καπιταλισμός, ιμπεριαλισμός. Τα μαθήματα του Νίκου Πουλαντζά στο Πάντειο το 1977* [State, social classes, capitalism, imperialism. Nicos Poulantzas' lectures at Panteion 1977]. Papazisis.
Poulantzas N., Miliband R. & Faye, J.-P. (1981). *Προβλήματα του σύγχρονου κράτους και του φασιστικού φαινομένου* [Problems of the contemporary state and of the phenomenon of fascism]. Themelio.
Psalidopoulos, M. (1999). *Πολιτική οικονομία και Έλληνες διανοούμενοι. Μελέτες για την ιστορία της οικονομικής σκέψης στη σύγχρονη Ελλάδα* [Political economy and Greek intellectuals. Studies on the history of economic thought in contemporary Greece]. Typothito.
Psarras, D., & Karidas, D. (2019, September 2). *A revolutionary from the OECD – the Castoriadis-Poulantzas Debate*. Retrieved April 13, 2022, from https://www.versobooks.com/blogs/4427-a-revolutionary-from-the-oecd-the-castoriadis-poulantzas-debate
Psychopedis, K. (1992). Dialectical theory: Problems of reconstruction. In W. Bonefeld, R. Gunn, & K. Psychopedis (Eds.), *Open Marxism. Volume I: Dialectics and history* (pp. 1–53). Pluto Press.
Psychopedis, K. (1993). *Ο Max Weber και η κατασκευή εννοιών στις κοινωνικές επιστήμες* [Max Weber and concept formation in the social sciences]. Kentavros.
Psychopedis, K. (1994). *Ιστορία και μέθοδος* [History and method]. (L. Sakali, Trans.). Smili. (Original work published 1984).
Psychopedis, K. (1999). Η απόφαση για θεωρία στη θεωρία της απόφασης του Παναγιώτη Κονδύλη [The decision for theory in Panagiotis Kondylis' theory of decision]. *Nea Estia, 1717*, 498–513.
Psychopedis, K. (2001). Ο Νίκος Πουλαντζάς και η πολιτική μέσα στη μέθοδο (Προβλήματα στρουκτουραλιστικής επιστημολογίας στο έργο του Νίκου Πουλαντζά) [Nicos Poulantzas and politics within method (Problems of structuralist epistemology in the work of Nicos Poulantzas)]. In A. Rigos & C. Tsoukalas (Eds.), *Η Πολιτική Σήμερα: Ο Νίκος Πουλαντζάς και η Επικαιρότητα του Έργου του* [Politics Today: Nicos Poulantzas and the relevance of his work] (pp. 142–151). Themelio.
Psychopedis, K. (2002). Το ανορθολογικό στοιχείο στην ελληνική θεωρητική σκέψη [The element of irrationalism in Greek theoretical thought]. In K. Psychopedis (M. Angelidis, Ed., 2011) (pp. 311–328). *Ήσσονα κριτικά* (Minor critical [texts]). Nisos.

Psychopedis, K. (2003). Μερικά πράγματα που θυμάμαι από το Κέντρο Κοινωνικών Επιστημών Αθηνών (προ του 1967) [Some things I remember from the Athens Centre of Social Sciences]. In I. Lambiri-Dimaki (Ed.), *Κοινωνικές επιστήμες και πρωτοπορία στην Ελλάδα 1950–1967* [Social Sciences and novelty in Greece 1950–1967] (pp. 425–430). Gutenberg.

Psychopedis, K. (2008). Το πρόβλημα της κοινωνικοεπιστημονικής εξήγησης στην κοινωνιολογία του Τάλκοτ Πάρσονς [The problem of social-scientific explanation in Talcott Parsons' sociology]. In Maglaras, V. (Ed.), *Τάλκοτ Πάρσονς. Καπιταλισμός και αξίες: Τα πρώιμα κείμενα* [Talcott Parsons. Capitalism and values: The early texts] (pp. 169–183). Nisos.

Rigos, A, & Tsoukalas, C. (Eds.). (2001). *Η Πολιτική σήμερα: Ο Νίκος Πουλαντζάς και η επικαιρότητα του έργου του* [Politics today: Nicos Poulantzas and the relevance of his work]. Themelio.

Rorty, R. (1991). *Essays on Heidegger and others. Philosophical papers. Volume 2.* Cambridge University Press.

Scott, J. (2020). *British sociology: A history.* Palgrave Macmillan.

Simopoulos, K. (1992). Μεθοδολογική αποδόμηση και αισθητική ανασύνθεση: μια κριτική παρουσίαση των μεθοδολογικών επιλογών βάσει των οποίων συγκροτείται η κοινωνικο-ιστορική επιστημολογία του Georg Simmel [Methodological deconstruction and aesthetic synthesis: a critical presentation of the methodological choices on the basis of which Georg Simmel's socio-historical epistemology is constructed]. *Axiologika, 3,* 7–55.

Taylor, C. (1983). Review: Die Entstehung der Dialektik: Eine Analyse der geistigen Entwicklung von Holderlin, Schelling und Hegel bis 1802. By Panajotis Kondylis. Stuttgart: Klett-Cotta, 1979. Pp. 729. *The Journal of Modern History, 55*(1), 100–102.

Tepstra, M. (2008). A decisionist approach to democratic political order. *Netherlands Journal of Legal Philosophy, 37*(2), 151–162.

Tsinorema, V. (1994). Επιστήμη και ορθολογικότητα. Τα αδιέξοδα του σχετικισμού στη σύγχρονη φιλοσοφία και κοινωνιολογία της επιστήμης [Science and rationality. The impasses of relativism in contemporary philosophy and sociology of science]. *Axiologika, 7,* 7–71.

Tsivakou, I. (2021) Διαβάζοντας το Πολιτικό και ο Άνθρωπος: Μια οντολογική προσέγγιση της επικοινωνίας [Reading the Political and Man: An ontological approach to communication]. In *Γκρίζο στο γκρίζο. Ο Παναγιώτης Κονδύλης και η κριτική του Διαφωτισμού* [Grey on grey. Panagiotis Kondylis and the critique of Enlightenment] (pp. 141–154). Enallaktikes Ekdoseis.

Veltsos, Y. (1989). *Προς τον Κορνήλιο Καστοριάδη* [Addressed to Cornelius Castoriadis]. Plethron.

Wagner, P. (1994). *A sociology of modernity: Liberty and discipline.* Routledge.

Waters, M. (1994). *Modern sociological theory.* Sage.

CHAPTER 5

Greek Sociology's Interdisciplinary and Multi-paradigmatic Shift: 1990–2000

Abstract As Greece enters the 1990 affluent modernization, sociology develops from the centre to the periphery and from undergraduate to master's programmes. This chapter addresses sociology's institutional impetus but also extends to a thematic widening of sociological foci that span social change, demography, migration, gender roles, political parties and bureaucracy, social movements, ethnocentric narratives and diaspora, among many others. Further attention to sociology includes its media dissemination with the most important project being the filmed conversations of Veltsos and Tsoukalas with international sociologists and philosophers for the *Hellenic Broadcast Corporation* (ERT). On the level of sociological theory contributions, this chapter addresses Mouzelis' work and the reconstructive steps he proposes for sociological theory's renewal against the background of post-Marxism, sociological dualisms and post-modernism, making also references to Greece. What also emerges in the 1990s is the dual process of interdisciplinary bridges (mainly with history, anthropology) and of an internally growing multi-paradigmatic shift, often as a result of post-structuralist influence.

Keywords Interdisciplinarity • Mouzelis • Multi-paradigmatic shift • Tsoukalas • Veltsos

© The Author(s), under exclusive license to Springer Nature Switzerland AG 2022
S. Gangas, G. Lagoumitzi, *Sociology in Greece*, Sociology Transformed, https://doi.org/10.1007/978-3-031-16190-2_5

Reconstructing Sociological Theory: Nicos Mouzelis

Why begin a chapter about Greek sociology with Mouzelis' 1990 sociological theory programme that flourished in the UK? Mouzelis' work was propelled by what were then vivid calls towards transforming sociological categories (and to which he contributed), coupled to proposed guidelines for sociological theory's exit from real and perceived explanatory stalemates. Yet as we intimated in the previous chapter, Mouzelis' work abroad was never detached from the Greek context, as he also admits (see later in this section) and quickly became paradigmatic for Greek sociology (see, e.g. Lambiri-Dimaki's (2000, p. 134)).

In *Post-Marxist alternatives*, Mouzelis (1990) takes issue with a dualism that has shaped the sociological tradition since its inception. The Marxist versus non-Marxist dilemma is one that proves inadequate given Marxism's significant explanatory failures. Its tenacity by various acolytes in sociology seems, for Mouzelis, to be inversely related to Marxism's instances of conceptual and empirical fecundity. Surreptitiously, such rigidities 'neutralize the most fruitful aspects of the Marxist framework: its dialectical and holistic character' (1990, p. 173). Developing a heuristic typology of the Marxist proclivity to reductionism (voluntaristic 'agent to agent' reductionism, voluntaristic 'agent to structure' reductionism, structuralist 'structure to structure' reductionism and a 'structure to agent' reductionism of which Poulantzas offers a sophisticated variant), Mouzelis launches a meta-theoretical programme to transcend dualisms, built, however, on sociological dualisms' foundational materials (structure, agency). The book's last part traces Marxist reductionism's pitfalls to Greece's socio-political path to development. Focusing on a Greek Marxist and non-Marxist historiography around the explanation of the 1909 Goudi coup (see Chap. 1), Mouzelis deems as fallacious the inbuilt rigorism of each approach at the expense of multi-factor (political, economic, cultural [technologies, ideologies, religion, art]) explanations that for him reveal the relative autonomy of a Greek oligarchic polity. Instead of explaining the 1909 coup as a 'bourgeois revolution', this 'must be seen primarily as an essentially politico-military revolt which brought about an important change in the relations of domination, this change playing a crucial role in eventually transforming the relations of production a decade or more later' (139). Thus, the pincers of materialist reductionism of base (Marx) and Parsonsian culturally induced functionalism seem equally ill-suited as explanatory models and subsequent programmes.

As companion to that book, Mouzelis now makes a clarion call for a return to sociological theory's non-haughty (as opposed to epistemologically or conceptually a priori claims to completeness of sociological categories) craftsmanship in concept formation that owes to Merton (and later to Bourdieu). Thus, *Back to sociological theory* (1991) welcomes a reorientation shift to sociology's proper theoretical underpinnings, bracketing as it were any automatic quest for epistemological presuppositions and justifications. Reductionism and reification emerge as non-dualist 'solutions' even in sophisticated attempts like Giddens' structuration theory which aims to eschew the difficulties of dualism with a shift to the duality of 'agency and structure'. Partially questioning sociology's attachment to dualisms (during the same period dualist sociology was criticized by Holmwood & Stewart, 1991), Mouzelis resorts to the ontological foundation of categories, reproducing polarities even as he proffers to show that 'the notions of duality and dualism are both necessary for distinguishing, on the paradigmatic level, how actors orient themselves to rules and resources as a virtual order. They are equally necessary on the syntagmatic level, for stressing the asymmetrical, differential contribution of actors to the reproduction and transformation of a social system's structural properties' (1991, p. 39). Providing a subtly analytical topography of sociology's other dualisms (individual-society, micro-macro, social integration-system integration), Mouzelis warns against reiteration of sociological fallacies like reification, anthropomorphism and teleology of which Durkheimian and Parsonsian functionalisms share generous portions. Similarly, reductionisms of sorts ('downward' as in neo-Marxist underdevelopment theories or 'upward' as in Weber's human personality-driven explanation of capitalism's genesis or in rational-choice Marxism) prove equally debilitating for sociological theory's sensors to social reality's multi-dimensionality. It is apposite for the section on the interdisciplinary shift of sociology that Mouzelis ends the book with a further consideration of historical sociology's approach that reveals the groundwork, as it were, in what Mouzelis' proposed architectonic (170–171) is: the meta-theoretical ('third-order') level and its dialectical search for validation alongside sociology's theoretical/empirical ('second-order') growth and against the 'first-order' enunciation of sociology's historical groundwork in how actual actors in real social settings pursue concept formation and observe their own recipe skills in (re)making social orders.

Delving even deeper into the problem of sociological theory's future in *Sociological Theory: What Went Wrong?* Mouzelis' 'conceptual pragmatism'

(1995a, pp. 8–11) resists attachment to a priori valid sociological paradigms. Crucial here is the strategy of complexifying dualist rigidities, such as macro and micro, which should be approached under an 'onion-like systems-within-systems' (26) holism that is geared towards differentiation. Maintaining sociology's call for a 'relative autonomy' Mouzelis rebuts post-structuralist (Foucault) and other (rational-choice theory) paradigmatic infiltrations that elide discipline boundaries. At the same time, he hopes to alert sociologists to antinomies that stem from mutually exclusive approaches to concept formation and explanation of social reality. The most telling examples are Parsonsian functionalism and Elias' figuration sociology. For Mouzelis, each model must accommodate what the other provides (social holism in Parsons' deductive model, interactional interdependence in actual social settings for Elias), recognizing social reality's non-reducible multi-dimensionality. Emulating Durkheim's and later Giddens' 'new rules of sociological method', Mouzelis provides a set of prescriptions (154–159) on what sociology should avoid, what it should not conflate and how it can retain its distinctive standpoint next to other disciplines (it must be noted that such a prescriptive set is not without strains, considering the fact that non-foundationalism and anti-essentialism may unduly ignore or repel pragmatically fecund and differentiated essentialist reconstructions). Applying Bourdieu's non-hierarchical model of the different types of capital to himself and to his father's habitus in the transition from village life (Amfiklia) to rural town (Lamia) and then to an urban metropolis (Athens), Mouzelis (160–172) places them in a matrix of socio-spatial niches that include Switzerland, the United Kingdom (from Geneva to LSE and then to the University of Leicester and back to LSE) and link different types and degrees of economic, social and cultural capital. In a sense, he vindicates the perception of his frequent and meaningful rapport with Greece (168).

INTERDISCIPLINARITY: SOCIOLOGY'S IDENTITY ALREADY IN DOUBT?

Interdisciplinary work had been on the Greek sociological map even at a time when the discipline had only attained an institutionally at least pre-paradigmatic profile. For example, Nicolaou lists fields like jurisprudence, economics, philosophy, history, religion, psychology, education and art along with Marxist literature as ones from which 'the contribution that many individual scholars [...] made to sociology' sets the foundation for 'future closer interdisciplinary cooperation' (1974, p. 27, but see also p. 81). If we consider, however, the discipline's boundaries which, as we intimated in Chap. 4, proved challenging for accounts of Greek sociology (even in the case of Castoriadis' and Poulantzas' calibre), the 1990 impetus for such boundary collaborations and crossings tends to adumbrate a period of sociology proper that is sandwiched between the pre-paradigmatic state (sociology up to the late 1970s) and a rapidly assimilated multi-paradigmatic impetus.[1]

Koniordos (2010, p. 183) locates this tension, for example, in the late 1970 reception of Poulantzas in Greece and the oscillation between 'sociologizing Marxism' and 'Marxist sociology'. But cutting deeper into the structural reasons for the strained osmosis between sociology and other disciplines, one encounters sociology traversing a road towards institutionalized subject-matter autarky to be strewn with demarcation ambiguities. For Koniordos, sociology's growth seems to have been undermined both from a relative lack of expert faculty on the supply side and an unusual readiness on the demand side to recruit Department of Sociology faculty from neighbouring disciplines. This inbuilt heterogeneity created, for Koniordos (186), strains in adaptation to the subject of sociology and the discipline's degree of integration, both on the ground of undergraduate instruction and in terms of organizational efficiency. Moreover, it consolidated patterns (often under the rule of law) for subject-matter (specialism) shifts (if specialisms were considered barriers to a faculty member's research development) and proliferation of specialisms alien to sociology yet housed under sociology departments (189, n.18) that further obfuscated sociology's distinctive identity in theory, method and scope. In short, sociology quickly fell prey to

---

[1] Indicative of the state of social sciences' fuzzy boundaries is the case of the premier philosophy journal *Deukalion*. It featured, as in the 1975 (13) issue, contributions from Tsoukalas, Veltsos and Vergopoulos, among others. *Deukalion* welcomed and published articles of sociological focus even during the 2000s, despite its nearly exclusively philosophical (even analytical) orientation. Less rigorous in its selection breadth, since it was not patterned as a scholarly journal, but with sociological articles featured was *Synchrona Themata* (Contemporary Issues). In the 1990s, for example, Lambiri-Dimaki and Lipowatz published sociologically relevant articles.

'entryism' (188n.16), a neologism that is tantamount to a cronyistic strategy, often of a political intent. [2]

This anomaly is also shared by Psychopedis (1990, pp. 281–282) who adds the cases of welding or mixing between disciplines in conjunction to the social sciences' own internal struggles for administrative and curricular autonomy. The debate over disciplines' boundaries flared up in the 1990s. Lambiri-Dimaki (1997, p. 21) confirms the boundary fluidity and the shift to an interdisciplinary rather than to a clearly demarcated sociological focus among sociology publications in the 1990s. We have already seen how Castoriadis' works and certainly Kondylis' relevant to sociology books (see Chap. 4) have been largely ejected from the sociological 'rubric'. Examples of the potential for interdisciplinary systematic conversations are to be found in Mouzelis who while professor at LSE continued to contribute to the formation of a sociological discourse in Greece. At a time when Mouzelis, as we saw, sought to fortify sociology, he was quick to review Lambiri-Dimaki's (1989) book *Sociology and History*. For Mouzelis, Lambiri-Dimaki discerns a growing convergence between sociology and history (scope of phenomena studied, methodologies, interpretive schemes). While defending the 'general' character of sociology versus history's focus on specific actors, Lambiri-Dimaki repels any attempt at a full absorption of one field by another, for example, in the case of historicism and sociologism. Despite these identified merits, Mouzelis points to currently unbridgeable gulfs between history and sociology evinced in ethnomethodology and in phenomenological sociology which brush aside 'second-order' theories, priming instead actors' 'first-order' theories (2002, pp. 306–307). He identifies a trend in sociology to muster history with a view to merely embellish theory with empirical facts. Clarifying that such opportunistic uses of history (he refers critically (307) to Comte, Spencer and their epigones) are not discerned in Weber or in the best traditions of historical sociology (B. Moore, R. Bendix, T. Skocpol, M. Mann), Mouzelis hopes to mutually inform both fields; moreover, the proliferation of 'histories' and 'sociologies'

[2] In a letter of 20 April 2008 addressed to the rectors of all universities, to all sociology faculty and to prospective applicants for sociology positions, copied also to the *Hellenic Ministry of Education and Religious Affairs*, the *Hellenic Sociological Society* (HSS) had alerted all recipients as to the degree of deviation from sociology per se due to the great number of incoming faculty from 'related' fields. Beyond practical proposals that would safeguard the profession and academic profile of the Greek sociologist, the letter appealed to applicants' 'academic ethos' (See HSS, 2008).

raises an additional barrier to such convergence and what Mouzelis would welcome to be a more 'adversarial' than 'consensual' approach in Lambiri-Dimaki's argument (308). The spirit and substance of his review were pursued later with an argument in favour of historical sociology (Mouzelis, 1994a).

Equally engaging are Mouzelis' critical reflections on the 'new anthropology' in the context of its linkages to sociology, linguistics, psychoanalysis, history and philosophy. Taking his cue from important social anthropology works about contemporary Greece, he embarks on a qualified critique of markedly non-essentialist notions of gender in the transition from androcentrism to feminism in radical constructivist discourses (Mouzelis, 2002, pp. 332–339). Some of these arguments challenge the integration-driven approach to Greek rituals in the work of John Campbell as opposed to Michael Herzfeld's interaction-founded explanations.[3] Drawing on seminal Greek anthropological work by Papataxiarchis and Paradellis, Mouzelis revisits the disciplines' boundary drawing, now between anthropology and sociology. Commenting on international anthropological work about Greece, Mouzelis discerns a comparative approach with no recourse to a systematic study of structural transformations and how these elicit social transformations. This is a sociological lacuna in the 'new anthropology' (342–346) that calls, according to Mouzelis, for holistic models that connect the local, the regional and the nation-state dimensions to the global.

SOCIOLOGY IN PUBLIC AND VIRTUAL SPACES

With already three sociology programmes established in universities and colleges (see Chaps. 2 and 3), the development of the discipline aligned with a state-supported tendency to proliferate university faculties and departments in the Greek periphery. This development witnessed the establishment of a fourth sociology department at the University of the Aegean (Mytilini, Lesvos) in 1999. Furthermore, in 1998 sociology had its first master's programme established at Panteion University. It was

---

[3] See, indicatively, the insightful analysis on Cretan sheep thieves and the invocation/non-invocation of the state in face of local moralities (and their collapse) (Herzfeld, 1997, p. 8) which, tellingly, can be said to represent an overarching syndrome in contemporary Greek people's histrionic relationship to the state and its absence from the daily affairs of those who exploit this absence to perpetuate local networks of patronage.

organized by Nota Kyriazis who was also the director of the programme, and it featured collaborations with numerous foreign academic institutions, primarily in the UK and France, including the University of Edinburgh (with John Holmwood having played an important role in the program in different facets of its establishment) and L'Institut d'Études Politiques de Paris. The MA in 'Social Exclusion and Minorities' in sociology with pathways in criminology and in psychology developed a course structure that sought to combine theoretical and methodological orientations while reflecting the importance of engaging theoretically with social research.[4] As a first master's programme in sociology in Greece, it provided a solid bridge between undergraduate curricula and PhD-level studies.[5]

The incorporation of sociology in university curricula was immediately fraught with the problem of textbook and reading availability in Greek to support coursework for Greek students. Fluency in English language became a prerequisite for the newly launched MA programmes in sociology in the late 1990s, yet undergraduate programmes could not feasibly require such fluency. Given the then scant availability of translated works by the classical founders (with the exception of Marx) and of contemporary sociological theory as well as influential works in sociology specialisms, the only available option was to quickly move to textbook authorship.[6]

Sociology Journals and Research Centres

In the early 1990s, the National Centre of Social Research was jeopardized under the then New Democracy administration. It faced imminent cuts (advocated by the then minister of Industry, Energy, Technology and Commerce Andreas Andrianopoulos (see Hellenic Parliament Minutes, 1992, pp. 7753–7754)), leading to a prospective funding of 1/3 of what it used to be reserved for the Centre. According to Lambiri-Dimaki (2000,

---

[4] The importance of theoretically informed social research is a key theme in Kyriazi's work (see Kyriazis, 1999).

[5] The initiative of awarding honorary PhDs to major sociologists came late to Greece, and thus opportunities to boost interest in sociology proved scant on this front. For example, in 1999, Robert K. Merton was awarded an honorary PhD from the Department of Political Science and Public Administration National Kapodistrian University of Athens.

[6] Tsaoussis (see Chap. 3) covered pressing student needs for many years (Tsaoussis, 1991). Tatsis for his part shouldered much of the pedagogy mission with repeated imprints of his two-volume sociology textbook (Tatsis, 1989, 1991). Later, of course, Greek translations of UK and US textbooks, as well as a spectacular increase in English-language fluency among student cohorts, diminished the space for Greek sociologists' efforts on this side of undergraduate student needs.

p. ix), Costas Simitis (later Prime Minister of Greece under the PA.SO.K administration) and Nikos Christodoulakis (later Minister for Development and Minister for Economy and Finance under PA.SO.K administrations) had a catalytic role in defending the Centre and its prolific output. Its reconstruction coincided with the Centre's directorship under Pavlos Sourlas from 1993 to 1995. Nikiforos Diamandouros became its director from 1995 to 1998 before becoming the first Ombudsman for Greece. During the 1990 publications from the Social Sciences Centre (EKKE) (research volumes and articles in the *Greek Review of Social Research*) (see references section for web link)) focused on theory, social change and localities, forms of social exclusion, migration-related studies, urban and rural sociology, social networks and solidarity and ageing, also expanding to less researched areas like cinematic pornography, tourism and youth and the sociological taxonomy of professions.

Beyond the Centre's publications, the journal *Forum of the Social Sciences (To Vima ton Koinonikon Epistimon)* retained a marked sociological focus, proving resilient in face of adversities (see also the volume 18 (70) 2018 issue in memoriam issue to Pantazis Terlexis and his work on Max Weber), and it is still in print with biannual issues. *New Sociology* was founded by Meletis Meletopoulos (who had studied with Jean Ziegler), and its first issue was published in early 1988. Mouzelis and Tsoukalas sat briefly on the journal's editorial board (only until the fall of 1988). Among the journal's highlights were the April 1991 exclusive interview with Tom Bottomore (Issue 13), the 1989 issue 6 tribute to Poulantzas and the Panagiotis Kondylis exclusive interview to Spyros Koutroulis (Issue 25, 1998).

Theory and Society (Theoria kai Koinonia) was also another short-lived journal directly relevant to sociology. For example, the May 1990 issue 1 featured essays by Tsoukalas, Kondylis, Metaxopoulos and Lipowatz, while the December 1990 issue 3 featured essays by Demertzis on theories of power, Karabatzaki-Perdiki[7] on Durkheim and Metaxopoulos on Poulantzas. The March 1991 issue 4 featured a Mouzelis article on Habermas.

---

[7] Karabatzaki-Perdiki had an affiliation to the University of Ioannina where she was teaching philosophy. Yet her PhD thesis at East Anglia University has a marked sociological interest (she was also a speaker in the 1991 symposium on Poulantzas at Ioannina) examining Durkheim and Plato through Gouldner (Karabatzaki-Perdiki, 1988). What this indicates for us today is a relative poverty (for an exception, see Lekkas, 1988) among Greek sociologists to rethink early sociologists through the lens of classical Greek thought. See, for example, McCarthy (2003).

In 1990–1991 a department of Social Policy and Social Anthropology was established at Panteion University under Tsaoussis' directorship. It housed a new research unit, the *Research Centre of Social Morphology and Social Policy* (KEKMOKOP) that managed soon to develop an impressive database of publications in social sciences, many of which focus on Greece. In 1992 at the University of Thessaly, the *Laboratory for Social Studies and Opinion Polls* was launched under the directorship of sociologist Pantazis Terlexis.

Greek TV's Mission Impossible: Disseminating Sociology to a Wider public Public (1)

With the rapid proliferation of private TV broadcasting stations in Greece in the early 1990s and their quick emulation of models from US and European TV shows, one type of programme that prevailed was the panel discussion. These panel shows ranged considerably in terms of quality as they soon became an opportunity for self-promotion, inflated rhetoric that thrived on negation and 'manufactured' agitation under the pretext of diversity (for these and other strategies, see Constantopoulou, 2011, pp. 47–49). This sort of 'tele-socialization' (Luhmann, 2000, p. 78) primed, even under the guise of the value of discussion and consensus and hard-to-deescalate 'conflicts' (28). Themes of such panel discussions were drawn from the national and international news. The premium was placed on issues that revealed chronic or ephemeral pathologies of Greek society and its diplomacy. In such panels, sociologists had minimal contribution (unlike interventions made by them in the press). While this qualified neglect protected most sociologists from falling prey to populist and distorted speech situations, the underside was a progressive impression that sociologists (as opposed to psychologists, economists, political scientists, lawyers, theologians, journalists, novelists and artists, among others) had no relevant professional judgement to provide. By default, even for those occasions where the discourse in such panels had available some preconditions for intellectually robust yet accessible for the layperson exposition of ideas, sociologists' mark was hardly discernible both on the demand and supply side of this communicative circuit. The advent of television and the dissemination of a post-modern relativization of rationality are acknowledged by Lambiri-Dimaki (1997, pp. 19–20), but there is no further trace, in her otherwise valuable chronicle of Greek sociology up to the 2000, of Greek sociology's representation on Greek TV, particularly when flowing from sociologists' initiative.

A bright exception to what was quickly to become a McDonaldized TV environment was the dedication to serve pedagogical and intellectual missions, mostly—if not exclusively—by programmes produced by the *Elliniki Radiofonia Tileorasi* (Hellenic Broadcasting Corporation) (ERT). Based on an idea by sociologist Yiorgos Veltsos[8] and with the collaboration, primarily by Constantinos Tsoukalas (other collaborators included Kostas Vergopoulos, Foteini Tsalikoglou and Yangos Andreadis), ERT initiated a series of episodes (usually around 50 minutes each) titled *In the Paths of Thought* that focused on major intellectual profiles in the social sciences and the humanities. It is a major contribution to the visibility and dissemination of renowned sociologists and philosophers at a time when their work was mostly unavailable in translation and both Veltsos and Tsoukalas drew on their own social and cultural capital, primarily, in France to make the series possible. Thus, from 1993 until the end of the decade, they interviewed Agnes Heller, Julia Kristeva, Noam Chomsky, Hélène Cixous and André Gorz, among many others. In this stellar list, sociologists have had more than a modest representation. Our sociology chronicle addresses those interviews that present the greatest sociological interest for debates that unfolded in Greek sociology too and also make some reference to Greece. This series goes against the perception of a 'sociological silence' (Constantopoulou, 2011, pp. 45–46) on TV.

The earliest sociological entry par excellence was the series' interview with Niklas Luhmann (1992). The interview was held in the island of Samos with Luhmann's ascetic disposition being shot against sun-lit but humble backgrounds (a pier, non-conspicuous gardens, a local tavern, a modest beach, a chapel). Luhmann was in Greece on the occasion of a conference organized by the University of the Aegean on 'Culture, Knowledge, Communication in Systems' (July 1992), and he had given a paper on the 'ecology of non-knowledge'. In that interview Luhmann presents in broad strokes the logic of systems theory based on the difference between 'system' and 'environment', his controversy with Habermas, the

---

[8] Yiorgos Veltsos (then Professor of Sociology at Panteion University) had already contributed to the media visibility of sociology (and social theory) since the 1980s. For example, he presented a 26-minute tribute to Michel Foucault on the occasion of the latter's death in 1984. That TV show was part of the series *Periskopio* (ERT News, 1984). ERT also devoted a biopic to sociologist Vassilis Filias (Filias, 1994).

codes of the mass media, the search for a function of religion in complex social systems, the need to restructure the concept of democracy to avoid paradoxes ('the people rule the people') and utopian formulations of it as well as the project of developing a 'hyper-theory' that would be interdisciplinary in scope and logic, incorporating not only sociology but also linguistics, biology and cybernetics, among other fields. Such hyper-theory and the specialisms that it summons find in the sociology of Niklas Luhmann, according to the show's narrator, a classical thinker next to Durkheim, Weber and Parsons.

Tsoukalas' interview with Pierre Bourdieu (1995) was held at the College De France. The episode includes brief extracts from performances of Bourdieu's plays, inspired from his work on social suffering. Discussing with Tsoukalas the issue of autonomy in contemporary academia, Bourdieu perceives a relevant threat for sociology: caught between the positive and mathematical sciences and the domain of politics, media and policy, sociology should draw on its rich resources to sustain its distinctive discourse and political purpose in promoting autonomy while not being cut off from state or even corporate funding. (Here Bourdieu draws on one of his own research projects that was funded by Kodak yet had additional theoretical interest on the level of practice and negotiations between actors.) Pointing to secrecy as an index of heteronomy, Bourdieu hails the public sphere of ancient Greece that marked an opening towards relative autonomy. (This argument, as we saw in Chap. 4, is reminiscent of Castoriadis' emphasis on the ancient Greece's democratic imaginary.) While sociologists, for Bourdieu, cannot substitute the people in the struggle against heteronomy, they can prevent the pattern of silence from becoming canonical. To this purpose, he informs Tsoukalas about the project of the European review *Liber*, which he conceives to be a practical instrument of internationalization and about its forthcoming publication in Greek. Regarding Greece as an intellectually international resource, he considers Tsoukalas' rejoinder that the Greek language is virtually incomprehensible in the international academic community. Insisting on the imperative that people should be capable of expressing ideas in their own language, Bourdieu wishes to resist what he calls the vulgar Anglicanization and homogenization of academic discourse. Means to accomplish this desideratum of a non-homogenized internationalization attuned to national traditions and practices are, for Bourdieu, the scholarly translations of original books/articles written in Greek.[9]

The interview with Lyotard (1992) is indicative of the impact he exerted on Veltsos' own thought (see the subsequent remarks on Veltsos' *Non-Sociology* book). Lyotard refers in passing to the 1960s disillusionment, mentioning the Castoriadis and Lefort *Socialisme ou Barbarie* group. He then moves to a sharp rescuing of sociality through an analysis of Kant's *sensus communis* as a summon to everyone's participation in the aesthetic judgement and then as a regulative idea for an ideal mode of social organization. Suggesting that, for him, 'Greece' is a word that is symbolically far too laden, he considers classical Greece as the birthplace of philosophy and politics; the latter point marks a contradistinction between Heidegger's pre-political *Volk* and Greece's *demos*, namely, the people within the polity, which Lyotard considers to be Greece's great accomplishment. Ironically, for Lyotard, the birthplace of political autonomy succumbed to imperial occupations, and thus what captures Greece best is this tragic predicament whereby a rich heritage was followed by centuries of Greece's deprivation of it. Appositely, he concludes by the evocative image of Greeks as 'pauperized princes'.

Veltsos visited Jacques Derrida in France and secured special permission to have the latter's 29 January 1992 seminar at the École Des Hautes Études video-recorded. While the brief prologue with Derrida is mainly on the linguistic trope 'différance' and its Greek equivalent (as introduced by Veltsos, namely, διαφορά to διαφωρά) and the epilogue addresses normativity and decision, the sole sociological interest that surfaces during Derrida's lecture, devoted mainly to the Czech philosopher Jan Patočka, is at the point where Derrida makes a departure from the notion of deconstruction to what for Veltsos is a theory of institutions. Yet Derrida's middle section in the seminar about 'institutions' revolves around the critique of an instrumental modernity and its fall towards an inauthentic mode of Being (a Heideggerian motif). The most telling sociological enunciation here reflects Derrida's (1993) remark that the technological mind-set does not 'neutralize' the religious dimension. Rather, in its

---

[9] One year later at a University of Athens conference, Bourdieu (2003 [1996]) made gallant allusions to his philhellene affection (*hexis* anticipating *habitus*, the attachment to the Greek culture, language, monuments and landscapes, democracy vs. demagogy) using the honour bestowed on him to engage in a reflection on the role of the university by means of a discourse anchored in classical Greek notions.

tendency towards 'adiaphorization' (a motif in Zygmunt Bauman), it latently reinstalls the demonic into the core of a new individualism based on will to power. The demonic is now tantamount to the human as a social being able to harness, as Derrida interprets Patočka, an unprecedented release of cosmic forces; that is, as if the human being were a machine. In this individualism of roles what predominates is the simulated (and quantifiable) equality under a single 'social mask' (interestingly, a motif in Ernst Jünger's metaphysics of the *Typus*) that dissimulates 'mystery'. Connecting this thread of Derrida's deconstruction to the significance of 'différance' as applied to sociology, Veltsos caps the episode by making a remark about 'différance' as in institutional trope at Panteion University (to which he was then teaching). Deconstruction is not, for Veltsos, a means to efface the university which, for him, remains an 'unshakable' institution. Rather, the 'dysfunctionality' of the university in general as an institution (its manipulative processes as an organization [Veltsos uses the noun 'crematorium' [10]]) reveals its functions as a machine that constantly 'invents' on the basis of the deferring principle of 'différance'.[11]

Hoping to secure a joint interview with Gilles Deleuze (who tactfully declined due to his heavy illness) and Félix Guattari, Veltsos interviewed the latter at his house in Paris. Guattari (1992) quickly points out that he had visited the Leros Psychiatric Hospital (in operation from 1957 to 1995) and some suburban Athens hospitals, witnessing the then appalling conditions of patients' hospitalization. But beyond this consideration of the patient as an excluded entity who suffers from societal disciplinary normality, the psychiatric patient for Guattari poses questions about social relations in general, making the idea of schizophrenia relevant to what Guattari names the 'social good', which summons us as it were to learn more about our personal paralogisms. This notion of marginality that is embodied (and represented) by the schizophrenic patient is occluded in market and media-induced narratives, while the entire continents (e.g. Africa) remain marginal. He views society as dualist (caught between a

---

[10] Obviously, we do not endorse this label for any Greek university or for the university as an institution at large even if it is equally obvious that Veltsos' penchant for linguistic puns and their figurative connotations suggest the 'frame' through which this statement should be interpreted and is similar to the sweeping remarks by Heidegger (and Derrida) on productionist metaphysics. For continental sociology's 'linguistic turn' under Derrida and others, see Romanos (2014).

[11] For a similar call to sociology to consider Derrida's philosophical trajectories of 'différance' and confront its own reductionist proclivities, see Mavridis (1999, p. 579).

capitalist aristocracy and the mass) with lapses into pseudo-societies (e.g. subcultures, counter-cultures), yet even within the seemingly amorphous mass, non-intellectual mutations constitute shapes (and tides) of resistance that could, potentially, lead to new 'universal values'. Half-jokingly he says to Veltsos that contemporary Greece is perceived as Europe's 'bad student', yet such taunting collective disposition displays a recalcitrant complexity at odds with Franco-German prototypes of normality and compliance. This was Guattari's last media appearance before his untimely death on 29 August 1992.

Very prescient to current developments in a complex world marked by eruptions of war is the 1995 interview Edgar Morin (then Director of the *French National Social Science Centre*) gave to Tsoukalas. Morin (1995)—whose parents belonged to the Jewish diaspora and had lived in Thessaloniki which until World War II had a prominent Jewish community—presents his interests around the problem of complexity that stems from modernity's fragmented and technical logic. He invokes a normative ecumenism that is loosely tied around a species-being substratum that is common to humans, introducing pertinently the notion of 'homeland-earth' (*terre-patrie*). Morin draws quickly on examples of odious reductions of complexity. The Greeks' persecution by the Turks, the latter from the Serbs, the break-up of Yugoslavia. This phenomenon of Balkanization seems, for Morin, to be the imminent risk for Europe and the tragedy of its people, being incapable of living together. Rebutting the dilemma of optimism versus pessimism posed by Tsoukalas, he modifies the question around the axis between amphiboly and faith. Drawing on Pascal's wager with regard to the existence of God, he mentions as its secular manifestation the Greco-Persian wars and the unlikely probability of a Greek victory. At this juncture he makes the analogy between classical Athens and Grozny in Chechnya in the estimated calculus of probabilities, alongside with the low probability of an Allied victory in World War II. Stressing his own activism in resistance, Morin inverts once more the hope/despair dialectic sharing the elation felt with the collapse of the Berlin Wall in contrast to the USSR's problems being unfrozen and melting into a new eruption of barbarity.

Although not particularly instructive in any connections to Greece, Tsoukalas' conversation with Jean Baudrillard (1995) in the latter's apartment must be noted for its density even if Baudrillard simplifies the argument for the purposes of the show. Epigrammatically, Baudrillard touches on a global system's saturation point which has suspended *durée*;

in such post-historical experience of time, the individual experiences her life free of conflicts and dualities but rather as a terminal in a closed-circuit technological cloud. Individuals act-out, yet all judgement between criteria has been obfuscated in an atonal (or monotonous) world of 'adiaphorization'. To Tsoukalas' reservation about the relevance of Baudrillard's descriptions for the millions of those who are dispossessed (and thus for them objects are still relevant as use values and not as sign values), Baudrillard retorts with disarming neutrality: he describes the world he belongs to and not the world of people who do not belong to this world or have been excluded from it. Those who are excluded must determine on their own the degree of relevance of Baudrillard's descriptions. Even if the logic of the system leads to global integration, in reality it is marked by internally diagonal ruptures caused by antagonistic forces. He sees the world to suffer a dualist tension between a system of excess (hyper-reality) and a system of penury and deprivation. Resisting Heidegger's view of technology as a demonic power, Baudrillard deems more promising a standpoint of irony towards technology which renders it an 'enigmatic space', namely, beyond the simultaneity of messages and the telescopic effacement of the distinction between the ridiculous and the tragic. When Tsoukalas insists on Baudrillard's own moral position, the response is that there is indeed a moral standpoint that he endorses that goes against his own descriptions.

At a time of a current shift to de-colonizing sociology (e.g. Bhambra & Holmwood, 2021), the series' interview with Edward Said (1994) (taken in the US by Stathis Gourgouris and Giorgos Chouliaras and with Tsoukalas' own interventions to Said's comments being shot in Greece) sheds light on what in the sociology of Greece remains a desideratum. After explaining the main thesis on Orientalism, the discussion is moved swiftly by Said to the case of Greece. The standardly reproduced value-laden rift between Hellenes and barbarians is for Tsoukalas one axis of relevance, yet Said establishes an elective affinity between the predicaments of the contemporary Greek and the contemporary Arab/Muslim: their voices are by and large occluded by the discourse on classical Greece and classical Islam, respectively. While classical Greece as the cradle for democracy has a privileged position in a global discourse of world history, for Said, issues of continuity and hybridity emerge in a people whose identity has been shaped (and transformed) through wars and occupations and yet such people maintain a distinctive history and language.

Moreover, the discourse on the Greek classical ideal is by and large detached from the wider Mediterranean context and brackets the relations between Greeks and Semites, Africans, Asians as well as the ongoing tensions with Turkey. Said suggests that degrees of Greek science and commerce have had reciprocal infiltration conduits with other cultures. In the contemporary world, contemporary Greece (e.g. its politics) is generally neglected. Resorting to an autobiographical anecdote, Said draws on his own hybrid roots since his father's family had been initially Greek-Orthodox [12] underlining the familiar chords that Cavafy's poetry struck in him and how it shaped his literary interests. Adding to this, Tsoukalas notes that classical Greece has been largely a construct of the West. The West draws from the ancient Greek pool key ingredients for its own distinctive identity and its concomitant claims to universality but with no intrinsic need to connect to it, genealogically. The problems that stem from such trajectories are more acute for modern and contemporary Greece which struggles for a relatedness orientation by reference to the West's construct of its own classical roots. Exacerbated by the stereotypical dualism of a rationalist West and a non-rational East, Greece's relationship to Byzantine culture is also elided since for the West's narrative Byzantium belongs to the East. Rather than aligning with the nineteenth-century beginning of European nation-state narratives of identity, Greece, for Tsoukalas, confronts constantly the tension of having to return to the classical 'beginnings' to cope with the void of Greek identity due to an equivocal Byzantine legacy.

Within a social and intellectual capital geography that includes Mouzelis in the United Kingdom, Kondylis and Psychopedis (who were not sociologists but did contribute to the discipline in Greece) in Germany and Veltsos and Tsoukalas in France, it is significant that only the latter sought by means of mass media: (a) to connect social theory, after the institutionalization of sociology in Greece in the 1980s, to the catalysts that shaped it internationally in what was mostly French sociology and social theory and (b) to re-introduce such brief encounters to a Greek audience at a time when such debates and hitherto unavailable works by these scholars had just begun to be more widely available. Evidently, the post-modern constellation in Greece (Veltsos) and left-wing sociology

---

[12] In Greek sociology, research on Greek Orthodoxy is not as undeveloped as it may seem. See, for example, Kokosalakis (1996).

(Tsoukalas) upheld higher standards of excellence than what 'modernist' critics of post-modernity had estimated with regard to the compatibility between sophisticated concept dissemination and TV images.[13]

Multi-paradigmatic Post-Modernism: Veltsos' Non-sociology

The multi-paradigmatic shift in Greek sociology and its overlap with neighbouring disciplines had to grapple with a recalibration of the normative component that undergirds the discipline (at least in the wide perception of its practitioners). Yiorgos Veltsos' book *Non-Sociology: Analytics of the Post-Modern* reflects best this trend which was not limited to Greek sociology.[14] Although Veltsos' book was published in 1988, it highlights the burgeoning 1990s' spell of post-modernism and its impact on Greek sociology. Consistent with post-modernism's linguistic turn and with its appeal being triggered by Marxism's disillusionment (among other Grand narratives' alleged decline) in the absence of viable alternatives to consumer society, Veltsos' book was not only the culmination of his 1970 links between sociology and language. Rather, it marked the indeterminate zone that sociology cannot claim to contain, associated by Veltsos with various eruptions of indeterminacy in sociological categories (see also Chap. 3). This accommodation of the indeterminate is reflected in the book's layout which ignores citation orthodoxies and provides quotes and references in its margins, thus de-centring the 'authority' of the text's structure. Veltsos objects to the search for the social bond in

---

[13] In Veltsos' conversation with Hélène Cixous (1995) in France and her brief memoir of her friendship with Nicos Poulantzas and his wife Annie Leclerc (and her prominent role in promoting feminism in France), there is an initial apostrophe on the cinematic gaze and the beauty of the cinematic image in contrast to TV's levelling effect on human imagination (i.e. emptying tragic phenomena of their immanent tragedy). Veltsos admits that the show is not addressed to a wide audience, but he conceives 'what is sent to Greece through the [video-recorded] frame' as 'a letter of suffering', admitting its low spectatorship numbers. In the prologue to the show, Veltsos says that unlike the usual invitation extended to 'philosophers and sociologists' this particular episode will feature a scholar whose work eschews classification.

[14] For example, in German sociology, it was Helmut Schelsky and Friedrich Tenbruck who launched the short-lived 'anti-sociology' (but not post-modern) criticism of the discipline (see Moebius, 2021, pp. 99–100).

action; instead, the social bond should be deferred (also) to the phrase (for such an effort in the work of classical sociology, see Green, 1988). The crisis of sociology is:

> to be condemned not to think beyond its own 'reconstructions', forced to retreat in face of new asymptotic hypotheses, obliged to announce the broadening of what until now it excluded, bound from a theory of knowledge that cancels itself and from a mode or writing that is tautologous, it surrenders its place to a non-sociology, to a palimpsest that witnesses its own crisis through the recurring coatings of heterogeneous texts. (Veltsos, 2005 [1988], p. 68)

With sociology's quest for social facts, social structures, class relations and, in short, for social totality, being relegated to 'fictions', the mode of rescuing sociology's legacy is through dissensus and the archaeology of the 'trace'. This incessant involution of sociology to non-sociology is, for Veltsos (104–105), akin to Bourdieu's sociology of sociology that brings to the fore sociology's limitations and contours. In this sense, the 'sociological judgement' fails to represent diversity because it lacks the categories (and the words) to convey the multitude of intersection points between individuality and meaning, namely, the zone of 'indeterminate lived experience elements of the social' (154). In its aid, one can hope to configure a non-sociology through the prism of Kant's 'analytic of the sublime' in the *Critique of Judgment* that transfers the universal capacity of judgement to the 'particular' itself and its infinite ramifications. Yet simultaneously other sociologists distanced themselves from post-modern discourses and specifically from Veltsos' non-sociology. Demertzis thus (1989, pp. 21–22) wonders about the necessity of a 'postmodern sociological reason' which seems at pains to sustain the project of human emancipation and to deal with the structural, normative and cultural challenges posed in the contemporary world, along those that stem from Greece's late and hasty encounter with modernity (the latter erroneously equated, for Demertzis, with modernization).

Greek Sociology's Steady Growth

Despite the multi-paradigmatic impetus that was to swirl Greek sociology, especially under post-structuralist French thought and the admittedly elastic spine of the discipline's maturation in Greece, the 1990s generated noticeable work across many sociology specialisms, namely, gender (Papageorgiou-Lymperis, 1992; Moussourou, 1993), urban sociology (Kouvelis, 1993; Nikolaidou, 1993) and population studies, connecting theory to empirical research (Kyriazis, 1992) and to epistemological debates (Coniavitis, 1993). Crucial in the 1990s were the Centre's contribution to the sociology of the family, migration, social networks and social exclusion (see, indicatively, Maratou-Alipranti, 1991) and the sociology of ageing (Teperoglou, 1989). The still unexplored field of the sociology of knowledge was applied to the sociology of education (itself a focus of a KEKMOKOP volume by Kokosalakis & Tsaoussis, 1999) and its epistemological foundations (Kouzelis, 1992). The sociology of deviance had also important studies to contribute as in Astrinakis' (1991) work on youth subcultures that combined British theory with the Greek experience of working-class youths. The issue of ideology became prominent (Doxiadis, 1992; Lipowatz & Demertzis, 1994), particularly through a Marxist historical sociology (see, e.g. Lekkas (1996) on nationalism). The pathologies of the Greek state and society invited sustained sociological focus (Samatas, 1993) as well as the standing reflection on the status of the Greek university (indicatively only, see Samatas, 1991), including the long-standing controversy about the public university and a prospective establishment and recognition of private universities (Chletsos, 1990).[15] This was part of a wider reflection and

---

[15] In Chap. 2 we have seen one occasion that illustrates that the intersection of human capital between public universities and colleges can sometimes be remarkable in terms of accomplishment of quality outcomes in curriculum delivery and research, influence on the societal community and the global division of intellectual labor. Relevant sociological views include Durkheim, for example, who defends the state's role in supervising non-state-administered schools but argues against rigid prohibitions since the degree of intervention cannot be determined 'once and for all' (1956, p. 80). Similarly, the role of the fiduciary and of influence in society demands that 'higher education is legitimately seen as a relatively open system with regard to general exchanges with communities' and between 'private and public institutions' (Parsons & Platt, 1973, pp. 358–359). Analogous arguments towards such bridge-building and ensuing legitimations can be reconstructed from Habermas' alerts against 'the instrumentalization of the law' to the extent that it ceases to consider agents' experiences of 'repression and disrespect', failing thus to monitor collective goal achievement 'against the project of non-instrumentalizable rights' (1998, pp. 429–430). A Luhmannesque understanding of social system complexity would probably accommodate binary (public-private) codes as conditions for education's functional differentiation (this, e.g. could include a doubling of the code within the system as a public not-for-profit and private not-for-profit/private-for-profit code) that resist homogenization reforms either on the education or on the economy sub-systems side of society (see, e.g. Baraldi & Corsi, 2017, pp. 110–111).

reconsideration of the statist coordination of Greek universities including the Constitution Article 16 prohibition of private university education in Greece (see Petmesidou, 1998, p. 378) and the pathologies of the statist approach and the Janus-faced impact of Law 1268/1982 on various facets of university life, structure and the social sciences in particular (Petmesidou, 1998, pp. 368–369).

A significant shift to the sociological study of migration started taking place as a response to the massive influx of immigrants from the Balkans and from Eastern Europe since 1990 (see the seminal study by Kassimati, 1992). Subsumed under the broader rubric of social exclusion (Psimmenos, 1995), such studies prepared the ground for subsequent focus on migration and its intensification in Greece during the 2000s. Demographic studies too (see, e.g. Lambiri-Dimaki & Kyriazis, 1995) were often embedded in wider research programmes (e.g. under the aegis of the *Giovanni Agnelli Foundation*) and focused largely on the Mediterranean region of Europe and Greece's demographic topography in terms of fertility rates, urbanization and the rural population, health services, demography and social security, employment and education opportunities as well as Greece's prospects at the 2000 threshold.[16] Tourism from a sociological perspective begun to be considered in the wider context of employment studies (Tsartas, 1991). The latter field also extends to the medical professions (Chiotakis, 1998), for example, in a state-coordinated organized medicine, struggling with pathologies of personal patronage connections, endemic to low-trust societies, that override its collective mission (see Colombotos & Fakiolas, 1993). Labor relations and growth proved standing topics (Papaioannou, 1997) as well as society's broader interchange with law, justice and ethics (Lambiri-Dimaki & Papachristou, 1993).

PA.SO.K's 1980s' embrace of populism (that was generated, as it were from 'above' under the charismatic leadership of Andreas Papandreou (Mouzelis, 1994b, pp. 14–15)) quickly led to the need for further sociological scrutiny in light of an emerging polarization between populism's advocacy for immediacy in policy design and implementation, a diminution of meritocracy (see Mavrogordatos, 1997) under reductionist notions of equality and of a friend-enemy distinction that occludes (and

---

[16] Such prospects of considering 2000 a threshold era that legitimizes a holistic appraisal of Greek society's path towards further modernization and correlated to processes of political legitimation had appeared since the late 1980s (see, e.g. Kyrtsis, 1988).

pulverizes) substantive struggles under false dichotomies (see, e.g. Mouzelis, Lipowatz & Spourdalakis (1989) as well as Costas Simitis' introduction to their volume). Sotiropoulos (1994, 1996) did a systematic study of populism during the 1981–1989 era of Papandreou's domination of Greek politics and the formulation of a rhetorical discourse that was quickly to neutralize the radical Left's arsenal. Thus, the 'contract with the people' and the call for 'change' just prior to the PA.SO.K electoral triumph in 1981 (1996, pp. 50–51) became buzzword pillars to a new populist hegemony in PA.SO.K's winding road between egalitarian welfare reforms[17] and the 'creation of an administrative elite' (97). The aborted attempt to routinize charisma (55–57) was about to lead to a paradigm shift for PA.SO.K and its subsequent 'modernization' reforms by Costas Simitis, while Terlexis (1996) takes recourse to Weber in discussing the problem of bureaucracy in contemporary nation-states in light of a tradition that revisits Hegel, Marx along with Michels and Mosca in what is a meticulous reconstruction of Weber's pessimism regarding individual integrity in the backdrop of the problem of *Sittlichkeit* and its sociological reconstruction. Generally, political sociology found fertile ground (see Marantzidis, 1998) for development beyond Marxist studies' hegemony.

The mission to maintain sociology's boundaries was manifested in Tatsis' systematic efforts to keep alive the tradition of classical sociology and to replenish contemporary sociological theorizing accordingly. Drawing on his earlier theoretical background on Marx, Durkheim (Tatsis & Zito, 1974) and Weber (Wallimann et al., 1980) and his sustained exposure to generally neglected in Greece strands of American sociology, Tatsis (1992) made a noticeable venture in delineating Dahrendorf's *homo sociologicus* refracted as it were through Parsonsian systems theory, Homans' exchange-theory, interactionism (Blumer) and conflict sociology.

---

[17] Sotiropoulos (1994, 1996) accounts for a number of laws passed by PASOK, often questioning their positive or groundbreaking nature. Law 1268/1982 regarding higher education reform and university governance is unaccounted for with none of its Janus-faced implications being mentioned. For these, see Mavrogordatos (2012) including the later obstacles against the Law 4009/2011 higher education reform that attempted to rectify abuses of Law 1268/1982. Problems that have solidified in the Greek public university are also highlighted by Tsoukalas, a rather radical sociologist. Tsoukalas points to the free-rider mentality mix of credentialism, misguided accumulation of graduates in a then largely inert public administration and civil service along with student-corporatist trade-offs within the niche of a 'public rent-allotting system' (1995, pp. 209–210).

The end of the nineties is processed in newly configured fin-de-siècle codes, diagnostics, projections and assessments amid recondite millenarian imagery (for a pun on such disaster-laden semantics about the year 2000 doomsday threshold, see, in passing, Tsoukalas, 1995, p. 193).[18] Yet there is a marked sense of transcending the binary political codes that shaped the twentieth century, and Greece is no exception, despite its modernization lags. Thus, in a contribution to a volume titled *Greece prepares for the twenty-first century*, Mouzelis (1995b) no longer sees as paradoxical any potential convergences between the (liberal) Right and the (progressive) Left, advocating a modernization path for Greece tied, however, to mediating values, institutions and collective interests that would resist crude and spasmodic emulations of pre-planned modernization patterns and processes. Such mediated modernization will, for Mouzelis, effectively confront Greek pathologies like servility and a life-world's retreat (to adopt Habermas terminology) into a privatized consumerism.[19] Tsoukalas, for his part, finds the repeated calls to 'modernization' plethoric and 'monotonous' (1995, p. 192). Explaining the Greek syndrome of law-defiance and anomie in face of undigested and intentionally resisted 'rationality' discourses in what is also a perceived hegemony of the West whereby Greece constitutes a recalcitrant case that makes the populist-invoked 'essence of Greekness' tantamount to 'an eclectic and original synthesis of libertarian and anarchic individual capacities' (200), Tsoukalas musters comparative statistical evidence on wage earners and employees and excavates the Greek socio-historical substratum that consolidated 'opportunistic economic buccaneering to organized market warfare' (205). Such strategic rationality was by no means limited to socially disadvantaged classes; rather, for Tsoukalas, it permeated the very ethos of Greeks' approach to 'professional ethics' and societal integration, culminating in a paradoxical equation of moral codes and free-rider practices. It may as well be asserted that Tsoukalas already anticipates the

---

[18] Tsoukalas' (1991) criticisms of idols like neoliberalism, the rigid welfare state and consumer society are suffused with Poulantzas' thought (p. 15).

[19] In the same volume, Kyriazis lauds the PA.SO.K reforms in ending gender discrimination, strengthening legislation against sexual violence, enhancing social security provisions, including an extension of agricultural pensions to women (1995, pp. 282–283). Generally, the EU framework of rights and equality is deemed instrumental in accelerating and embedding gender equality, yet she notes that surveys conducted in Greece tend to reveal attachment to a patriarchal coding of certain professions at the micro-level (296–297).

Janus-faced destiny of the free-rider mind-set that a looming yet gloomy 'end of growth' (211) predicament is just around the corner with sociocultural and economic 'aftereffects'.

There is, however, an optimistic flipside in the nineties which in itself marks an index of sociology's growth. With Lambiri-Dimaki's second part of the trilogy of the sociology in Greece published in 1997 (for a presentation and brief assessment of this trilogy, see Chap. 6) and possibly in inverse direction to her optimism-pessimism spectrum (Lambiri-Dimaki, 1997, p. 21), sociology in Greece is now mature enough to reflect on its own institutional, paradigmatic, theoretical and empirical presuppositions as well as to confront its setbacks. Publications about Greek sociology (to which we also gratefully rely for our sociological relay marathon in this book) intended to make the discipline's history and development better known in Greece (Kyrtsis, 1996; Lambiri-Dimaki, 1997) and abroad (Lambiri-Dimaki, 1996; Kassimati, 1998; Kokosalakis, 1998; Kyrtsis, 1998) and mark a turning point in the discipline's self-evaluation capabilities, enabling its practitioners to not renege on such promising reflexivity.

References

Astrinakis, A. (1991). Νεανικές υποκουλτούρες. Παρεκκλίνουσες υποκουλτούρες της νεολαίας της εργατικής τάξης: η βρετανική θεώρηση και η ελληνική εμπειρία [Youth subcultures. Deviant subcultures of working-class youth: The British theory and the Greek experience]. Papazisis.

Baraldi, C., & Corsi, G. (2017). *Niklas Luhmann: Education as a social system*. Springer.

Baudrillard, J. (1995). Conversation with Constantinos Tsoukalas. In Στα Μονοπάτια της Σκέψης [In the paths of thought]. ERT (Ellinikí Radiofonía Tileórasi A.E (Hellenic Broadcasting Corporation)). Archive number: 0000006777. Retrieved May 8, 2022.

Bhambra, G. & Holmwood, J. (2021). *Colonialism and modern social theory*. Polity.

Bourdieu, P. (1995). Interview to Constantinos Tsoukalas. In Στα Μονοπάτια της Σκέψης [In the paths of thought]. ERT (Ellinikí Radiofonía Tileórasi A.E (Hellenic Broadcasting Corporation)). Archive number: 0000006790. Retrieved January 24, 2022, from https://archive.ert.gr/6790/

Bourdieu, P. (2003 [1996]). Conférence à l' Université d' Athènes, 14 Octobre 1966 (extrait). In I. Lambiri-Dimaki (Ed.), Κοινωνικές επιστήμες και πρωτοπορία στην Ελλάδα 1950–1967 [Social Sciences and novelty in Greece 1950–1967] (pp. 55–59). Gutenberg.

Chiotakis, S. (1998). Για μια κοινωνιολογία των ελεύθερων επαγγελμάτων: επιστημονική επαγγελματοποίηση των ιατρικών υπηρεσιών [For a sociology of freelance professions: Scientific professionalization of medical services]. Papazisis.
Chletsos, M. (1990). Δημόσια και ιδιωτικά πανεπιστήμια. Συνύπαρξη ή αντιπαράταξη [Public and private universities. Coexistence or Opposition]. In *Το πανεπιστήμιο στην Ελλάδα σήμερα* [The university in Greece today] (pp. 92–102). Sakis Karagiorgas Foundation.
Cixous, H. (1995). Interview to Yiorgos Veltsos. In Στα Μονοπάτια της Σκέψης [In the paths of thought]. ERT (Ellinikí Radiofonía Tileórasi A.E (Hellenic Broadcasting Corporation)). Archive number: 0000006783. Retrieved May 25, 2022, from https://archive.ert.gr/6783/
Colombotos, J., & Fakiolas, N. (1993). The power of organized medicine in Greece. In F. Hafferty & J. McKinley (Eds.), *The changing medical profession: An international perspective* (pp. 138–149). Oxford University Press.
Coniavitis, T. (1993). Πλουραλισμός στην κοινωνιολογία. Μεθοδολογική προσέγγιση [Pluralism in sociology. A methodological approach]. Odysseas.
Constantopoulou, C. (2011). Η μεταμοντέρνα κατάσταση: Τεχνικός πολιτισμός, κοινωνιολογική σιωπή και τηλεοπτική φλυαρία [The postmodern condition: Technical culture, sociological silence and TV-chatter]. In L. Maratou-Alipranti, M. Thanopoulou, A. Teperoglou, & E. Fronimou (Eds.), *Όψεις της κοινωνιολογίας στην Ελλάδα σήμερα. Τιμητικός τόμος στη μνήμη της Ιωάννας Λαμπίρη-Δημάκη* [Facets of sociology in Greece today: *Festschift* in Ioanna Lambridi-Dimaki's memory] (pp. 43–55). Sakkoulas.
Demerztis, N. (1989). Κουλτούρα, νεωτερικότητα, πολιτική κουλτούρα [Culture, modernity and political culture]. Papazisis.
Derrida, J. (1993). Interview to Yiorgos Veltsos/Seminar at the Ecole Des Hautes Etudes. In Στα Μονοπάτια της Σκέψης [In the paths of thought]. ERT (Ellinikí Radiofonía Tileórasi A. E. (Hellenic Broadcasting Corporation)). Archive number: 32INCHEMB1851.
Doxiadis, K. (1992). Υποκειμενικότητα και εξουσία. Για τη θεωρία της ιδεολογίας [Subjectivity and power. On the theory of ideology]. Plethron.
Durkheim, E. (1956). *Education and sociology* (S. D. Fox, Trans.). The Free Press (Original work published 1922).
ERT (Ellinikí Radiofonía Tileórasi A.E) (Hellenic Broadcasting Corporation). (1984). Ένα μικρό αφιέρωμα στον Μισέλ Φουκώ [A short tribute to Michel Foucault]. In Περισκόπιο (Periskopio) (with the assistance of Giorgos Veltsos). ERT (Ellinikí Radiofonía Tileórasi A.E (Hellenic Broadcasting Corporation)). Archive number: 325316.
Filias, V. (1994). Autobiographical documentary. In Μονόγραμμα (Monogram). ERT (Ellinikí Radiofonía Tileórasi A.E (Hellenic Broadcasting Corporation)). Archive number: 0000073098. Retrieved April 16, 2022 from https://archive.ert.gr/73098/

The Greek Review of Social Research. National Centre of Social Research. Retrieved May 20, 2022., from https://www.ekke.gr/en/services/grsr

Green, B.S. (1988). *Literary methods and sociological theory. Case studies of Simmel and Weber*. The University of Chicago Press.

Guattari, F. (1992). Interview to Giorgos Veltsos. In Στα Μονοπάτια της Σκέψης [In the paths of thought]. ERT (Ellinikí Radiofonía Tileórasi A.E (Hellenic Broadcasting Corporation)). Archive number: 32INCHEMB1707.

Habermas, J. (1998). *Between facts and norms: Contributions to a discourse theory of law and democracy* (W. Rehg, Trans.). MIT Press (Original work published 1992).

Hellenic Parliament. (1992, June 19). Πρακτικά Βουλής [Parliamentary minutes]. Retrieved June 1, 2022, from https://www.hellenicparliament.gr/UserFiles/a08fc2dd-61a9-4a83-b09a09f4c564609d/199206_%CE%A3%CE%A5%CE%9D%CE%9F%CE%94%CE%9F%CE%A3_%CE%92_%CE%A3%CE%A5%CE%9D_%CE%A1%CE%9D%CE%A3%CE%A4%60_19_%CE%99%CE%BF%CF%85%CE%BD%CE%AF%CE%BF%CF%85_1992.doc

Hellenic Sociological Society. (2008, October 20). Letter to the Rectors of the Greek Universities to the Heads of Sociology Departments, to faculty with specialisms in the domain of sociology, to faculty election committees. (Private document).

Herzfeld, M. (1997). *Cultural intimacy: Social poetics in the nation-state*. Routledge.

Holmwood, J., & Stewart, A. (1991). *Explanation and social theory*. Macmillan.

Karabatzaki-Perdiki, H. (1988). *Individual and society in Plato and Durkheim: A comparative and critical analysis*. Thesis submitted for the degree of Doctor of Philosophy, in the School of Economic and Social Studies: University of East Anglia.

Kassimati, K. (1992). Πόντιοι μετανάστες από την πρώην Σοβιετική Ένωση: Κοινωνική και οικονομική τους ένταξη [Pontian immigrants from the former Soviet Union: Their economic and social integration]. Ministry of Culture (in association with Panteion University and KEKMOKOP).

Kassimati, K. (1998). Development of social research in Greece: Problems, trends and prospects. *International Sociology, 13*(3), 345–358.

Kokosalakis, N. (1996). Orthodoxie grecque, modernité et politique. In G. Davie & D. Hervieu-Léger (Eds.), *Identités religieuses en Europe* (pp. 131–152). La Découverte.

Kokosalakis, N. (1998). Politics and Sociology in Greece, 1950-1998. *International Sociology, 13*(3), 325–343.

Kokosalakis, N., & Tsaoussis, D. (Eds.). (1999). *Non-official higher education in the European Union*. Gutenberg.

Koniordos, S. (2010). Η συζήτηση για τη δημόσια κοινωνιολογία και η κοινωνιολογία στην Ελλάδα [The discussion of public sociology and sociology in Greece]. In M. Kousis, M. Samatas, & S. Koniordos (Eds.), *Εξουσία και κοινωνία. Δωρήματα* στον Κωνσταντίνο Τσουκαλά [Power and society: Offerings to Constantine Tsoukalas] (pp. 227-250). Kastaniotis.

Kouvelis, A. (1993). Housing conditions and residential areas in great Greek urban centres. In N. Genov (Ed.), *Society and environment in the Balkan countries: Proceedings of Conference organized with the collaboration of UNESCO's Social and Human Science Sector* (pp. 117-143). Regional and Global Development.

Kouzelis, G. (1992). Από τον βιωματικό στον επιστημονικό κόσμο. Ζητήματα κοινωνικής αναπαραγωγής της γνώσης [From the lived to the scientific world. Issues of social reproduction of knowledge]. Kritiki.

Kyriazis, N. (1992). Αναπαραγωγή του πληθυσμού. Θεωρητικές προσεγγίσεις και εμπειρικές έρευνες [Population reproduction. Theoretical approaches and empirical studies]. Gutenberg.

Kyriazis, N. (1995). Feminism and the status of women in Greece. In D. Constas & T. Stavrou (Eds.), *Greece prepares for the twenty-first century* (pp. 267-301). The Johns Hopkins University Press.

Kyriazis, N. (1999). Η Κοινωνιολογική έρευνα. Κριτική επισκόπηση των μεθόδων και των τεχνικών [Sociological research: A critical review of methods and techniques]. Ellinika Grammata.

Kyrtsis, A-A. (1988). Πολιτική νομιμοποίηση και οικονομικός εκσυγχρονισμός [Political legitimiation and economic modernization]. In E. Katsoulis, T. Giannitsis, & T. Kazakos (Eds.), *Η Ελλάδα προς το 2000. Πολιτική και κοινωνία, οικονομία, εξωτερικές σχέσεις* [Greece toward 2000. Politics and society, economy, foreign affairs] (pp. 17-34). Papazisis.

Kyrtsis, A-A. (1996). *Κοινωνιολογική σκέψη και εκσυγχρονιστικές ιδεολογίες στον ελληνικό μεσοπόλεμο* [Sociological thought and modern ideologies in the Greek interwar period]. Nisos.

Kyrtsis, A.-A. (1998). Greek interbellum modernizers and the 'sociological idea'. *International Sociology, 13*(3), 311-324.

Lambiri-Dimaki, J. (1989). *Κοινωνιολογία και ιστορία: ομοιότητες και ιδιαιτερότητες* [Sociology and history: similarities and special features]. Papazisis.

Lambiri-Dimaki, J. (1996). Sociology in Greece: Trends and prospects. *South European Society and Politics, 1*(1), 121-130.

Lambiri-Dimaki, J. (1997). "Εισαγωγικό Σημείωμα" [Introductory Note]. In I. Lambiri-Dimaki (Ed.), *Η Κοινωνιολογία στην Ελλάδα σήμερα, 1988-1996*, Τόμος Β' (με κείμενα 47 συγγραφέων) [*Sociology in Greece Today*. Vol. II (with texts from 47 authors)] (pp. 11-31). Papazisis.

Lambiri-Dimaki, I. (2000). *Για την κοινωνιολογία* [For sociology]. Sakkoulas.

Lambiri-Dimaki, I., & Kyriazis, N. (Eds.). (1995). *Η ελληνική κοινωνία στο τέλος του 20ου αιώνα* [Greek society at the end of the 20th century]. Papazisis.

Lambiri-Dimaki, I & Papachristou T. (1993) *Κοινωνία, δίκαιο, ηθική. Πέντε κείμενα* [Society, right, ethics. Five texts]. Sakkoulas.

Lekkas, P. (1988). *Marx on classical antiquity. Problems of historical methodology*. Palgrave Macmillan.
Lekkas, P. (1996). Η εθνικιστική ιδεολογία. Πέντε υποθέσεις εργασίας στην ιστορική κοινωνιολογία [The nationalist ideology. Five working hypotheses in historical sociology]. Katarti.
Lipowatz, T., & Demertzis, N. (1994). Δοκίμιο για την ιδεολογία. Ένας διάλογος της κοινωνικής θεωρίας με την ψυχανάλυση [Essay on ideology. A dialogue between social theory and psychoanalysis]. Odysseas.
Luhmann, N. (1992). Interview. In Στα Μονοπάτια της Σκέψης [In the paths of thought]. ERT (Ellinikí Radiofonía Tileórasi A.E (Hellenic Broadcasting Corporation)). Archive number: 32INCHEMB1740.
Luhmann, N. (2000). *The reality of the mass media* (K. Cross, Trans.). Polity Press (Original work published 1996).
Lyotard, J-F. (1992). Interview. In Στα Μονοπάτια της Σκέψης [In the paths of thought]. ERT (Ellinikí Radiofonía Tileórasi A.E (Hellenic Broadcasting Corporation)). Archiv number: 32–73882.
Marantzidis, N. (1998). Πολιτική κοινωνιολογία και ελληνική πολιτική κοινωνιολογία [Political sociology and Greek political sociology]. *New Sociology, 25*, 54–58.
Maratou-Alipranti, L. (1991). Γυναικείες σταδιοδρομίες και οικιακή εργασία. Η περίπτωση των γυναικών της Αθήνας [Female careers and domestic labor. The case of women in Athens]. *To Vima ton Koinonikon Epistimon, 1*(4), 69–91.
Mavridis, I. (1999). Απορία και νόμος στη σκέψη του Ζακ Ντεριντά [Aporia and law in the thought of Jacques Derrida]. *Nea Estia, 1713*, 553–585.
Mavrogordatos, G. (1997). From traditional clientelism to machine politics: The impact of PASOK populism in Greece. *South European Society and Politics, 2*(3), 1–26.
Mavrogordatos, G. (2012, May 24). Styx and stones. *The Times Higher Educational Supplement*, (2051), 34.
McCarthy, G. (2003). *Classical horizons: The origins of sociology in ancient Greece*. State University of New York Press.
Moebius, S. (2021). *Sociology in Germany. A history*. Palgrave Macmillan.
Morin, E. (1995). Interview to Constantinos Tsoukalas. In Στα Μονοπάτια της Σκέψης [In the paths of thought]. ERT (Ellinikí Radiofonía Tileórasi A.E (Hellenic Broadcasting Corporation)). Archive number: 0000006780.
Moussourou, L. (1993). Γυναίκα και απασχόληση. Δέκα ζητήματα [Women and employment. Ten issues]. Gutenberg.
Mouzelis, N. (1990). *Post-Marxist alternatives: The construction of social orders*. Macmillan.
Mouzelis, N. (1991). *Back to sociological theory: The constructions of social orders*. Macmillan.
Mouzelis, N. (1994a). In defense of 'grand' historical sociology. *The British Journal of Sociology, 45*(1), 31–36.

Mouzelis, N. (1994b). *Ο εθνικισμός στην ύστερη ανάπτυξη* [Nationalism in late development]. Themelio.
Mouzelis, N. (1995a). *Sociological theory. What went wrong? Diagnosis and remedies.* Routledge.
Mouzelis, N. (1995b). Greece in the twenty-first century: Institutions and political culture. In D. Constas & T. Stavrou (Eds.), *Greece prepares for the twenty-first century* (pp. 17–34). The Johns Hopkins University Press.
Mouzelis, N. (2002 [1994]). *Από την αλλαγή στον εκσυγχρονισμό. Κριτικές παρεμβάσεις: Πολιτική, κοινωνία, πολιτισμός, θεωρία* [From change to modernization. Critical interventions: Politics, society, culture, theory]. Themelio.
Mouzelis, N., Lipowatz, T., & Spourdalakis, M. (1989). *Λαϊκισμός και πολιτική* [Populism and politics] (with an introduction by C. Simitis). Gnosi.
Nikolaidou, C. (1993). *Η κοινωνική οργάνωση του αστικού χώρου* [The social organization of urban space]. Papazisis.
Papageorgiou-Lymperis, Y. (1992). The women's movement and Greek politics. In J. Bystydzienski (Ed.), *Women transforming politics: Worldwide strategies for empowerment* (pp. 67–79). Indiana University Press.
Papaioannou, S. (1997). Μετά τα «όρια της ανάπτυξης» τα «όρια της εργασίας» [After the "limits of growth", then the "limits of labor"?]. In I. Lambiri-Dimaki (Ed.), *Η Κοινωνιολογία στην Ελλάδα σήμερα, 1988–1996*, Τόμος Β' (με κείμενα 47 συγγραφέων) [Sociology in Greece Today. Vol. II (with texts from 47 authors)] (pp. 377–387). Papazisis.
Parsons, T., & Platt, G. M. (1973). *The American university.* Harvard University Press.
Petmesidou, M. (1998). Mass higher education and the social sciences in Greece. *International Sociology, 13*(3), 359–384.
Psimmenos, I. (1995). *Μετανάστευση από τα Βαλκάνια. Κοινωνικός αποκλεισμός στην Αθήνα* [Migration from the Balkans. Social exclusion in Athens]. Papazisis.
Psychopedis, K. (1990). Οι κοινωνικές επιστήμες στο σημερινό ελληνικό πανεπιστήμιο [Social science in the Greek university today]. In K. Psychopedis (M. Angelidis, Ed., 2011) (pp. 279–287). *Ήσσονα κριτικά* [Minor critical texts]. Nisos.
Romanos, V. (2014). The 'linguistic turn' and continental sociology: The question of agency and structure. In S. Koniordos & A. A. Kyrtsis (Eds.), *Routledge handbook of European sociology* (pp. 98–115). Routledge.
Said, E. (1994). Interview. In *Στα Μονοπάτια της Σκέψης* (In the paths of thought). ERT [Ellinikí Radiofonía Tileórasi A.E (Hellenic Broadcasting Corporation)]. Archive number: 0000008057. Retrieved May 18, 2022, from https://archive.ert.gr/8057/
Samatas, M. (1991). Παράγοντες και συνέπειες του πανεπιστημιακού γραφειοκρατισμού [Factors and consequences of university bureaucratization].

In *Το πανεπιστήμιο στην Ελλάδα σήμερα* [The university in Greece today] (pp. 215–227). Sakis Karagiorgas Foundation.

Samatas, M. (1993). Debureaucratization failure in post-dictatorial Greece: A sociopolitical control approach. *Journal of Modern Greek Studies, 11*(2), 187–217.

Sotiropoulos, D. (1994). Bureaucrats and politicians: A case study of the determinants of perceptions of conflict and patronage in the Greek bureaucracy under PASOK rule, 1981-1989. *The British Journal of Sociology, 45*(3), 349–365.

Sotiropoulos, D. (1996). *Populism and bureaucracy: The case of Greece under Pasok 1981–1989*. University of Notre Dame Press.

Tatsis, N., & Zito, G. (1974). Marx, Durkheim and alienation: Toward a heuristic typology. *Social Theory and Practice, 3*(2), 223–243.

Tatsis, N. (1989). *Κοινωνιολογία. Ιστορική εισαγωγή και θεωρητικές θεμελιώσεις. Τόμος Πρώτος* [Sociology. Historical introduction and theoretical foundations. Volume I]. Odysseas.

Tatsis, N. (1991). *Κοινωνιολογία. Κοινωνική οργάνωση και πολιτισμικές διεργασίες. Τόμος Δεύτερος* [Sociology. Social organization and cultural processes. Volume Two]. Odysseas.

Tatsis, N. (1992). *Γνωστικές προσωπογραφίες. Σύγχρονες θεωρητικές μορφοποιήσεις του κοινωνιολογικού ανθρώπου* [Cognitive profiles. Contemporary theoretical configurations of *homo sociologicus*]. Odysseas.

Teperoglou, A. (1989). *Η ηλικιωμένη γυναίκα στην Ελλάδα. Μια κοινωνιολογική προσέγγιση* [The elderly woman in Greece. A sociological approach]. *Social Research Review, 75*, 170–183.

Terlexis, P. (1996). *Διευθυντικές ολιγαρχίες. Γραφειοκρατία, κράτος και κοινωνική οργάνωση* [Directorate oligarchies. Bureaucracy, state and social organization]. Papazisis.

Tsaoussis, D. (1991). *Η κοινωνία μας. Οργάνωση, λειτουργία, δυναμική* [Our society. Organization, function, dynamics]. Gutenberg.

Tsartas, P. (1991). *Τουρισμός και αγροτική πολυδραστηριότητα* [Tourism and multiactivity]. EKKE.

Tsoukalas, C. (1991). *Είδωλα πολιτισμού. Ελευθερία, ισότητα και αδελφότητα στη σύγχρονη πολιτεία* [Idols of civilization. Freedom, equality and brotherhood in contemporary polity]. Themelio.

Tsoukalas, C. (1995). Free riders in wonderland; or, of Greeks in Greece. In D. Constas & T. Stavrou (Eds.), *Greece prepares for the twenty-first century* (pp. 191–219). The Johns Hopkins University Press.

Veltsos, G. (2005 [1988]). *Η Μη-κοινωνιολογία. Αναλυτική του μετα-μοντερνισμού* [Non-sociology. Analytics of post-modernism]. Nefeli.

Wallimann, I., Rosenbaum, H., Tatsis, N., & Zito, G. (1980). Misreading Weber: The concept of 'Macht'. *Sociology, 14*(2), 261–275.

CHAPTER 6

Sociology in Greece After 2000: The Discipline in Face of Crises

Abstract The last chapter addresses recent institutional and thematic trajectories of sociology in Greece. From a collective euphoria stemming from Greece's Eurozone membership, the Olympic Games held in Athens in 2004, the country's remarkably high growth rates and sociology's increasing international visibility and networking to Greece's unprecedented vulnerability during the Great Recession, sociology not only engaged in diagnostics but proved capable of generating new problem shifts. The *National Centre for Social Research* publications on crisis, democracy, the rise of far-right parties, social solidarity and the Covid-19 pandemic reflect this state of uncertainty. Other foci are local societies, youth, the Internet and social inequality, the memory of crisis, globalization, the Greek Welfare State, social transformation in rural Greece, migration and social exclusion, surveillance during the Olympic Games craze as well as theoretical work with international scope that builds bridges across sociological paradigms, reinterprets the classical founders of sociology, reconstructs normativity and has a voice in recently articulated fields like the sociology of emotions. Mouzelis' and Tsoukalas' most recent books are briefly addressed. The currently existing sociology departments are mapped along with the translations and the sociological journals landscapes.

Keywords Crisis • International shifts • Mouzelis • Sociology departments • Tsoukalas • Values

The Crisis in Greece and the Crisis of Sociology?

At the dawn of the twentieth-first century, Europe had to reassemble its composure as the Yugoslav wars were bitterly coming to an end in nation-state erosion and new nation-state formations, NATO bombings on European soil, ethnic cleansing and genocidal murder (Mann, 2005), unbeknown to Europe's post-World War II march to peace, prosperity and social justice. With the Eurozone established on New Year's Day of 1999, national and cultural traumas (Alexander, 2012) seemed to await catharsis in the pool of unprecedented growth rates and 'end of history' elation narratives as the West seemed to have effectively exorcised the demons of Spenglerian decline (Bauman & Donskis, 2013). As the 9/11 disaster shattered 'end of history' tranquility into smithereens, the subsequent wars in Iraq and Afghanistan along with the spectrally viral (Baudrillard, 2012) global terrorist escalation (Al Qaeda, IS) that followed posed additional anxiety and boundary confusion over uses and misuses of 'axis of evil' binaries (Bernstein, 2005). The post-2008 Great Recession and its discontents marked a major blow to neoliberalism's mythologies (Piketty, 2017) yet with a marked realization that TINA ('there is no alternative') destinies unleashed an unpredictably procrastinating *interregnum* era (Streeck, 2016). Coupled to the experience of nationalism's resurgence (including Brexit) and far-right extremism in Europe, the Covid-19 pandemic undermined the last vestiges of normality. As the Russian invasion of Ukraine is currently unfolding since February 2022 and a humanitarian and an energy crisis are already on the world's doorstep, for a mere twenty-two years into the new century, such compression of crises makes Beck's (2012) 'world in turmoil' diagnostics a euphemism.

Greece has had its own share of involvement and vulnerability in the twenty-first-century crises and global shifts in wealth, power and geopolitics. The affluent late 1990s and early 2000s optimism that culminated in the 2004 Olympic Games hosted in Athens for the first time since 1896 were quickly dissolved as Greece was hit the hardest from the Great Recession's domino effects in Europe. On 23 April 2010 and filmed against the tranquil waterfront of the remote island of Kastellorizo, a humbled George Papandreou (the then Greek prime minister) made a televised message to the Greek people about the imminent bailout package from the IMF, the Eurogroup and the European Central Bank. With deficits having soared to nearly $300 billion and a downgrading of Greek bonds to 'junk', the country entered a long period of austerity disciplining, pension and welfare scheme cuts, massive social unrest, capital controls, unprecedented government coalitions (left wing SY.RI.ZA with the National Patriotic Alliance of Independent Greeks) and political fermentation, culminating in the rise of neo-Nazi criminal organization Golden Dawn and its representation in the Greek parliament (from 2012 to 2019) (see Ellinas, 2013).

Greek sociologists (like most of their international colleagues) had not foreseen any of this.[1] The Great Recession and its manifestation in the Greek crisis exposed the bold conjecture lacuna in sociology and other social sciences like economics yet with a largely under-perceived sense of the discipline's own explanatory crisis. Rather, this state of shock called for retrospective explanations even as the crisis was still in place (Tsoukalas, 2012). An important volume (Zamparloukou & Kousis, 2014) in this direction addressed the political consequences and causes of the crisis, the implosion of hitherto 'functional' models of growth in Greece, the social impact in terms of a widening inequality, rising unemployment and underemployment with taxing pressure on middle-class incomes. Addressed were also the wider causes of the recession like neoliberal market deregulation, growth of inequality between the European North and the European South, populism and clientelism (as argued by Mouzelis' contribution), low-trust society (Koniordos), the impact on education (Fotopoulos), the crisis in Greece's political system (see also the recent explanation offered by Tsirigotis on Greek *partitocrazia*, namely, the party-state rule geared to populism and 'disjointed corporatism' (2019, p. 158)) and the deregulation of the typical middle-class Greek family's socioeconomic security pillar like home ownership.

Greece's Crises: In Search of the 'Intermediate' Way?

Sociologists felt the need (and the imperative) to continue engagement with the public sphere and to reach lay audiences with critical interventions on then current issues through short pieces on the Greek press. Regarding Mouzelis who published in 2002 a collection of such interventions in the newspaper *To Vima* from the late 1980s to the early 2000s, it is important to identify the sociological compass that guides the explanatory/critical validity of such interventions. In the volume's almost programmatic introduction, Mouzelis states that the collection of essays

---

[1] Sociologists may have to learn from Kondylis' different approach which engages in bold conjectures. His remarkably accurate explanation of the power (in)balances that could lead (as it turned out) to Russian aggression in Eurasia, including EU's myopia, as he claims, and US-backed NATO expansion towards the East is a pertinent case in point (Kondylis, 1998, pp. 117–118).

should be seen through the lens of a differentiated modernity. Salient here 'from a sociological standpoint' is the differentiation of 'distinct institutional fields (economic, political, social, cultural), with each field having—potentially, at least—its own dynamics, logic and values' (2002, p. 13). While different configurations of societies can emerge from the coordination and rapprochement between such institutions, Mouzelis contends that 'any attempt by any field to dominate others, thus any attempt at abolishing the values and the particular logic of a field has dysfunctional and pathological for the social whole consequences: it leads to statism/party domination, market domination, theocracy etc.' (13). Conjuring a logic of balanced coordination, Mouzelis' imagery of progress in modernity entails 'the secure balance between the economic field (in which the values of productivity/competitiveness prevail), the political field (values of democracy/human rights), the social field (values of solidarity and "difference") and the cultural field (values of self-realization and respect of "difference")' (13). Mouzelis embraces a neo-Weberian systems-theory approach which draws on Parsonsian normativism but stresses the autonomy of each system (or field in Bourdieu's paradigm) in a fashion that recalls Luhmann's incommensurability between autopoietic systems. In Mouzelis' scheme, however, Luhmann's post-humanist normative neutrality is abandoned. Rather, Mouzelis' synthesis elides the systemic interchanges between institutional spheres or systems (as in Hegel, Durkheim or Parsons) as opposed to an overarching core of values that runs through, as it were, all institutional configurations; instead of mediations between general values and specific codes that stem from the value relevance and particularism of each institutional sphere, each institutional field is somehow tied to immanent to it normative values.

Mouzelis' interventions traverse the fields of political structures in Greece, Greek foreign policy, international relations, modernization, civil society, culture and lifestyles.[2]

---

[2] Mouzelis (1994) wrote a short monograph on the rise of nationalism that is exclusively devoted to the early Macedonian naming dispute (1991–2019) through the wider lens of Greece's placement in a late development/underdevelopment modernity. Locating the roots of this 'culture war' in the attritive struggle between what Diamantouros called 'underdog' and a modernization culture (1994, pp. 17–19), Mouzelis sees the Macedonian controversy as a manifestation of nationalist resurgence within a modern nation-state that is marked by weak civil society (35–52). Through this lens he holds in check the then Greek Orthodox Church's nationalist populism (as opposed to contemporary bridge-building religiosity) as well as the 'amoral familism' coined by anthropologist Edward Banfield (1958) that afflicts Greek institutions (Mouzelis, 2003).

A trope that surfaces is a 'third way' argumentation. In politics this takes the shape of advocating a renovated and pragmatic social democracy as opposed to the sterile alternatives of neo liberalism and voluntarist leftist radicalism. This trope of the third option has also a heuristic function in a cartography of issues beyond the themes of social justice and social differentiation (see, e.g. the scheme of the 'pro-Western' perspective, the pro-Serbian perspective and the 'third viewpoint' on the issue of Yugoslavia's balkanization in light also of NATO's military intervention (100–104)). Back to the field of Greek politics, Mouzelis energizes the 'intermediate' trope to make a clarion call for resisting the 'Scylla of reckless populism' and the 'Charybdis of Thatcherite modernization' (187).

Greek Sociology's Struggle for a Public Audience

The Journals Landscape

The economic crisis and its social discontents challenged the viability of the few sociological reviews in circulation. The longest running sociological review of *Nea Koinoniologia* (New Sociology) came to an end with Issue 46 in 2010. Some of its 2000 highlights included the tribute to Castoriadis (Issue 31, 2000), an exclusive interview with Richard Münch (Issue 38, 2004) and Jean Ziegler (Issue 39, 2004), the reprints of the *Sociological Review* issues 1 to 6 (years 1945–1946) (Issue 40, 2005), an exclusive translation for the journal by Christian Papilloud[3] on Gurvitch (Issue 41, 2005), the review's exclusive interview with Alain Touraine (Issue 43, 2006–2007) and the extended and detailed tribute to Castoriadis' early years and affiliations in Greece (Issue 44, 2008). The journal's international network of collaborations (e.g. *American Sociological Review*, *Revue Suisse de Sociologie*) did not prevent its demise. In the journal's eulogy, its editor-in-chief and founder, sociologist Meletis Meletopoulos (2010), regrets the short-lived but stellar editorial board and praises publisher Victor Papazisis' support despite adversities. With the notion of crisis being ascribed to several factors (the dire economic crisis and human capital renewal challenges, as a result of a corresponding 'decline' that was imputed to education in Greece in toto, but was hardly demonstrated, the shift to online outlets, but not to a missed potential for enhancing the journal's scope and scholarly rigor), the review's farewell

---

[3] Christian Papilloud is a major Simmel scholar affiliated to the *Simmel Studies* journal.

anthologizes valuable highlights like those already mentioned, less persuasive cultural diagnostics and polemics as well as the review's standing focus on Greek history, geopolitical challenges and national identity (Kondylis' body of work in this direction has been paradigmatic for late *New Sociology*'s interpretive lens).

Interdisciplinary work proliferated as well as work that aimed towards delineating the boundaries within sociology. Journals like *Social Cohesion and Development* converged with sociology on a number of occasions (see, indicatively, Karakioulafi, 2007; Kantzara, 2016; Xypolitas, 2017). The journal *Science and Society: Review of political theory and ethics* was launched in 1998 and continues to publish annually until now. Mouzelis, Demertzis, Lipowatz, Koniordos and Panayotopoulos[4] are among those who give to this interdisciplinary journal a solid sociological profile; the journal includes an interesting 'Rereading the classics' section which provides opportunities to rediscover neglected founders of the discipline. Similarly, the *Hellenic Review of Political Science* launched in 1993 featured articles by Tsoukalas, Mouzelis, Demertzis, Alexandropoulos and Psimmitis, among others.

The Translations Landscape

Conducive to sociology's dissemination in Greece has been the steady proliferation of translated works in sociology. Early and mid-twentieth-century eclectic translations of work by Sombart, Lévy-Bruhl, Simmel, Freyer and Durkheim (e.g. Papalexandrou, 1927) among others, lacked introductions or postscripts by the then translators and editors. This dry terrain which reflected the unsystematic state of sociology in Greece continued until the late 1980s. While Marx's translated major works have had ample attention, largely due to the political appeal of Marxism among intellectuals in disciplines outside sociology, Weber, Durkheim and Simmel have received less attention. Tsaoussis was a consultant in the 1980 book series *Sociological Library* (Gutenberg Publishers) that published in Greek works by Gurvitch, Bottomore, Weber, Durkheim, H. Michel and Lefebvre, among others, at a time when very few books of basic sociology were available in translation. The works of Durkheim are by now mostly available in translation, yet no translation of *The Division of Labour in*

---

[4] In 2012 Panayotopoulos launched the *Social Sciences* tri-lingual journal which promotes a Bourdieu-esque problematic.

Society and *The Elementary Forms of Religious Life* exists. Max Weber's *Economy and Society* was made available in six volumes, meticulously translated and edited by Thanasis Giouras for Savalas Publishers. Georg Simmel's *The Philosophy of Money* has not been fully translated with only long extracts from some chapters being available in translation. However, as Demertzis and Lipowatz (2006, p. 24) note, 'a milestone in the publications annals' in Greece is 'the translation of some important' essays by Simmel (2004).

Kondylis (see Chap. 4) was the editor of the book series *Modern European Civilization* (Nefeli Publishers) which featured a number of translated works from sociology like Elias, Sombart, Freyer, D. Bell and Sennett. The selection of titles confirm Kondylis' hard-to-dispute sociological interest. Kondylis also founded the book series *Philosophical and Political Library* (Gnosis Publishers) which featured translations of important works in sociology by Sorel, Granet, Aron, Nisbet, Michels and Mannheim's *Ideology and Utopia*. The last sociological title in the series that was announced was Durkheim's *Suicide*, but it was never completed due to Kondylis' untimely death. Kondylis' prolific output and sustained dialogue with sociology included sociology works by A. Hauser, L. L. Schücking and L. Kofler he translated for Kalvos Publishers.

The bulk of American sociology remained for many decades unavailable to Greek readers. As Lambiri-Dimaki claims, 'Ethnomethodological research has not gained ground among Greek sociologists' (1996, p. 129). Towards making known this tradition to Greek audiences a collection of translated essays appeared in the early 2000s (Kalfopoulos, 2003), featuring essays by Garfinkel, Psathas, Blumer, Schütz, Lazarsfeld and Astrinakis, among others. Regarding interactionist sociology's visibility, four Goffman books were published by Alexandria Publishers from 1996 to 2012. A further breakthrough was the overdue translation of Talcott Parsons' early essays and of *The Structure of Social Action* in an admirable effort by Vassilis Maglaras to render Parsons' jargon accessible.

Nurturing Bourdieu's appeal in Greece, Nikos Panayotopoulos (see, e.g. 1999) who had been a member of the European Review of Books *Liber* and has studied with Bourdieu edited many of his translated works in Greek. Sociology's increasing development and visibility led inevitably to a wider scope from the classical founders to contemporary sociology. Thus, at least one work from every major contemporary social theorist is by now available in translation.

Greek TV's Mission Impossible: Disseminating Sociology to a Wider Public (2)

Tsoukalas[5] and Veltsos continued the TV series *In the Paths of Thought* in the 2000s and the 2010s. The gamut of interviewed thinkers (including Élisabeth Badinter, Clifford Geertz, Maurice Godelier, Michael Walzer) featured sociologists, but the spark of the 1990s shows was somewhat extinguished. Immanuel Wallerstein's (2001) interview is about the world system theory and its relevance for the accumulating crises of capitalism. Little is said about Greece except a passing reference to PA.SO.K's social-democratic control of the state within the context of social-democracy's victories, considering also that, as he claims, aspects of the social-democratic programmes have been adopted by conservatives too. In 2001 Tsoukalas interviewed Luc Boltanski in what was a concise summary of the *New Spirit of Capitalism* with Boltanski (2001) identifying Karl Polanyi (for an explanation of the Greek austerity crisis through Polanyi, see Markantonatou, 2014) and Max Weber as the inspiration behind the dissection of contemporary capitalism's appropriation of the 1968 artistic critique. Similarly reticent on any bridges to the Greek reality was Tsoukalas' conversation with Frances Fox Piven (2003) about the dismal inequality increase in the US under the wider climate of societal securitization. The interview with David Harvey (2005) was held at the City University of New York on the topic of neoliberalism. Although there is only a passing reference by Harvey on Greece in that it is also moving towards the political right, when questioned by Tsoukalas about Europe, Harvey makes an interesting remark in terms of sagacity about neo-conservative societal militarization and mentions as an example the probability of a future 'flu pandemic'.

Far more relevant to the Greek context is Tsoukalas' 2001 interview with Paul Kennedy (then Yale University professor of history) and Stanley Aronowitz (then State University of New York professor of sociology). The conversations are structured around the United States and its socio-political transformation under globalization. Not unexpectedly, Aronowitz emphasized how he and Peter Bratsis resort to Poulantzas to argue that nation-state and national capital have not withered away in global

---

[5] Tsoukalas' contribution to sociology through this series is among the reasons that led to the honorary PhD awarded to him on 6 June 2007 by the University of Crete (see Kousis et al., 2010, p. 13).

capitalism.[6] For Aronowitz IMF, WTO and the World Bank boards are occupied by finance ministers who stem from the nation-state constellation and legitimize political directorate alliances. Connecting proposals for a universal basic income (UBI) and a shorter working day to the contemporary constitution of the *polis*, Aronowitz's cavalier disposition makes an interesting pun when he resorts to neoliberalism's dismantling of the *polis*. This, for him, renders citizens 'idiots', qualifying the noun with the Greek etymology: *idiōtēs* (private persons, ignorant persons) (for the etymology and meanings in Greek, see Dimitrakos, 1970, p. 698). Aronowitz couples this meaning to what is for him a lamentable route of higher education (in the US and elsewhere) towards specialization. Kennedy picks up the thread to express his scepticism on a Janus-faced EU, driven by cooperation and competition. Drawing on the digital divide as an index of the new shape of inequality, he is alarmingly prescient, making a disconcerting prognosis, since such inequality gaps make the 'East German skinheads who do not have a job and do not have very good education qualifications or Ukrainian skinheads for that matter' an 'explosive and combustible material' (Aronowitz & Kennedy, 2001). Applauding Tsoukalas for this programme initiative, Kennedy hopes that it can make an even tiny contribution in disseminating this kind of understanding to the public.

Recent Developments and Mouzelis' and Tsoukalas' Latest Works

The proliferation of works in sociology in the 2000s focused on filling gaps in the textbook and reader market, extending the discipline's theoretical and methodological scope in Greece and research on diverse sociology specialisms. For example, Tatsis (2004) updated the discussion about late modernity with a useful book on sociological profiles (e.g. Giddens, Bell, Touraine, Habermas, Luhmann, Castells) around the axis

---

[6] Aronowitz summarizes this argument which must have been taking shape at the time of this interview, published subsequently in 2002 in a volume on Poulantzas that he and Peter Bratsis edited and to which Tsoukalas had contributed a book chapter (Tsoukalas, 2002) on the idea of differentiated levels of the state apparatus. In a sense, Tsoukalas anticipates the core-periphery dependency, even if Italy, Spain and Greece had social-democratic governments (2002, p. 234). He also sheds light on how 'interterritorial bribes' are incorporated into a tacit practice of EU-induced capitalism. This phenomenon may strike familiar chords to the Greek public with regard to bribery scandals that surfaced a bit later, like the SAIC-Siemens and the Olympic phone-tapping scandals (see Samatas, 2014, pp. 47–83).

of a modernity that is intertwined with social change. He also continued to familiarize Greek sociologists with the Chicago School (Tatsis & Thanopoulou, 2009), before embarking at a hermeneutics of consumer society (Tatsis, 2021). Modernity's Janus-faced promises and failures were handled with by now sufficient expertise to justify volumes that traversed classical and contemporary sociological theory to post-modernism (see, e.g. Koniordos, 2010b). Antonopoulou (2011), for her part, revisited the classical founders with an important treatise on the social content of philosophical materialism (Antonopoulou, 2000) as part of Greek sociology's focus on the sociology of knowledge, as in the case of Nagopoulos (2003, 2015). Other theoretical trajectories offered valuable insights into the reception of seminal sociology works, like Durkheim's *The Elementary Forms of Religious Life* (see, for instance, Acheimastos, 2019).

Seminal at the beginning of the 2000s was Frangoudaki's monograph on the Greek language question from the 'perspective of sociology' (Frangoudaki, 2001, p. 13). Examining the politically charged controversy between *katharevousa* (purist) and *demotiki* (demotic) (reactionary/conservative and progressive/enlightened, respectively), Frangoudaki provides a hermeneutic framework in order to discern in language controversy a struggle for shaping national identity. This, for her, conflates national identity with purist Greek versus a logic of *demotic* pollution (particularly during the Greek junta), considering also its concomitant evaluation by various political and intellectual constituencies and a proclivity to an 'excessive normativity' (99) in language's role not only in lay locutions but also in scholarly discourses, detached from context.

Migration studies which had generated important sociological foci in the 1990s maintained that impetus (see, e.g. Psimmenos and Kassimati (2003), Katsas (2013), Fouskas (2012)), extending it also to the international scope of migration studies indicatively (Papadopoulos et al., 2018). Quickly the focus on migration and inclusion/exclusion mechanisms specialized on gender with emphasis on Balkan and Eastern Europe migrant women (Kassimati & Moussourou, 2007; Kampouri, 2007; Thanopoulou, 2007; Psimmenos & Skamnakis, 2008; Zachou & Kalerante, 2010). Furthermore, Pontic-Greek diaspora was systematically approached through the notion of trauma (Lagoumitzi, 2011, 2020). The family received sustained attention in light of women's entry into the labour force and in relation to the rise of single-parent families (Mousourou, 2006), supplemented by work on the under-researched problem of age and ageism in Greece (Mousourou, 2005).[7] This shift to the domain of gender grappled with the still stereotypical perception and depiction of women on Greek TV (Nina-Pazarzi & Tsangaris, 2008) or TV's own underdevelopment in the Greek periphery (Panagiotopoulou, 2004). Social media was soon to initiate sociological interest, theoretical (Constantopoulou, 2013; Leverrato & Leontsini, 2008) and empirical. On the latter, Pleios (2015) conducted a survey among 500 Facebook users, investigating the correlation between use and the experience of the Great Recession in Greece and capitalism's links to information society (Pleios, 2016). Other fields and foci that continue to flourish are sociological methodology (Kyriazi, 2011), the sociology of leadership (Nikolaou-Smokoviti, 2004), labour relations (Lytras, 2000), sociology of education (Kelpanidis, 2002; Pyrgiotakis, 2000; Koniordos & Fotopoulos, 2010), symbolic networks (Chtouris, 2004), sociology of religion (Sakellariou, 2022), political sociology (Moschonas, 2018; Pappas, 1999), bureaucracy (Serafetinidou, 2012), electoral sociology (Nikolakopoulos, 2010), civil society (Papaioannou & Serdedakis, 2001), social trust (Koniordos, 2010a) and social movements (Alexandropoulos, 2001). Studies in the interdisciplinary fuzzy border continued in the domain of psychology (Alexias & Bletsos, 2009; Lipowatz, 2021), social anthropology (Papataxiarchis et al., 2009), constitutional law and the sociology of law (Kontiadis, 2006; Tsaoussi, 2013), criminology (Daskalaki et al., 2000) and social policy (Stratigaki, 2007).

The Centre of Social Research continues its prolific output. Since the 2000s the *Greek Review of Social Research* addressed oral histories, social change and urban segregation, crime and criminal justice, the macro-micro impact of the economic crisis in Greece, aspects of gender precariousness, disciplinary society, NGOs, social stratification, the sociology of culture, the sociology of religion, sociology of agriculture and rural life, the Muslim communities in Thrace, social solidarity, the far right's recourse to social media and a special issue (2020, (154)) on the Covid-19 pandemic. Important is the initiative to publish issues exclusively in English (see, e.g. the 144 (1), 2015 Special Issue: Politics, Democracy and Digital Cultures edited by Afouxenidis or the 136 (3), 2011 Special Issue:

---

[7] Many of these studies coincided with the burgeoning research activity at KEKMOKOP (see Mousourou & Kassimati, 2004). EU-funded research projects like IAPASIS (*Informal Administration Practices and Shifting Immigrant Strategies*) or EURONAT (under the *European University Institute*) (Europe and the Nation in Current and Prospective Member States: Media, Effects and Civil Society (2001–2004)) had also a marked sociological interest. For relevant synopses see the 2006 1(1) issue of *Social Cohesion and Development*.

Contemporary Social Inequalities, edited by Psimmenos). Notable are also the Centre's periodic volumes on *The Social Portrait of Greece* published in 2006, 2010 and 2012 combining analyses with metrics on social exclusion, poverty, employment, social and political integration.

Like the 1990s reflexive efforts on Greek sociology, the 2000s honoured some of its major representatives. Relevant tributes to Lambiri-Dimaki (Maratou-Alipranti et al., 2011, Afouxenidis & Alexakis, 2006) to Tsoukalas (Kousis et al., 2010), and to the Centre of National Research (Lambiri-Dimaki, 2003) growth and its vicissitudes[8] affirm Greek sociology's quest for legacies.

A discourse on values (see also end of Chap. 4) was taken up in various directions.[9] Mouzelis (2002, pp. 349–354; 355–360) contributed to it in bringing to the fore the issue of 'value conflicts'. Adhering to the explanatory modality of a middle-range position between the extremes of an unattainable today value idealism and of a debilitating relativism, he proposes a third solution towards a comparative-historical and evolutionary approach. Undoubtedly, there is a modernist outlook in Mouzelis' discourse on values, yet he qualifies his evolutionism with a logic of global differentiation in how societies combine 'global values' in unique ways. This happens against a backdrop of fundamentalist resurgences and of imbalanced development in those values' scope. Mouzelis considers cosmopolitan values not only as desirable convergences among different peoples but also conditions for the planet's sustainability.

Relevant here are the findings of the World Value Survey (WVS) for Greece (see Koniordos, 2018) which drew on data collection among 1200 respondents in 2017. Conducted in conjunction with the National Centre of Social Research and the research and policy institute *diaNEOsis*, the Greek survey relied on variables like social values, social well-being, social capital and trust, economic values, corruption, security, post-materialist values, science and technology, religion, ethics and norms, political participation and political culture. In many respects, Greece appears to be in a state of a not yet completed transition from tradition to modernity (Koniordos, 2018, p. 110). Other important conclusions are the decline

---

[8] From May 2009 and until the Fall of 2011, as the Great Recession hit Greece, the Centre was subject to reform announcement for mergers that would jeopardize the public dimension of social research (Maratou-Alipranti et al., 2011, p. xi, n.1).

[9] Psychopedis' *Axiologika* legacy continued to inspire scholars in philosophy and political science (see Faraklas, 2013) and sociology (see Gangas, 2004, 2020).

of trust in its strong correlation to the Great Recession's debilitating impact in Greece, the acknowledgement of corruption mostly imputed to the state and to public officials and less to the respondents' own entanglement in everyday networks of corruption and the correlation between less educated strata's positive evaluation of security as opposed to more educated strata's appreciation of freedom. Generally, Greece seems to have receded, compared to the 1999 European Value Study (EVS-3) and the 2008 EVS-4, in terms of its then shift to post-materialist values, regressing after the WVS-7 survey to a 'rather materialist' position (114). A subsequent volume of relevant studies and interpretative work on the WVS appeared recently (Koniordos, 2021). Among its many significant contributions, we can note Tsaoussis' chapter which presents Greece as an open society, yet with 'mild anomie' (for this phrase see Koniordos, 2018, p. 79 and 79, n14), but subject to an introvert conservatism (Tsaoussi, 2021). This assessment of Greece and its values was preceded by the exhaustively informed volume on social trends in Greece from 1960 to 2000 (Charalambis et al., 2004), which entails studies of a shift to modern values but with traditional normative loads still being invoked. Particularly instructive is Charalambis' (2004) introduction which is a concise chronicle of socio-political traits of Greek society, including challenges and setbacks such as Greece's burgeoning privatization schemes, the role of the mass media and their unwarranted influence and power over the political system, the decentralization impetus (largely boosted through EU funds) that creates new local networks of patronage and power-wielding niches, an underground economy that is incumbent upon the public administration, xenophobia due to a lack of immigration-receiving culture, an imagined community of linearly and purist nationality and clientele networks based on kin and cronies.

Mouzelis' Late Works

Mouzelis' quest for bridge-building (a Parsonsian motif) across dualistic patterns culminates in *Modern and Postmodern Theorizing: Bridging the Divide* (2008, p. 5). Mouzelis challenges the validity of the alleged rift between the modern and the post-modern constellations. Preferring the designation 'late modernity', he emphatically asserts the Parsonsian system's continuing relevance as a powerful categorical resource to which sociological theory should by no means turn its back. If we try to configure Mouzelis' project in terms borrowed from Lakatosian epistemology, we can suggest that its 'negative heuristic' aims to keep open the sluices between sociological binaries (macro-micro; agency-structure)—sociological theory's hard core as it were—while the 'positive heuristic' expounds sociological theory's fruitfulness by reconstructing categories so as to avoid theoretical compartmentalization and to enable the articulation of novel perspectives. In a dense exposition, Mouzelis traverses sociological theory in its entirety, but perhaps more representative is his attempt (217–224) to reconcile the methodological desideratum of holism as an explanatory (rather than an ontological) project and thus rescue it from post-modern attacks on its essentialist connotations in face of ever contingent, fragmentary and context-dependent discourses. The image of the bridge-building effort as opposed to paradigmatic silos is what informs Mouzelis' open holism. Moments of this explanatory programme include the action-structure repulsion of conflation in favour of a balanced consideration of each paradigm's relative merits and the safeguarding of theoretical concepts from tendencies to subordinate rival paradigms, to transcend binaries or to abolish them as post-modern theorizing hopes to accomplish. Similarly, the macro-micro continuum should be rethought in holistic but anti-essentialist terms (as opposed to, say, functionalist teleology), having as a compass Lockwood's system and social integration explanation levels (255–257).[10] Equally spirited is the claim against economy-based of culture-based reductionism. Here the articulation of conceptual tools that are open to the political, social and cultural institutional spaces is welcomed if these abandon explanatory and categorical apriorism and leave to empirical reality the tribunal's role for theoretical fruitfulness (Lakatos again).

Mouzelis' (2018) latest book (published only in Greek) attempts to provide a feasible reconstruction of social-democracy's scope and potential. In a sense, it marks no deviation from his theoretical articulations. Challenging contemporary Marxist accounts of capitalism's crises, Mouzelis maintains that although capitalism is unsustainable in the long run (2018, p. 19, 162), no signs of implosion (Streeck) or periphery zone capital accumulation exhaustion (Wallerstein) are likely to emerge. For all their systematic exposition and acuity, such radical Marxist narratives underestimate capital's potential to generate self-corrective mechanisms that rekindle processes of social-democratic control of markets. This is

---

[10] The Lockwood-Goldthorpe British tradition in empirical sociology has yet to receive proper attention in Greece.

presented as capital's reaction to global risks, eliciting synergies between the major agents of capital accumulation and geopolitical control (72). Moreover, Mouzelis (41–46) mobilizes the argument of capitalist system's own geopolitical differentiation into a neoliberal sub-system (United States), a social-democratic sub-system (EU) and an authoritarian capitalism sub-system (China). While EU's institutional weakening is hard to deny, Mouzelis hopes to undergird its historical acme (1945–1975) towards a new paradigm of nation-state integration founded on autonomy. The history of heteronomous shapes of integration includes (1) clientele-based networks that flourished in the context of oligarchical parliamentarism and (2) populism (a standing sociological focus of Mouzelis since his 1970 work). Opposed to this, shapes of autonomous integration are crystallized in the perspective 'where differentiated institutional spaces of a contemporary social scheme coordinate not by leveling, but, rather in a balancing way' (128). As neoliberal paradigms prevailed since the 1980s and coupled to the Great Recession years, social democracy faces the challenge of replenishing and adjusting its potential. Mouzelis believes that a social democracy that vies for de-colonizing civil society is the most promising path for resisting global neoliberalism's discontents with conditions for its success, being the elimination of unemployment based on a third pole (beyond the standard employment and education opportunities) (171–172) like remunerated service work.

Tsoukalas' Recent Diagnostic Sociology

For his part, Constantinos Tsoukalas is less sanguine about the scope of freedom in contemporary societies, including Greece. In his recent and dense book on *Invisible Leviathan*, Tsoukalas (2020) adheres to a format that is removed from sociological orthodoxies but draws on sociology and from neighbouring disciplines. The picture that emerges given modernity's collapse of normative promises is an *interregnum* plateau. This stretches from modernity's contradictions including paradoxes of democracy, a post-normative system that is gradually emerging, the corrosion of a privatized morality, the shrinking of the public duties, the Hayekian liberalization-instrumentalization of human agency as well as the opportunistic twist to human sociation (2020, p. 461). What, for Tsoukalas, is no longer tenable is the holism from Hegel to Parsons (131–132). In this post-humanist invisible Leviathan that invokes values no more, has no discernible source and musters no legitimation (27), its victims seem uncannily to be the agents of their own oppression. Interestingly enough, Tsoukalas' confessed bewilderment (24–25) over the outcomes of his grand synthesis of those intellectual currents and structural changes that shape a quest towards praxis seems to move closer to Castoriadis' stoic anticipation of a new imaginary.

The sense of crisis that had become a recurring trope for sociological diagnostics and interventions could not have omitted the Covid-19 pandemic's traces and traumas. In a book that could be considered as addendum to the heavy-handed *Invisible Leviathan*, Tsoukalas (2021) looks at the consequences of the pandemic and stretches to a reappraisal of the notion of normality, both as a sociological concomitant of the Enlightenment and its holist illusions and as a practical desideratum that found its way in the public discourse. Tsoukalas detects in the pandemic's rupture a political potential that had until then been occluded under 'normality', 'a voluntarist techno-optimism' and an 'arrogant systemic confidence' premised on the fiction of a perpetual 'progress of growth' (2021, pp. 47–48).

Tsoukalas' impressionist method weaves around the pandemic a pattern of 'crisis' which eschews explanatory closure. This is particularly true in an era where 'crises spill over from one sphere to another' (123). Rather than taking recourse to rigid and one-dimensional claims to clarity, Tsoukalas believes that 'under certain circumstances a liquid and flexible "creative ambiguity"'[11] (143) could yield better insights and outcomes in face of overwhelming contradictions. Yet he turns this trope on its head, as the 'meta-political' Leviathan is everywhere visible in its operations but can never be located, relying on a sort of 'authoritative ambiguity' (145). Next to the breach in the everyday-interaction proximity and distance between agents, Tsoukalas elevates the pandemic's semantics to the possibility of replenishing the political in face of wider geopolitical shifts (Trumpism, authoritarian Russia and China, liminal India, middle-range delusional projects of Turkish expansion to the Aegean or of North Korean nuclear pyrotechnics, Iranian and Saudi Arabian fundamentalisms, EU vacillations of sorts) (149) and, ultimately, to heightening the 'antagonism' between economy and politics. Less prone to cultural diagnostics through a political

---

[11] The expression 'creative ambiguity' is a reference to the Greek economist, former SY. RIZ.A government finance minister and current General Secretary of MeRA25 Yanis Varoufakis' rhetorical trope during the then government's negotiations with the IMF, the European Commission and the European Central Bank over bail-out austerity measures in Greece. Tsoukalas served as an MP for SY.RIZ.A from January 25, 2015 to August 28, 2015.

lens but equally tuned to the traumatic impact of the pandemic on culture, Demertzis and Eyerman (2020), for their part, configure the Covid-19 pandemic as a total social fact that is global, risky and uncertain, mediated by media dramatizations and aestheticizations of trauma.

The Sociology of Sociology in Greece: The Work of Lambiri-Dimaki

In 2002 Lambiri-Dimaki completed the visionary trilogy on *The Sociology in Greece Today* (1987a, 1997a, 2002a). Conceived as a marathon project that spanned fifteen years, featuring samples of work from 113 sociologists, it also adumbrated the context of a prospective sociology of Greek sociology. She notes initially a Hellenocentric orientation among the sociologists featured in the first volume with little comparative sociology orientation and even less attempts at a holistic study of Greek society (Lambiri-Dimaki, 1987b, pp. 45–46). While the then underdeveloped state of sociology in Greece seems to reflect a 'crisis' in the discipline, the image that surfaces with regard to the causes of such perceived crisis is even more Balkanized, adducing issues of theoretical/explanatory adequacy and a polysemic sociological jargon (then definitely in a pre-paradigmatic shape) (47). To the critical question of Greek sociology's morphology (and existence even), Lambiri-Dimaki adopts unfortunately an unrealistic measuring rod (US, British, French and German sociology) that leads her to commit to what is an a priori disadvantageous for Greek sociology comparison (1997b, p. 23). It seems that regional-oriented comparisons elide her account. In conjunction with sociology's largely Hellenocentric orientation, the language barrier and what she regards as dubious claims to originality in theoretical work, the picture seems dismal. Delving deeper into the sociology of Greek sociology, the last volume in the trilogy adopts a Bourdieu-inspired pattern which despite its fruitfulness risks structuralist closures.[12] Coupling habitus to the heuristic recourse

---

[12] Bourdieu-inspired calls for a 'realpolitik of sociological reason' (Panayotopoulos, 2020) and for a 'social history' of Greek sociology's 'theoretical and methodological legacy' (99) risk invalidating in an a priori mode (and with no references to specific works or Greek sociologists) an unidentified corpus of work (often labelled as being 'poseur' or 'vulgar' (99)) without having exhausted these works' claims to validity and explanatory fruitfulness. Debunking hierarchical sociological reason in this fashion risks regress to 'ressentiment' criticism; more importantly, even the castigated 'Grand Theorist' (85–92) syndrome has problem-solving potential, recognized by Panayotopoulos, but diluted amid polemics of what is an effort at a spirited defense of sociology's autonomy (against heteronomous shapes like journalistic anti-intellectualism (21)).

to Mannheim's 'generations', Lambiri-Dimaki sketches two generations of Greek sociologists drawn from their PhD award era. What emerges is the spell of Western thought and with 110 out of the 113 sociologists included in the trilogy to have been wholly or in part schooled abroad and having thus formed a 'cosmopolitan consciousness' (2002b, p. 66). The 1960s and the 1970s are marked by a political sub-generation (the 'Polytechnic' uprising generation) drawn to activism, Marxism and optimism towards social progress. This seems to be superseded by the 1980 and 1990 'crisis of sociology' perception as a concomitant of the crises in the welfare state (neoliberal reforms) and in Enlightenment values (e.g. post-modernism). Her conjecture is that the younger generations enter sociology with greater scepticism regarding the scientific and rational validity of the discipline (75–76).

Yet the dualism she discerns (1997b, p. 21) between an older generation of sociological 'optimism' and a younger generation's rather 'pessimistic' outlook towards sociology's potential must be taken with caution. For all its merits, the reading of sociology's bifurcation in optimistic or pessimistic outlooks or to theory-driven versus empirically oriented research could be prone to structuralist rigorism and of unduly entrenched approaches to the institutionalization and legitimacy of sociology in Greece. Habitus dispositions that may seem mutually incompatible may have more intersection points than initially assumed as well as capabilities for broadening the identity perspective and disposition-induced practices in the academic world.

We have already detected Lambiri-Dimaki's attempt to deal with the seemingly recalcitrant inclusion of Mouzelis (given his UK career), and the same approach is to be found in Koniordos and Kyrtsis (2014) in an important volume on European sociology that lacks, however, references to Castoriadis and Poulantzas across all authors' contributions (such category loops our Chap. 4 reconsiders and, hopefully, mends), while in its regional sociologies section devotes no chapter to Greek sociology.[13]

---

[13] However, it breaks new territory in amplifying the intersection points that would warrant a regional account of a sociological tradition written by a sociologist of that region. Thus, Kyrtsis' (2014) chapter on British sociology sets a promising precedent for such projects in an increasingly hybridized network of national traditions. He also makes a passing reference (2014, p. 402) to Greek sociology's development and its dependence of European traditions including the post-1980 British tradition that shaped the conceptual map and networks of many Greek sociologists. (We consider ourselves too as epigones of the British sociology habitus.)

Further International Reach[14]

Despite constraints associated with the weak public support for sociological research in Greece, the struggle for an identity of the discipline, the inertia of research productivity relying exclusively on the Greek language as well legal entrenchments across the public/private tertiary education that pose barriers to professional sociology[15] and, moreover, block the strengthening of the sociologists' collective consciousness, signs of work produced towards an international audience are not insignificant. Indeed, injunctions to Greek sociologists to 'create a local/global nexus, in order to transfer the dynamics of their local community to international sociological fora' must develop, according to Kyrtsis, alongside efforts to 'integrate into the community of Greek, but not ethnocentric, discourses those foreign colleagues who do not prefer folkloristic and ethnocentric curiosities' (1996, p. 11).[16] Part of the problem here is what Kyrtsis correctly notes as the 'handicap' of the Greek language and its extinction from any international niche of sociology, which, however, seems to lock sociology in Greece between local ethnocentrism (see also Kokosalakis, 1998, p. 338) and transnational segmentation of the discipline.

Increase in Greek sociology's international networking, visibility and contribution has been emphatically stated by Lambiri-Dimaki who suggests that 'Greek sociology is likely to become in time even more open to outside influences, more comparative and better-known abroad' (1996, pp. 129–130). At a time, however, when the global division of sociological labour and the curricula of traditional centres of gravity in the discipline's influence capital become de-colonized, such calls may retrieve the reverse

---

[14] International reach pertains also to affiliations in research committees (e.g. in ISA and ESA) as well as organization of international conferences in Greece. An example of the latter is the 2008 *Sociology for the Twenty-First Century* conference by the Department of Sociology at the University of Crete with speakers, among others, Derek Layder, Margaret Archer, Chris Rojek and George Ritzer.

[15] For Koniordos (2010c, p. 190–192) professional sociology is a precondition for public sociology to flourish.

[16] Such bridge-building with Greek sociology's diaspora could network with Michalis Lianos (2020) (University of Rouen), Iraklis Dimitriadis (2022) (University of Milan), Dimitris Michailakis (2003) (Linköping University), Evangelia Tatsoglou (2009) (Saint Mary's University), Apostolis Papapastos (2012) (Södertörn University), Victor Roudometof (2016) (University of Cyprus), Leonidas Cheliotis (2011) (LSE) and Athanasia Chalari (2017) (University of Northampton & Visiting Senior Fellow at the *Hellenic Observatory*, LSE), among others.

trend, legitimizing the dependency relations and orientation that we have discussed in the first chapters of this book.[17] Yet, given the problems that we outlined, such drive towards recognition, networking and influence with such centres is not unwarranted.[18] Since the mid-2000s contributions of international visibility ranged from sociological theory to nationalism and gender (Halkias, 2004), rural society in face of globalization (Kasimis & Papadopoulos, 1999) and Koniordos' (2001) seminal historical sociology study of the artisans. Moreover, Demertzis (2020) has systematically contributed towards establishing the sociology of emotions, drawing in the groundbreaking work he had published with Lipowatz (Demertzis & Lipowatz, 2006). In that work, they had applied 'ressentiment' to Greek populism by recourse to its ideal-typical accentuations in conjunction with empirical and content analysis data from the PA.SO.K hegemony of the press yet detecting such roots in the post-World War II petty bourgeoisie and the colossal junta poisoning of the Greek collective conscience with 'ressentiment'. Building on these merits, Demertzis (2011) opens once more the field of negative emotions to the context of the Greek Civil War: 'As a totalizing social event the Greek civil war can be described as a cultural trauma because it affected collective memories, group consciousness, and the organizational principles of Greek society, redirecting its orientation for several decades' (2011, p. 146). His programmatic call for a *Political Sociology of Emotions* (2020), as it marks the 'end of the "emotions-proof" period in sociology' (Demertzis, 2020, p. xii), enriches the hitherto available accounts of populism, including barriers that make the imperative of forgiveness difficult to accomplish, given the still hard-to-untangle distinction between perpetrators and victims (156–157). Demertzis' research programme on 'ressentiment' marks a fruitful shift in sociology, coinciding

---

[17] By contrast, Kokosalakis (1998, p. 338) expresses a need for Greek sociology to draw on the Greek cultural context and, resisting potential labels attached to it as 'reactionary' or 'conservative', to forge a potentially new epistemological break beyond relativism and rationalism, positioned against a tendency to 'imitate' dominant sociological paradigms from the discipline's core gravitation centers (US, French, German and British sociology). While contact with such traditional centers is vital and welcomed, there is a risk of comparative maximalism if Greek sociology is only (and, expectedly, unfavorably) compared to these traditions.

[18] Younger sociologists working in Greece draw on postgraduate studies capital that was accrued to them abroad. For example, Panagiotou (2017) draws partially on Mouzelis' theoretical work in studying GMOs (genetically modified organisms), while Giannakopoulou (2021) who is responsible for the safekeeping and publication of part of David Frisby's unpublished notes and essays as well as editor of the University of Glasgow David Frisby website) applies Frisby's ideas to urban sociology.

also with parallel concerns on the sociology of emotions (see also Gangas, 2020, Chap. 5), and it vindicates Lembesis' pre-war sociological intuition on modernity's 'ressentiment' syndromes (see Chap. 1). Work on the classical founders (e.g. Gangas, 2004) started to gain visibility in normative reconstructions of Simmel, while Gangas' work (2007, 2009) on Hegel and Durkheim was considered by Axel Honneth (2011, p. 327; 2021, p. 21) who further probed the Durkheim-Hegel rapprochement. Even more recently, Gangas (2020) opened a systematic dialogue between sociological theory and the capability approach of Amartya Sen and Martha Nussbaum in the book *Sociological Theory and the Capability Approach*.[19] In this work Gangas suggests that normative essentialism through the capability approach can powerfully inform sociological notions of agency and recalibrate more productively alienation narratives; at the other end, sociology must be considered by the capability approach to enrich the latter's relative paucity on institutions as configurations of freedom, on values and on the coupling of capability approach's claims to identity broadening with sociological theories that explain how identities regress to fundamentalism.

Generally, the placement of Greece as a focus of research and explanation in a wider regional, EU and global setting has further propelled interdisciplinary niches of sociological relevance (i.e. Alipranti, 2021 on family values, Demertzis, 1997 on political culture, Psalidopoulos, 2013 on economics in Greece) which confer a sociological optic (along other perspectives from social sciences and the humanities) on the history of Greece, its politics, economy and society.[20]

The 'Hellenic Sociological Society'

The establishment of the *Hellenic Sociological Society (HSS/EKE)* was long overdue. Launched in 2007 with Nikos Tatsis as its first president its focus is on the study of social phenomena and problems in Greece and globally

---

[19] This work has already gained attention in a 'basics' sociology book as part of 'sociological visions' (see Plummer, 2022, p. 241).

[20] Such is the focus and composition of the *Hellenic Observatory* at the London School of Economics under Kevin Featherstone, established in 1996 with the creation of the Eleftherios Venizelos Chair of Contemporary Greek Studies (for research under its auspices, see Arapoglou & Gounis, 2017) and the affiliate *Hellenic Foundation for European and Foreign Policy* (ELIAMEP) (see, e.g. Frangoudaki, 2003; Fokas, 2018).

the dissemination of sociology in educational programmes in Greece, the support of Greek sociologists and the attempt to provide relevant and useful knowledge to Greek society and its publics. The *HSS* was quick to organize (initially annual) conferences in Greece (seven until now) bringing together not only sociologists from all specialisms but opening its fora to academics and professionals from neighbouring disciplines. Among its highlights include the international conference on Max Weber (30–31 May 2008), co-organized with the Department of Sociology at Panteion University and the Department of Political Science at the University of Crete with Wolfgang Schluchter, among the keynote speakers. A colloquium on civil society with Peter Waldmann as keynote speaker followed in 22 May 2009, an international conference (5–7 November 2009) on *Risk society and challenges of the twenty-first century* with Ulrich Beck as keynote speaker, while the HSS had active involvement and support toward the organization of the 13th Conference of the European Sociological Association (ESA) held in Athens in the summer of 2017.

The *HSS* need for further differentiation across specialisms is patterned after the format of international associations like the *ISA*. The *HSS* numbers currently ten thematic groups (sociology of education, gender and society, sociological/social theory, sociology of culture and mass media, sociology of work, sociology of migration, methodology of the social sciences, sociology of health and medical sociology, sociology of religion and military sociology). In 2014 the *HSS* launched *The Greek Sociological Review* which has published up to now eight issues. Its inaugural issue had its main focus the crisis (with important contributions by Mouzelis, Kyrtsis, Tatsis, Romanos and Kokosalakis, among other distinguished contributors). In a sense it was a resonant announcement of transcending the crisis through explanation while still immersed into its debilitating consequences. The international networking of the *HSS* and the journal's editorial board could prove promising in enhancing invitations for original articles by major international sociologists. These would complement the topics addressed by Greek contributors and would enhance further bridge-building with the international community and with national or regional sociology fora.

The Current Profile of Sociology Departments in Greece

As the presence of sociology modules in Greek secondary education has once again been demeaned (sociology appeared as a core course in 1984;

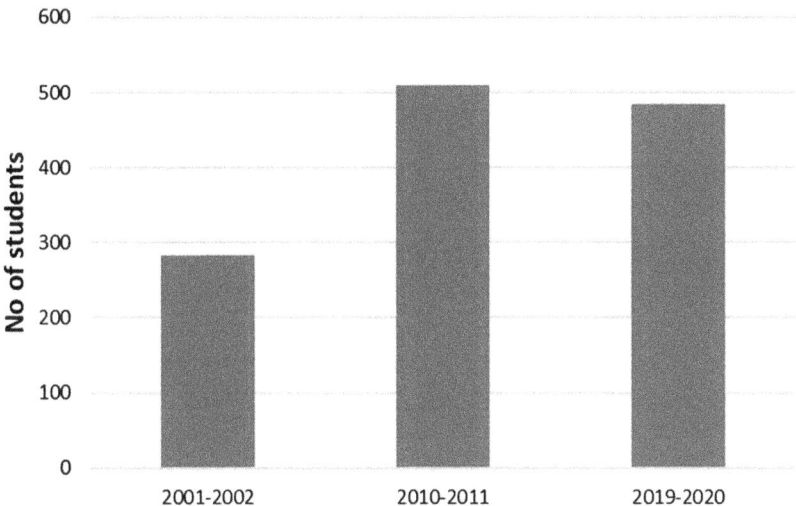

Fig. 6.1 Total degrees in sociology (Bachelors, MScs, PhDs)

then as of 1997, it became elective until 2001 when it was restored to core, but as of school year 2021–2022, sociology will not be subject to examination in the Panhellenic examinations towards entry into the Greek public university),[21] sociology proves resilient but with a professional status in need of deeper institutionalization and wider recognition.

Still, student intake guarantees viability and makes short but steady steps forward. As Figs. 6.1 and 6.2 indicate,[22] there is a clear increase of postgraduate students from 2001 to 2010. This could be seen as a promising trend since postgraduate studies involve more conscious decisions and

---

[21] This decision was protested by the *Hellenic Sociological Society* (see HSS 21 October 2020 announcement titled 'The pandemic and the need for sociology at https://www.hellenicsociology.gr/nea-tis-eke/i-pandimia-kai-i-anagki-tis-koinoniologias. Retrieved 5 August 2022). The *British Sociological Association* President Susan Halford wrote also a letter of protest and petition to the Greek Minister of Education about the closure of sociology in high schools (see https://es.britsoc.co.uk/bsa-president-writes-to-the-greek-minister-for-education-about-the-closure-of-sociology-in-high-schools-2/. Retrieved 5 August 2022).

[22] Due to data limitations (compiled mostly from the *Hellenic Statistical Authority* but also from those provided by the *Hellenic Ministry of Education and Religious Affairs*), these figures and tables cannot be used for a rigorous statistical inference which is beyond the scope of this book. They should be merely interpreted as annual snapshots that might indicate a trend over the two decades.

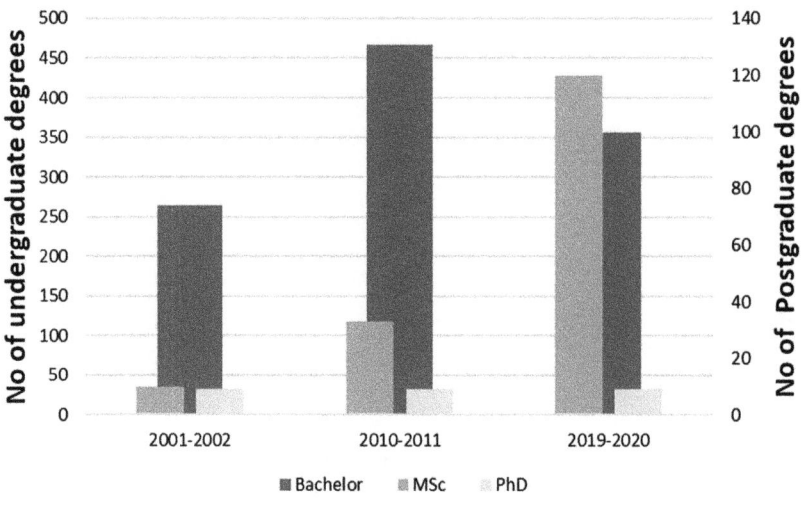

Fig. 6.2 Breakdown by degree

Table 6.1 Degrees in sociology per university and degree

University	2001			2010			2019		
	Bachelor	MSc	PhD	Bachelor	MSc	PhD	Bachelor	MSc	PhD
Panteion	211	10	8	298	14	7	219	31	4
Aegean	0	0	0	80	14	2	76	78	3
Crete	53	0	1	89	5	0	61	11	2
Total	264	10	9	467	33	9	356	120	9

commitment. There is a small decrease in undergraduates from 2010 to 2020 which might be related to undergraduate students during the Great Recession's impact in Greece looking for areas that might furnish better employment opportunities.

These figures if seen in terms of each university's enrollment cohorts (see Tables 6.1 and 6.2) suggest a significant increase in MA postgraduate students at the Aegean University from 2010 to 2020. This impressive increase may be related to the 2015 migration wave on the basis of which a new postgraduate programme was launched on *Management of migratory and refugee flows in Europe*.

Table 6.2 Change in the no. of students of sociology per university and degree

University	From 2001 to 2010			From 2010 to 2019		
	Bachelor	MSc	PhD	Bachelor	MSc	PhD
Panteion	41%	40%	-13%	-27%	121%	-43%
Aegean	–	–	–	-5%	457%	50%
Crete	68%	–	-100%	-31%	120%	–
Total	77%	230%	0%	-24%	264%	0%

Among these trends a new sociology Department was established at the *National and Kapodistrian University of Athens* operating since academic year 2019–2020, hence the absence of relevant data. It offers though a module on *Sociology in Greece* developed and taught by Sokratis Koniordos. The *American College of Greece*'s sociology BA (Hons) is validated since 2011 by the Open University, UK and its programme also attracts study abroad students, mostly from the US.

The picture that emerges, therefore, is one that reflects sociology's steady institutional growth in terms of student enrollment but still in need of further consolidation on a number of fronts: (a) cultural recognition in Greece to align sociology's history and accomplishments with its public perception; (b) professional sociology's further development in line with a political climate that does not regard social relations to be tantamount to individual choices based on market rationalities and is able to coordinate this perception of the discipline with market demands in terms of opportunities that arise but also of recurring market discontents; (c) development of robust departmental profiles with greater international visibility with a view to attract exchange programme students and to balance solid sociology curricula the interdisciplinary openings of which would not jeopardize or concede sociology's autonomy; (d) enhancement of academic and professional legitimacy across all institutions where sociology is taught and practised and which demonstrate quality standards that are comparable across tertiary education in Greece and abroad; and last but not least (e) the extension of sociology's discursive scope with diverse publics.

Acknowledgements We are grateful to Petros Varthalitis for his invaluable assistance with statistical data and tables and figures design.

References

Acheimastos, M. (2019). Εισαγωγή στις 'Στοιχειώδεις μορφές του θρησκευτικού βίου' του Εμίλ Ντυρκέμ [Introduction to Émile Durkheim's 'The elementary forms of religious life']. ΜΙΕΤ.

Afouxenidis, A., & Alexakis, M. (Eds.). (2006). Πολιτική κοινωνιολογία: έξι κείμενα αφιερωμένα στην Ι. Λαμπίρη-Δημάκη [Political sociology: Six texts dedicated to I. Lambiri-Dimaki]. Papazisis.

Alexander, J. (2012). *Trauma. A social theory.* Polity.

Alexandropoulos, S. (2001). Θεωρίες για τη συλλογική δράση και τα κοινωνικά κινήματα. Πρώτος τόμος [Theories on collective action and social movements]. Kritiki.

Alexias, G., & Bletsos, C. (2009). Η ιατρική εξουσία στα όρια ζωής και θανάτου. Μια ψυχο-κοινωνιολογική ανάλυση [Medical authority in the life-death borders. A psycho-sociological analysis]. *The Greek Review of Social Research, 130*(3), 49–74.

Alipranti, L. (in cooperation with Gountsidou, V.). (2021). Family change and family values in Greece. In I. Albert, M. Emirhavizovic, C.-N. Shpigelman, & U. Trummer (Eds.) *Families and family values in society and culture* (pp. 165–185). Information Age Publishing.

Antonopoulou, M. (2000). Κοινωνική πράξη και υλισμός. Σπουδή στην κοινωνιολογία της γνώσης [Social praxis and materialism. Study in the sociology of knowledge]. Alexandria.

Antonopoulou, M. (2011). Οι κλασσικοί της κοινωνιολογίας. Κοινωνική θεωρία και νεότερη κοινωνία [The classical founders of sociology: Social theory in modern society]. Savallas.

Arapoglou, V., & Gounis, K. (2017). *Contested landscapes of poverty and homelessness in Southern Europe: Reflections from Athens.* Palgrave Macmillan.

Aronowitz, S., & Kennedy, P. (2001). Κάποιες σκέψεις για την Αμερική σήμερα [Some thoughts on America today]. Conversations with Constantinos Tsoukalas. Στα Μονοπάτια της Σκέψης [In the pathos of thought]. ERT (Ellinikí Radiofonía Tileórasi A.E (Hellenic Broadcasting Corporation)). Archive number: 0000076636.

Banfield, E. (1958). *The moral basis of a backward society.* The Free Press.

Baudrillard, J. (2012). *The spirit of terrorism* (C. Turner, Trans.). Verso (Original work published 2002).

Bauman, Z., & Donskis, L. (2013). *Moral blindness. The loss of sensitivity in liquid modernity.* Polity.

Beck, U. (2012). *Twenty observations on a world in turmoil* (C. Cronin, Trans.). Polity (Original work published 2010).
Bernstein, R. J. (2005). *The abuse of evil. The corruption of politics and religion since 9/11*. Polity.
Boltanski, L. (2001). Interview to Constantinos Tsoukalas. Στα Μονοπάτια της Σκέψης [In the pathos of thought]. ERT (Ellinikí Radiofonía Tileórasi A.E. (Hellenic Broadcasting Corporation)). Archive number: 0000076943.
Chalari, A. (2017). *The sociology of the individual: Relating self and society*. Sage.
Charalambis, D. (2004). Introduction. In D. Charalambis, L. Maratou-Alipranti, & A. Hadjiyanni (Eds.), *Recent social trends in Greece, 1960–2000* (pp. 1–24). McGill-Queen's University Press.
Charalambis, D., Maratou-Alipranti, L., & Hadjiyanni, A. (Eds.). (2004). *Recent social trends in Greece, 1960–2000*. McGill-Queen's University Press.
Cheliotis, L. (2011). For a Freudo-Marxist critique of social domination: Rediscovering Erich Fromm through the mirror of Pierre Bourdieu. *Journal of Classical Sociology, 11*(4), 438–461.
Chtouris, S. (2004). Ορθολογικά συμβολικά δίκτυα. *Global states και εθνικά χόμπιτ* [Rational symbolic networks. Global states and national hobbits]. Nisos.
Constantopoulou, C. (2013). L' imaginaire démocratique, les blogs en Grèce. In S. Dufoulon (Ed.), *Internet, ou la boîte à usage* (pp. 95–114). L' Harmattan.
Daskalaki, I., Papadopoulou, P., Tsamparli, D., Tsiganou, I., & Fronimou, E. (Eds.). (2000). *Εγκληματίες και θύματα στο κατώφλι του 21ου αιώνα. Αφιέρωμα στη μνήμη του Ηλία Δασκαλάκη* [Criminals and victims in the twenty-first century threshold. A tribute to the memory of Ilias Daskalakis]. EKKE.
Demertzis, N. (1997). Greece. In R. Eatwell (Ed.), *European political culture. Conflict of convergence?* (pp. 107–121). Routledge.
Demertzis, N. (2011). The drama of the Greek civil war trauma. In R. Eyerman, J. Alexander, & E. Butler Breese (Eds.), *Narrating trauma: On the impact of collective suffering* (pp. 133–161). Routledge.
Demertzis, N. (2020). *The political sociology of emotions: essays on trauma and ressentiment*. Routledge.
Demertzis, N., & Eyerman, R. (2020). Covid-19 as cultural trauma. *American Journal of Cultural Sociology, 8*, 428–450.
Demertzis, N., & Lipowatz, T. (2006). Φθόνος και μνησικακία. Τα πάθη της ψυχής και η κλειστή κοινωνία [Envy and 'ressentiment'. The passions of the soul and the closed society]. Polis.
Dimitrakos, D. (1970). *Νέον ορθογραφικόν και ερμηνευτικόν λεξικόν όλης της ελληνικής γλώσσης: Αρχαίας, μεσαιωνικής, καθαρευούσης, δημοτικής* [New spelling and interpretative lexicon of the entire Greek language: Ancient, medieval, puristic, demotic] (3rd ed.). Giovanis.
Dimitriadis, I. (2022). Migrants and undeclared employment within the European construction sector: Challenging dichotomous approaches to workers' agency.

Work, Employment and Society. https://doi.org/10.1177/095001 70211072777

Ellinas, A. (2013). The rise of Golden Dawn: The new face of the far Right in Greece. *South European Society and Politics., 18*(4), 543–565.

Faraklas, G. (2013). Νόημα και κυριαρχία. Νοηματική συγκρότηση και κριτική της κυριαρχίας [Meaning and sovereignty. Meaning-construction and criticism of sovereignty]. Hestia.

Fokas, E. (2018). The legal status of religious minorities: Exploring the impact of the European Court of human rights. *Social Compass, 65*(1), 25–42.

Fouskas, T. (2012). «Κοινότητες» μεταναστών και εργασιακή αντιπροσώπευση, Οι επιπτώσεις της χαμηλού κύρους εργασίας πέντε μεταναστευτικών ομάδων στη συμμετοχή στους εργασιακούς συλλόγους τους [Migrant "communities" and labor representation. The consequences of low-paid labor among five migrant groups in their labor union participation]. Papazisis.

Frangoudaki, A. (2001). Η γλώσσα και το έθνος 1880-1980. Εκατό χρόνια αγώνες για την αυθεντική ελληνική γλώσσα [Language and nation, 1880–1980. A hundred years of struggle towards an authentic Greek language]. Alexandria.

Frangoudaki, A. (2003). Greek education in the twentieth century: A long process towards a democratic European society. In T. A. Couloumbis, T. Kariotis, & F. Bellou (Eds.), *Greece in the twentieth century* (pp. 198–216). Frank Cass Publishers.

Gangas, S. (2004). Axiological and normative dimensions in Simnel's thought. *History of the Human Sciences, 17*(4), 17–44.

Gangas, S. (2007). Social ethics and logic: Rethinking Durkheim through Hegel. *Journal of Classical Sociology, 7*(3), 315–338.

Gangas, S. (2009). Hegel and Durkheim: *Sittlichkeit* and organic solidarity as political configurations. *Hegel-Jahrbuch, 1,* 222–226.

Gangas, S. (2020). *Sociological theory and the capability approach.* Routledge.

Giannakopoulou, G. (2021). Unmasking the *flâneur*. In G. Giannakopoulou, G. Gilloch, & G. (Eds.), *The detective of modernity: Essays on the work of David Frisby* (pp. 208–217). Routledge.

Halkias, A. (2004). *The empty cradle of democracy. Sex, abortion and nationalism in modern Greece.* Duke University Press.

Harvey, D. (2005). Interview to Constantinos Tsoukalas. Στα Μονοπάτια της Σκέψης [In the pathos of thought]. ERT (Ellinikí Radiofonía Tileórasi A.E. (Hellenic Broadcasting Corporation)). Archive number: 3132450.

Honneth, A. (2011). *Das Recht der Freiheit.* Grundriß einer demokratischen Sittlichkeit.

Honneth, A. (2021). Hegel and Durkheim: Contours of an Elective Affinity. In N. Marcucci (Ed.), *Durkheim & Critique* (pp. 19–41). Palgrave Macmillan.

Katsas, G. (2013). Ο "σκληρός πυρήνας" της ανεργίας, οι μετανάστες και ο κοινωνικός αποκλεισμός: Διερεύνηση των σχέσεων και των αντιθέσεων [The "hard core" of unemployment, immigrant and social exclusion: Investigation of relations and antitheses]. In M. Spyridakis (Ed.), Ανεργία και κοινωνική ανασφάλεια. Οψεις ενός εμμένοντος κινδύνου [Unemployment and social insecurity. Facets of a persistent danger]. pp. 105–120. Alexandria.

Kalfopoulos, K. T. (Ed.). (2003). Η Ποιοτική Παράδοση στις Κοινωνικές Επιστήμες [The Qualitative Tradition in the Social Sciences] (A. Michalakis, Trans.). Nisos.

Kampouri, E. (2007). Φύλο και μετανάστευση, τόμος Β΄. Η καθημερινή ζωή των μεταναστριών από την Αλβανία και την Ουκρανία [Gender and migration. Volume 2. The everyday-life of migrant women from Albania and Ukraine]. Gutenberg (in association with Panteion University and KEKMOKOP).

Kantzara, V. (2016). Education in conditions of crisis in Greece: An empirical exploration (2000-2013). *Social Cohesion and Development, 11*(1), 45–66.

Karakioulafi, C. (2007). Μεταμορφώσεις της εργασίας και της απασχόλησης και εξελίξεις στο πεδίο της κοινωνιολογίας της εργασίας [Changes in work and employment and recent developments in the field of sociology of work]. *Social Cohesion and Development, 2*(1), 43–51.

Kassimati, K., & Moussourou, L. (2007). Φύλο και μετανάστευση, τόμος Α΄. Θεωρητικές αναφορές και εμπειρική διερεύνηση [Gender and migration. Volume 1. Theoretical references and empirical investigation]. Gutenberg (in association with Panteion University and KEKMOKOP).

Kasimis, C., & Papadopoulos, A. (Eds.). (1999). *Local responses to global integration*. Routledge.

Kelpanidis, M. (2002). Κοινωνιολογία της εκπαίδευσης. Θεωρίες και πραγματικότητα [Sociology of education. Theories and reality]. Ellinika Grammata.

Kokosalakis, N. (1998). Politics and sociology in Greece, 1950-1998. *International Sociology, 13*(3), 325–343.

Kondylis, P. (1998). *Από τον 20ο στον 21ο αιώνα. Τομές στην πλανητική εποχή περί το 2000* [From the twentieth to the twenty-first century. Incisions on planetary politics around the year 2000]. Themelio.

Koniordos, S. (2001). *Towards a sociology of artisans: Continuities and discontinuities in comparative perspective*. Routledge.

Koniordos, S. (Ed.). (2010a). Κοινωνικό κεφάλαιο. Εμπιστοσύνη και κοινωνία πολιτών [Social capital. Trust and civil society]. Papazisis.

Koniordos, S. (Ed.). (2010b). Κοινωνική σκέψη και νεωτερικότητα [Social thought and modernity]. Gutenberg.

Koniordos, S. (2010c). Η συζήτηση για τη δημόσια κοινωνιολογία και η κοινωνιολογία στην Ελλάδα [The discussion of public sociology and sociology in Greece]. In M. Kousis, M. Samatas, & S. Koniordos (Eds.), Εξουσία και κοινωνία. Δωρήματα στον Κωνσταντίνο Τσουκαλά [Power and society: Offerings to Constantine Tsoukalas] (pp. 227–250). Kastaniotis.

Koniordos, S. (2018). Έκθεση παρουσίασης της ελληνικής εκδοχής του 7ου γύρου της παγκόσμιας έρευνας αξιών [Presentation report of the Greek version of the 7th round of the World Values Survey]. Retrieved June 13, 2022, from https://

www.dianeosis.org/wp-content/uploads/2018/09/WVS_Ekthesi_SKoniordos__Upd_250918.pdf

Koniordos, S. (Ed.). (2021). *Αξίες, πολιτισμικά πρότυπα και κοινωνικοί προσανατολισμοί στη σύγχρονη Ελλάδα* [Values, cultural patterns and social orientations in contemporary Greece]. Gutenberg.

Koniordos, S., & Fotopoulos, N. (Eds.). (2010). *Φτώχεια, ανισότητες και εκπαίδευση στο πλαίσιο της παγκοσμιοποίησης* [Poverty, inequalities and education in the context of globalization]. Centre of Development for Educational Policy of the General Confederation of Greek Workers.

Koniordos, S., & Kyrtsis, A. (2014). *The handbook of European sociology*. Routledge.

Kontiadis, X. (2006). *Δημοκρατία, κοινωνικό κράτος και Σύνταγμα στην ύστερη νεωτερικότητα* [Democracy, welfare start and the Constitution in late modernity]. Papazisis.

Kousis, M, Samatas, M., & Koniordos, S. (Eds.). (2010. *Power and society: Offerings to Constantine Tsoukalas.* Kastaniotis.

Kyriazi, N. (2011). *Η Κοινωνιολογική έρευνα. Κριτική επισκόπηση των μεθόδων και των τεχνικών* [Sociological research: A critical review of methods and techniques]. Pedio.

Kyrtsis, A. A. (1996). Greek sociology: Does it really exist? *The European Sociologist, 4,* 10–11.

Kyrtsis, A. A. (2014). The late ascent of the UK to a sociological great power: A comment from the margins. In S. Koniordos & A. A. Kyrtsis (Eds.), *The Handbook of European sociology* (pp. 391–406). Routledge.

Lagoumitzi, G. (2011). The uses of nostalgia in the 'imagination' of diaspora: The case of the new Pontic Greek refugees. In M. David & J. Muñoz-Basols (Eds.), *Defining and re-defining diaspora: From theory to reality* (pp. 25–40). Inter-Disciplinary Press.

Lagoumitzi, G. (2020). Narratives of trauma across generations of Pontic Greeks and their impact on national identity. In S. Magliveras (Ed.) *Agency and migration policy* (pp. 91–103) Transnational Press.

Lambiri-Dimaki, J. (Ed.) (1987a). *Η κοινωνιολογία στην Ελλάδα σήμερα,* Τόμος Α' (με κείμενα 30 συγγραφέων) [*Sociology in Greece Today*. Vol. I *Sociology in Greece today.* Vol. I (with texts from 30 authors)] (with texts from 30 authors)). Papazisis.

Lambiri-Dimaki, J. (1987b). Εισαγωγικά: Το χθες και το σήμερα της κοινωνιολογίας στην Ελλάδα [Introduction: yesterday and today of sociology in Greece]. In Lambiri-Dimaki, J. (Ed.). *Η κοινωνιολογία στην Ελλάδα σήμερα,* Τόμος Α' (με κείμενα 30 συγγραφέων) [*Sociology in Greece today.* Vol. I (with texts from 30 authors)] (pp. 15–53). Papazisis.

Lambiri-Dimaki, J. (1996). Sociology in Greece: Trends and prospects. *South European Society & Politics, 1*(1), 121–130.

Lambiri-Dimaki, J. (Ed.) (1997a). *Η κοινωνιολογία στην Ελλάδα σήμερα, 1988-1996, Τόμος Β'* (με κείμενα 47 συγγραφέων). [*Sociology in Greece today*. Vol. II (with texts from 47 authors)]. Papazisis.
Lambiri-Dimaki, J. (1997b). "Εισαγωγικό Σημείωμα" [Introductory note]. In Lambiri-Dimaki, J. (1997a). *Η κοινωνιολογία στην Ελλάδα σήμερα, 1988-1996, Τόμος Β'* (με κείμενα 47 συγγραφέων) [*Sociology in Greece today*. Vol. II (with texts from 47 authors)] (pp. 11–31). Papazisis.
Lambiri-Dimaki, J. (Ed.) (2002a). *Η Κοινωνιολογία στην Ελλάδα σήμερα. Η ολοκλήρωση της τριλογίας, 1959-2000, Τόμος Γ'* (με κείμενα 36 συγγραφέων) [Sociology in Greece today. The completion of the trilogy. Vol. III (with texts from 36 authors)]. Papazisis.
Lambiri-Dimaki, J. (2002b). Εισαγωγή: Η ολοκλήρωση της τριλογίας «Η Κοινωνιολογία στην Ελλάδα σήμερα»: Δύο γενιές Ελλήνων και Ελληνίδων κοινωνιολόγων στο δεύτερο μισό του 20ου αιώνα. Χαρακτηριστικά και συμβολές [Introduction: The completion of the trilogy «Sociology in Greece today»: Two generations of Greek sociologists in the second half of the twentieth century: Features and contributions]. In *Sociology in Greece today. The completion of the trilogy* Vol. III (with texts from 36 authors) (pp. 20–105). Papazisis.
Lambiri-Dimaki, J. (2003). *Κοινωνικές επιστήμες και πρωτοπορία στην Ελλάδα 1950–1967* [Social sciences and innovation in Greece 1950–1967]. Gutenberg/EKKE.
Leverrato, J.-M., & Leontsini, M. (2008). *Internet et la sociabilité littéraire. Éditions de la Bibliothèque publique d'information.* https://doi.org/10.4000/books.bibpompidou.197
Lianos, M. (2020). *Conflict and the social bond. Peace in modern societies.* Routledge.
Lipowatz, T. (2021). *Κριτική του μετανεωτερικού Λόγου. Τα παράδοξα του ατομικισμού* [Critique of postmodern Reason. The paradoxes of individualism]. Armos.
Lytras, A. (2000). *Κοινωνία και εργασία. Ο ρόλος των κοινωνικών τάξεων* [Society and labor. The role of social classes]. Papazisis.
Mann, M. (2005). *The dark side of democracy. Explaining ethnic cleansing.* Cambridge University Press.
Maratou-Alipranti, L., Thanopoulou, M., Teperoglou, A., & Fronimou, E. (2011). *Όψεις της Κοινωνιολογίας στην Ελλάδα σήμερα: Τιμητικός τόμος στη Ιωάννας Λαμπίρη-Δημάκη* [Aspects of sociology in Greece Today: Honorary Volume for Ioanna Lambiri-Dimaki]. Sakkoulas.
Markantonatou, M. (2014). Social resistance to austerity: Polanyi's 'double movement' in the context of the crisis in Greece. *Journal für Entwicklungspolitik, XXX*(1), 67–87. https://doi.org/10.20446/JEP-2414-3197-30-1-67
Meletopoulos, M. (2010). *Νέα Κοινωνιολογία, 1988-2010. Τέλος εποχής* [New Sociology, 1988–2010. End of an era]. Retrieved January 9, 2022, from http://www.newsociology.gr/teyxh/pdfs/telos.pdf

Michailakis, D. (2003). The systems theory concept of disability: One is not born a disabled person, one is observed to be one. *Disability & Society, 18*(2), 209–229.

Moschonas, G. (2018). European social democracy, Communism and the Ertfurian model. In W. Outhwaite & S. P. Turner (Eds.), *The SAGE handbook of political sociology* (pp. 516–547). Sage.

Mousourou, L. (2005). Εισαγωγή στην κοινωνιολογία των ηλικιών και των γενεών [Introduction to the sociology of age and generations]. Gutenberg.

Mousourou, L. (2006). Οικογένεια και οικογενειακή πολιτική [Family and family policy]. Gutenberg.

Mousourou, L. & Kassimati, K. (2004). Ζητήματα οικογενειακής πολιτικής. Θεωρητικές αναφορές και εμπειρικές διερευνήσεις [Issues of family policy. Theoretical references and empirical investigations]. Gutenberg (in association with Panteion University and KEKMOKOP).

Mouzelis, N. (1994). Ο εθνικισμός στην ύστερη ανάπτυξη [Nationalism in late development]. Themelio.

Mouzelis, N. (2002). Από την αλλαγή στον εκσυγχρονισμό. Κριτικές παρεμβάσεις: Πολιτική, κοινωνία, πολιτισμός, θεωρία [From change to modernization. Critical interventions: Politics, society, culture, theory]. Themelio.

Mouzelis, N. (2003). Η θρησκευτική διαμάχη. Σκέψεις ενός «μη ειδικού» [The religious controversy. Thoughts by a 'non-specialist']. Themelio.

Mouzelis, N. (2008). *Modern and postmodern social theorizing. Bridging the divide.* Cambridge University Press.

Mouzelis, N. (2018). Ματιές στο μέλλον. Καπιταλισμός, σοσιαλδημοκρατία, κοινωνικό κράτος [Gazing the future: Capitalism, social democracy, welfare state]. Alexandria.

Nagopoulos, N. (2003). Τα θεμέλια της κοινωνιολογικής γνώσης και οι κοινωνίες νεωτερικότητας: Η συμβολή του Max Weber στη σύγχρονη κοινωνιολογία της γνώσης [The foundations of sociological knowledge and societies in modernity: Max Weber's contribution to contemporary sociology of knowledge]. Kritiki.

Nagopoulos, N. (2015). Γνώση, μέθοδος και κοινωνική πράξη: Από τη γνωσιοθεωρία στην κοινωνιολογία της γνώσης [Knowledge, method and social praxis: From the theory of knwoledge to the sociology of knowledge]. Syndesmos Ellinikon Akadimaikon Vivliothikon (SEAV).

Nina-Pazarzi, E., & Tsangaris, M. (2008). Constructing women's image in TV commercials: The Greek case. *Indian Journal of Gender Studies, 15*(1), 29–50.

Nikolakopoulos, I. (2010). Από την επιταγή της ομοφωνίας στη λογική της πλειοψηφίας [From the consensus imperative to the majority logic]. In M. Kousis, M. Samatas, & S. Koniordos (Eds.), *Εξουσία και κοινωνία. Δωρήματα στον Κωνσταντίνο Τσουκαλά* [Power and society: Offerings to Constantine Tsoukalas] (pp. 295–301). Kastaniotis.

Nikolaou-Smokoviti, L. (2004). Business leaders' work environment and leadership styles. *Current Sociology, 52*(3), 407–427.

Panagiotopoulou, R. (2004). *Η τηλεόραση εκτός των τειχών. Η περιφερειακή και τοπική τηλεόραση στην Ελλάδα* [TV outside the walls. The regional and local TV in Greece]. Kastaniotis.
Panagiotou, A. (2017). *Structure, agency and biotechnology. The case of the Rothamsted GM wheat trials.* Anthem Press.
Panayotopoulos, N. (1999). The thinker of the 'primitive thought' of the thinkers of 'primitive thought'. *European Journal of Social Theory, 2*(3), 327–333.
Panayotopoulos, N. (2020). *Περί αυτονομίας. Για την ελληνική κοινωνιολογία* [About autonomy. On Greek sociology]. Kardamitsas.
Papadopoulos, A. G., Fratsea, L. M., & Mavrommatis, G. (2018). Governing migrant labour in an intensive agricultural area in Greece: Focusing on precarity, political mobilization and migrant agency at Manolada's fields. *Journal of Rural Studies, 64,* 200–209.
Papaioannou, S., & Serdedakis, N. (2001). Civil society and its enemies: The case of Greece. In A. Bron & M. Schemmann (Eds.), *Civil society, citizenship and learning* (pp. 204–222). LIT.
Papakostas, A. (2012). *Civilizing the public sphere: Distrust, trust and corruption.* Palgrave Macmillan.
Papataxiarchis, E., Topali, P., & Athanasopoulou, A. (2009). *Κόσμοι της οικιακής εργασίας. Φύλο, μετανάστευση και πολιτισμικοί μετασχηματισμοί στην Αθήνα του πρώιμου 21ου αιώνα* [Worlds of domestic labor. Gender, migration and cultural transformations in Athens in the early twenty-first century]. Alexandria.
Papalexandrou, K. (Trans.) (1927). Emile Durkheim: Τι είναι κοινωνικών φαινόμενον; (Emile Durkheim: What is a social fact?). *Αρχείον Οικονομικών και Κοινωνικών Επιστημών* (Archive of Economic and Social Sciences) 2(7), 151–161.
Pappas, T. (1999). *Making party democracy in Greece.* Macmillan.
Piketty, T. (2017). *Capital in the twenty-first century* (A. Goldhammer, Trans.). The Belknap Press of Harvard University Press (Original work published 2013).
Piven, F.F. (2003). Conversing with Constantinos Tsoukalas. *Στα Μονοπάτια της Σκέψης* [In the pathos of thought]. ERT (Ellinikí Radiofonía Tileórasi A.E (Hellenic Broadcasting Corporation)). Archive number: 0000076707. Retrieved May 18, 2022 from https://archive.ert.gr/76707/
Pleios, G. (2015). Facebook και κρίση: Εναλλακτική πληροφόρηση ή κοινωνική προσαρμογή [Facebook and the crisis: Alternative information or social adaptation?]. *Greek Sociological Review, 2–3,* 159–187.
Pleios, G. (2016). Communication and symbolic capitalism – Rethinking Marxist communication theory in the light of the information society. In C. Fuchs & V. Mosco (Eds.), *Marx and the political economy of the media* (pp. 98–137). Brill.
Plummer, K. (2022). *Sociology: The Basics* (3rd ed.). Routledge.
Psalidopoulos, M. (2013). Greece. In V. Barnett (Ed.), *Routledge handbook of the history of global economic thought* (pp. 68–76). Routledge.

Psimmenos, I., & Kassimati, K. (2003). Immigration control pathways: Organizational culture and work values of Greek welfare officers. *Journal of Ethnic and Migration Studies, 29*(2), 337–371.
Psimmenos, I., & Skamnakis, C. (2008). Οικιακή εργασία των μεταναστευτριών και κοινωνική προστασία. Η περίπτωση των γυναικών από την Αλβανία και την Ουκρανία [Domestic work of female migrants and social protection. The case of women from Albania and Ukraine]. Papazisis.
Pyrgiotakis, I. (2000). Εκπαίδευση και κοινωνία στην Ελλάδα. Οι διαλεκτικές σχέσεις και οι αδιάλλακτες συγκρούσεις [Education and society in Greece. Dialectical relations and intransigent conflicts]. Ellinika Grammata.
Roudometof, V. (2016). *Glocalization: A critical introduction*. Routledge.
Sakellariou, A. (2022). Η αθεΐα στην Ελληνική κοινωνία: Από την Ορθόδοξη θρησκευτική μνήμη στην άθεη θρησκευτική συνείδηση [Atheism in Greek society: From the Orthodox religious memory to the atheist religious conscience]. Papazisis.
Samatas, M. (2014). *The "super-panopticon" scandal of the Athens 2004 Olympics and its legacy*. Pella.
Serafetinidou, M. (2012). Το φαινόμενο της γραφειοκρατίας. Ιστορική αφήγηση (από την απολυταρχία στον κρατικό καπιταλισμό) [The phenomenon of bureaucracy. Historical narrative (from authoritarianism to state capitalism)]. Gutenberg.
Simmel, G. (2004). Περιπλάνηση στη νεωτερικότητα. Κοινωνιολογικά, φιλοσοφικά και αισθητικά κείμενα [Wandering in modernity. Sociological, philosophical and aesthetic texts] (S. Gangas & K.Th.Kalfopoulos, Eds.) (G. Sagriotis & O. Stathatou, Trans.). Alexandria.
Stratigaki, M. (2007). Το φύλο της κοινωνικής πολιτικής [The gender of social policy]. Metaihmio.
Streeck, W. (2016). *How will capitalism end? Essays on a failing system*. Verso.
Tatsis, N. (2004). Νεωτερικότητα και κοινωνική αλλαγή. Κοινωνιολογικές προσεγγίσεις [Modernity and social change. Sociological approaches]. Nisos.
Tatsis, N. (2021). Η καταναλωτική κοινωνία. Ερμηνευτικά θεωρήματα [Consumer society. Interpretive theorems]. Papazisis.
Tatsis, N., & Thanopoulou, M. (2009) Η κοινωνιολογία της Σχολής του Σικάγου [The Chicago School sociology]. Papazisis.
Tatsoglou, E. (2009). *Women, gender and diasporic lives: Labor, community, and identity in Greek migrations*. Lexington Books.
Thanopoulou, M. (2007). Φύλο και μετανάστευση, τόμος Γ'. Διαγενεακές σχέσεις και σχέσεις φύλου σε οικογένειες Αλβανών μεταναστών [Gender and migration, Volume 3. Intergenerational gender relations in families of Albanian immigrants]. Gutenberg (in association with Panteion University and KEKMOKOP).
Tsaoussi, A. (2013). Δίκαιο και συνεργατικότητα. Μια νέα προσέγγιση στην κοινωνιολογία του δικαίου [Right and cooperation. A new approach in the sociology of law]. Papazisis.

Tsaoussi, A. (2021). Οι ηθικές αξίες και νόρμες των Ελλήνων σύμφωνα με τον 7° γύρο της παγκόσμιας έρευνας αξιών: ήπια ανομία ή εσωστρεφής συντηρητισμός [The moral values and social norms of Greeks according to the 7th wave of the World Value Survey" Mild *anomie* or introvert conservatism?]. In S. Koniordos (Ed.), *Αξίες, πολιτισμικά πρότυπα και κοινωνικοί προσανατολισμοί στη σύγχρονη Ελλάδα* [Values, cultural patterns and social orientations in contemporary Greece] (pp. 95–125). Gutenberg.

Tsirigotis, D. (2019). The Greek puzzle: A socio-political analysis of the current Greek crisis. *International Area Studies Review, 22*(2), 148–167.

Tsoukalas, C. (2002). Relative autonomy and its changing forms. In S. Aronowitz & P. Bratsis (Eds.), *Paradigm lost: State theory reconsidered* (pp. 221–244). University of Minnesota Press.

Tsoukalas, C. (2012). *Ελλάδα της λήθης και της α λήθειας. Από τη μακρά εφηβεία στη βίαιη ενηλικίωση* [Greece of forgetfulness and un-forgetfulness [truth]. From the prolonged adolescence to the violent maturity]. Themelio.

Tsoukalas, C. (2020). *Ο αόρατος Λεβιάθαν. Δημοκρατία, δικαιοσύνη και ηθική στα χρόνια της κρίσης* [The invisible Leviathan. Democracy, justice and morality in the years of the crisis]. Polis.

Tsoukalas, C. (2021). *Το πολιτικό στη σκιά της πανδημίας* [The political in the shadow of the pandemic]. Kastaniotis.

Wallerstein, I. (2001). Interview to Constantinos Tsoukalas. *Στα Μονοπάτια της Σκέψης* [In the pathos of thought]. ERT (Ellinikí Radiofonía Tileórasi A.E (Hellenic Broadcasting Corporation)). Archive number: 0000076512. Retrieved January 25, 2022 from: https://archive.ert.gr/76512/

Xypolitas, N. (2017). Preparation / allocation / habituation: The holistic approach of migrant exclusion. *Social Cohesion and Development, 12*(1), 57–71.

Zachou, C., & Kalerante, E. (2010). Becoming a citizen: Albanian women's civic education and political engagement in Greece. In M. Abraham, E. N. Chow, L. Maratou-Alipranti, & E. Tastsoglou (Eds.), *Contours of citizenship: Women in a global/local world* (pp. 77–94). Ashgate.

Zamparloukou, S., & Kousis, M. (Eds.) (2014). *Κοινωνικές όψεις της κρίσης στην Ελλάδα* [Social facets of the Greek crisis]. Pedio.

Conclusion

The six chapters in this book adumbrated the history of sociology in Greece from the early 1900s until the current twenty-first century and its multifaceted challenges. The book chronicled Greek sociology at its inception; charted the precarious balance between sociology's uncertain academic physiognomy and the quest for empirical research; and discussed the process of Greece's modernization amid dependency after 1974 and until the 1990s when an impetus in sociological theory, research methods and sociology specialisms is discerned and continued unabated to the twenty-first century. Moreover, the book examined the sociological aspects of major Greek intellectuals abroad who enriched Greek sociology even if this enrichment stemmed often from other disciplines.

Sociology in Greece, despite an initially negligible output and profile amid Greece's slow modernization and dependency, showed remarkable degrees of replenishment, given its generally meagre incumbency in political, economic, professional and educational reforms. Oscillating between a misplaced self-sufficiency, solely within the periphery of Greek academia and the public, and a 'dependence'-induced humility toward the great sociological centres abroad, it often underestimated its own potential for synergies. For the latter the Castoriadis, Poulantzas and Mouzelis cases are instructive. They all shared their sociological capital as it were with their fellow sociologists in Greece, the students and the public. Other Greek sociologists (Tsoukalas, Veltsos) shared their 'international network' capital with the Greek public, while the 1990s–2020s sociology output contributed to strengthen universities and Greek sociology's visibility abroad; such instances testify to a culture of knowledge-sharing that could be further cultivated in face of still regressively stagnant ideological entrenchments that monopolize what the 'correct' discipline's practice is and evasively instrumentalise out of date institutional dichotomies. Greek diaspora sociologists also constitute a precious resource for such bridge-building and comparative broadening of sociological perspectives, best practices and institutional resources. Similarly, sociologists working in Greece sharpen the Greek society's sociological lens, working under adverse conditions of research support, despite EU openings in funded programmes and collaborations.

We have attempted, therefore, to do justice to the richness of Greek sociology, to its entanglement with institutional change amid turbulent and traumatic historical episodes and to its setbacks and its growing potential for international visibility and recognition. We discussed and brought to the fore work that has not received sufficient attention in the international historiography of our discipline, hoping that a 'de-colonized' reconstruction of sociology's multiple trajectories across nation-state history and global interconnectedness will balance cultural particularism and global relevance. We, of course, leave other proposals for the further development of Greek sociology to the community of fellow sociologists. We hope that our book re-opens this discussion.

Index[1]

NUMBERS AND SYMBOLS
9/11, 136
1922 *Democratic Manifesto*, 4
1967 coup d' état, 48

A
Acheimastos, Myron, 144
Adiaphorization, 118, 120
Adorno, Theodor, 75, 86n21
Aegean, xii, 150
Aeschylus, 74
Afghanistan, 136
Afouxenidis, Alex, 145, 146
Africa, 118
Agency, 68, 106, 107, 149, 155
Agonas, 81
Al Qaeda, 136
Alexakis, Emmanouil, 146
Alexander, Jeffrey, 136
Alexandropoulos, Stelios, 95, 140, 145
Alexias, Giorgos, 145
Alienation, 82, 83, 96, 155
Alivizatos, Nikos, 26n1, 40n26
Almond, Gabriel, 56, 57
Althusser, Louis, 80, 86, 88, 88n23, 96n30
Althusserian, 49, 57, 77
Ambéli, 34, 34n14
American College of Greece, xi, 28, 29, 159
American Sociological Review, 139
Amfiklia, 108
Amin, Samir, 51, 52
Anafi, 35
Anastasiadis, Giorgos, 4n6
Anatolia College, 28
Andreadis Group, 85
Andreadis, Stratis, 33
Andreadis, Yangos, 115

---

[1] Note: Page numbers followed by 'n' refer to notes.

Andrianopoulos, Andreas, 112
Anthropology, 18, 31, 111, 145
Anti, 81
Antonopoulou, Maria, 144
Arab/Muslim, 34n13, 120, 145
Arapoglou, Vassilis, 155n20
Aravantinos, Panagiotis, 2
Archer, Margaret, 153n14
Archive of Philosophy and Theory of Science, 9, 10n14
Archive of Sociology and Ethics, xi, 27, 67
Area studies, 31
Argyriadou, Eleni, 30, 31
Aristotle, 76n12
Aristotle University of Thessaloniki, 73n9, 74
Army, x, 4n5, 49, 79, 80
Arnason, Johann, 66
Aron, Raymond, 141
Aronowitz, Stanley, 142, 143, 143n6
Art, 14, 18, 28, 106, 108
Asia Minor, x, 7, 7n11, 13, 28, 34
Association Castoriadis, 77
Association of Greek Sociologists, 59
Astrinakis, Antonis, 124, 141
Athens, ix, xi, 2, 7, 13, 28, 29, 31, 36, 73, 74, 82, 83, 85, 108, 118, 119, 136, 156
Athens Center of Ekistics (ACE), 36n18
Athens Social Sciences Centre (KKEA), xi, 6, 26, 30–39, 30n11
Athens University, 7, 7n10, 9, 10, 16, 55, 117n9
Auschwitz, 76, 76n12
Autonomy, 5, 53, 54, 56, 66, 67, 70, 71n7, 73n9, 74, 78, 80, 106, 108, 110, 116, 117, 138, 149, 151n12, 159
Avgeridis, Manos, 48n1

Avghe, 81, 87
Axiologika, 66, 95–96, 146n9
Axiology, 83, 86

B

Backhaus, Hans-Georg, 86n21
Badinter, Élisabeth, 142
Bakhtin, Mikhail, 48n1
Balkanization, 36, 119, 139
Balkans, 76n14, 125, 144
Banfield, Edward, 138n2
Baraldi, Claudio, 124n15
Baran, Paul, 51
Bassakos, Pantelis, 74, 75
Baudrillard, Jean, 119, 120, 136
Bauman, Zygmunt, 118, 136
Beaton, Roderick, 2, 2n2
Beck, Ulrich, 136, 156
Beethoven, Ludwig van, 75
Beilharz, Peter, 66
Being, 76, 91n25, 117
Bell, Daniel, 141, 143
Bendix, Reinhard, 110
Bergson, Henri, 18, 71n8
Berlin, 2, 29
Bernstein, Edward, 3
Bernstein, Richard, 136
Bhambra, Gurminder, 120
Bibliographical essay, 38
Bitsakis, Eftichios, 74n10
Bletsos, Konstantinos, 145
Blumer, Herbert, 126, 141
Boltanski, Luc, 142
Bonefeld, Werner, 86
Bottomore, Tom, 56, 113, 140
Bourdieu, Pierre, 37, 38, 77n15, 107, 108, 116, 117, 117n9, 123, 138, 141
Bourgeoisie, 15, 49, 52, 53, 78, 79, 84, 85, 154

Bourgeois sociology, 78
Bournazos, Stratis, 4
Bratsis, Peter, 142, 143n6
Braudel, Fernard, 31
Brexit, 136
Burckhardt, Jacob, 75, 75n11
Bureaucracy, 53, 79, 126, 145
Burgel, Guy, 33, 35, 36, 39
Byzantine, 76n14, 121

C
Campbell, John, 27n5, 31, 34, 111
Capitalist societies, 78
Carmocolias, D. G., 30, 30n9
Castells, Manuel, 143
Castoriadis, Cornelius, xi, xiii, 27, 58, 59, 64–77, 64n1, 65n2, 76n13, 76n14, 77n15, 82, 87, 88, 88n23, 92, 95, 96, 109, 110, 116, 117, 139, 150, 152, 171
Cavafy, Constantine, 121
Centre of Marxist Studies and Research, 82
Certificates, 40, 40n26
Chalari, Athanasia, 153n16
Charalambis, Dimitris, 147
Chechnya, 119
Cheliotis, Leonidas K., 153n16
Chicago School, 144
China, 149, 150
Chiotakis, Stelios, 125
Chletsos, Michael, 124
Chomsky, Noam, 115
Chouliaras, Giorgos, 120
Christian/Christianity, 94
Christodoulakis, Nikos, 113
Chronotope, 48n1
Chtouris, Sotiris, 145
Church of Greece, 28
City University of New York, 142

Civil society, 10, 53, 67, 94, 138, 138n2, 145, 149, 156
Civil war, xi, xiii, 7, 7n11, 13, 26, 27, 38
Cixous, Hélène, 115, 122n13
Clarke, Simon, 77, 78, 86, 86n21
Class politics, 55
Class structure, 40, 50, 53–55, 78
Class struggle, 79n16, 81, 83
Clientele-based networks, 149
Clientelism, 94, 137
Client-patron discourses, 54
College De France, 116
Colombotos, John, 125
Communicative action, 72, 90
Communism, 26, 65
Communitarianism, 18n20, 26
Comprador capital, 52, 78, 85
Comprador capitalist class, 85
Comte, Auguste, 8–11, 110
Conflict theory, 90
Coniavitis, Thomas, 124
Conservative, 4, 26, 49, 80, 142, 144, 154n17
Constantine, King, x, 7n11
Constantopoulou, Christiana, 114, 115, 145
Consumerism, 51, 95, 127
Conze, Werner, 89
Corsi, Giancarlo, 124n15
Covid-19 pandemic, xiii, 136, 145, 150, 151
Creative ambiguity, 150, 150n11
Criminology, 16, 88, 112, 145
Crisis, x, xii, 3, 67, 74, 78, 81, 84–87, 123, 136–159
Critical Theory, 66, 73
Cultural formalism, 37
Cultural sociology, 38
Cyprus, xi, 39, 39n24, 48
Cyprus crisis, 49, 49n2
Czechoslovakia, xi, 85

D

Dahrendorf, Ralf, 126
Damianakos, Stathis, 31
Darstellung, 57, 58, 80, 81n18
Daskalaki, Iro, 145
Decisionism, 89, 90n24, 96n31
Deconstruction, 117, 118
Deleuze, Gilles, 118
Della Volpe, Galvano, 82
Delmouzos, Alexandros, 2
Delta, Penelope, 4
Demertzis, Nikos, 38, 113, 123, 124, 140, 141, 151, 154, 155
Democracy, xi, 26, 27, 40, 48–50, 48n1, 74, 79, 94, 95, 116, 117n9, 120, 138, 149
Democratic Defense, 5n7
Democritus University of Thrace, 74
Demoticist movement, 3n4
Demotiki (demotic), 144
Dependent industrialization, 52
Dependent integration, 55
Deree, vi, 30
Derrida, Jacques, 117, 118, 118n10, 118n11
Dertilis, Giorgos, 7n11
Deukalion, 109n1
Diamantouros, Nikiforos, 48n1, 49, 113, 138n2
DiaNEOsis, 146
Diavazo, 56, 81
Dictatorial exclusion, 55
Dictatorship, xi, xiii, 5n7, 13, 14, 17n17, 26n1, 40, 48, 52, 64n1, 78, 79, 87
Dictionary of Social Sciences, 38
Différance, 117, 118, 118n11
Dilthey, Wilhelm, 10, 14
Dimirouli, Foteini, 27
Dimitrakos, Dimitrios, 143
Dimitras, Elie, 36n19
Dimitriadis, Iraklis, 153n16
Dobratz, B.A., 6, 28

Dogmatism, 68
Donskis, Leonidas, 136
Dosse, François, 66n3
Dowry, 32
Doxiadis, Constantinos, 36n18
Doxiadis, Kyrkos, 124
Dragona, Thaleia, 38n21
Dragona, Thaleia, 38n21
Dragoumis, Markos, 18n20
Du Boulay, Juliet, 34, 34n14
Dualisms, 11, 72, 106, 107, 121, 152
Durkheim, Émile, 6, 8, 69, 70, 71n7, 72, 76n12, 80, 90, 96n30, 108, 113, 113n7, 116, 124n15, 126, 138, 140, 141, 144, 155

E

East, 35, 121, 137n1
Eastern Europe, 125, 144
École Des Hautes Études, 117
École Pratique des Hautes Études, 31, 83n20
Economics, vii, xii, 2, 4, 6, 16, 18n20, 32, 33, 35–37, 50, 51, 54, 58, 67, 78, 82, 94, 96, 96n29, 106, 108, 127, 128, 137–139, 145, 146, 155, 171
Education, v, vii, 3, 6n8, 29n8, 37–40, 39n24, 54, 59, 64, 74, 81, 89, 96, 108, 124, 124n15, 125, 126n17, 137, 139, 143, 145, 149, 153, 156, 159
Ekistics, 36n18
Elefantis, Angelos, 86n22, 87
Eleftheria, 81
Eleftheropoulos, Avrotelis (alias as *Eleftheros, Filolaos*), 7–18, 27, 38
Elias, Norbert, 108, 141
Ellinas, Antonis, 137
Elliniki Radiofonia Tileorasi (Hellenic Broadcasting Corporation) (ERT), 74, 115, 115n8

INDEX 177

Emmanouil, Artemis, 30
Empirical research, 26–41, 56, 93, 124, 171
Enclave form, 54–55
End of history, 10, 136
Engels, Friedrich, 79
Enlightenment, 38, 40, 90, 150, 152
Enrichment without modernization, 51
Epistemological break, 50, 154n17
Epistemology, 68, 70, 88, 90n24, 147
ERT, vi, vii
Essentialism, 48, 53, 155
Eurasia, 137n1
Eurogroup, 136
EURONAT (under the European University Institute), 145n7
Europe, xi, 36, 37, 78, 81, 87, 94, 119, 125, 136, 142
European Central Bank, 150n11
European Commission, 150n11
European Economic Market (EEC), 78, 85
European Sociological Association (ESA), 153n14, 156
European Union (EU), 127n19, 137n1, 143, 147, 149, 150, 155, 172
European Value Study (EVS), 147
Eurozone, 136
Evia, 34, 34n14, 35
Exarchou, Orietta, 28
Exchange-theory, 126
Eyerman, Ron, 151

F
Fakiolas, Nikos, 125
Fallmerayer, Jakob Philipp, 13
Family, 7, 30, 32, 34, 51, 56, 80, 121, 124, 137, 144, 155
Faraklas, George, 93n26, 146n9
Fascism, 78, 85

Faye, Jean-Pierre, 79n16
Featherstone, Kevin, 155n20
Feminism, 111, 122n13
Filias, Vassilis, 5n7, 37, 39, 52–53, 56, 57, 115n8
Filolaos Eleftheros, 27
Fokas, Effie, 155n20
Formal sociology, 90
Forum of the Social Sciences, 113
Fotopoulos, Nikos, 137, 145
Foucault, Michel, 108, 115n8
Foundationalism, 92
Fountoukou, Vera, 31
Fouskas, Theodoros, 144
France, ix, 31, 65, 66, 66n3, 74, 77, 78, 81, 84, 112, 115, 117, 121, 122n13
Frangoudaki, Anna, 38n21, 69n6, 144, 155n20
Frankfurt School, 86n21
French Institute in Athens, 73
French Institute in Thessaloniki, 74
French National Social Science Centre, 119
Fressard, Olivier, 66n3
Freud, Sigmund, 18
Freund, Julien, 93
Freyer, Hans, 140, 141
Friedl, Ernestine, 34
Frisby, David, 154n18
Functionalism, 79, 86, 86n21, 90, 106–108
Fundamentalism, 150, 155

G
Gangas, Spiros (*author*), 96, 155
Garaudy, Roger, 82
Gardikas, Konstantinos, 16
Garfinkel, Harold, 141
Geertz, Clifford, 142
Gemeinschaft, 11
German Idealism, 89, 96

Germany, 14, 37, 65, 66, 66n3, 80, 89, 96, 121
Gesellschaft, 11
Giannakopoulou, Georgia, 154n18
Giannaras, Christos, 87
Giddens, Anthony, 72, 96n30, 107, 108, 143
Gioka, T., 29, 33
Giouras, Thanasis, 141
Giovanni Agnelli Foundation, 125
Gkioka, Tina (also as Gkioka-Katsarou, Tina), 29
Gnosis Publishers, 141
Godelier, Maurice, 142
Goffman, Erving, 72, 141
Golden Dawn, xii, 137
Goldthorpe, John, 148n10
Gorz, André, 115
Goudi coup, 4, 106
Gouldner, Alvin, 113n7
Gounis, Kostas, 155n20
Gourgouris, Stathis, 120
Goutos, Michalis, 36, 39
Granet, Marcel, 141
Great Britain, 80
Great Recession, xiii, 136, 137, 145, 146n8, 147, 149, 158
Greek civil war, 27, 154
Greek Communist Party (KKE), x, 50, 82
Greek dictatorship, 52, 78, 79
Greek Enlightenment, 93n27
Greek junta, 79, 96n29, 144
Greek language, 94, 116, 144, 153
Greek Orthodox Church, 27, 78, 138n2
Greek Review of Social Research, 38, 40, 113, 145
Greek secondary education, 156
Greek shipping, 85
Greek society, 14, 18, 30n9, 32, 48n1, 50, 51, 65n2, 77, 84, 93–95, 114, 125n16, 147, 151, 154, 156, 172
The Greek Sociological Review, 156
Greek state, 51, 52, 84, 94, 124
Greek working class, 84
Green, Bryan, 123
Greveniti, 31
Grozny, 119
Guattari, Félix, 118, 119
Gulag, 76, 76n12
Gumplowicz, Ludwig, 15, 17
Gunn, Richard, 86
Gurvitch, Georges, 58, 139, 140
Gutenberg Publishers, 140

H
Habermas, Jürgen, 7n9, 66, 71n8, 72, 89, 90, 113, 115, 124n15, 127, 143
Habitus, 40, 84, 108, 117n9, 151, 152, 152n13
Halaris, Yiorgos, 95
Halford, Susan, 157n21
Halkias, Alexandra, 154
Haniotis, George, 40n27
Haritakis, Georgios, 6
Haritopoulos, Gerasimos, 71n7
Harth, Dietrich, 89
Harvey, David, 85, 142
Hauser, Arnold, 141
Havel, Vaclav, 76n13
Heberle, Rudolf, 11
Hegel, Georg Wilhelm Friedrich, 10, 11, 76n12, 81, 82, 84, 86n21, 96, 126, 138, 149, 155
Hegelian, 57
Hegelianism, 68n5
Heidegger, Martin, 67, 117, 118n10, 120
Heidelberg circle, 9–14
Hellenes, 120

Hellenic Broadcasting Corporation (ERT), vi, 74, 115, 115n8
Hellenic Foundation for European and Foreign Policy (ELIAMEP), 155n20
Hellenic Ministry of Education and Religious Affairs, 110n2, 158n22
Hellenic Observatory (LSE), 108, 110, 153n16, 155n20
Hellenic Review of Political Science, 140
Hellenic Sociological Society (HSS), vii, 110n2, 155–156
Hellenic Statistical Authority, 158n22
Hellenocentric orientation, 151
Heller, Agnes, 66, 115
Heller, Clemens, 31
Henri, Michel, 89
Henrich, Dieter, 89
Hermeneutics, 58, 90, 144
Herzfeld, Michael, 13, 31, 111, 111n3
Hirschon, Renée, 34
Historical sociology, 40, 55, 107, 110, 111, 124, 154
Historicism, 75, 91, 110
Hitler, Adolf, 14, 76
Holism, 72, 108, 148, 149
Holmwood, John, vi, 107, 112, 120
Homans, George C., 126
Honneth, Axel, 71n8, 155
Human geography, 35

I

I Kathimerini, 81
Ideological apparatus of the State, 80
Iliou, Filippos, 87
Imaginary institution, 69–74
Imaginary institution of society, 58, 69–73
IMF, 136, 143, 150n11
Imperialism, 78, 83, 85

Imvriotis, Yiannis, 83
Indeterminacy, 57, 58, 69, 70, 73, 75, 90n24, 91, 96, 96n31, 122
India, 85, 150
Individualism, 8–9, 14, 118
Industrialization, 27, 32, 33, 52, 94
Informal Administration Practices and Shifting Immigrant Strategies (IAPASIS), 145n7
Institut Géographique National de Paris, 35n17
Institutions, vi, 3, 4, 6n8, 12, 15, 28–30, 32, 39, 48, 55, 56, 58, 70, 75, 76n12, 76n14, 81, 82, 84, 86, 91n25, 96, 112, 117, 118, 118n10, 124n15, 127, 138, 138n2, 155, 159
Instrumentalization of the law, 124n15
Integration, 56, 73, 86, 92, 107, 109, 120, 127, 146, 148, 149
Interactionism, 72, 90, 126
Interdisciplinarity, 39, 108–111
International Sociological Association (ISA), 53, 59, 153n14, 156
In the Paths of Thought, 115, 142
Ioannina, 31, 113n7
Irakleion, 74
Iraq, 136
IS, 136
Isenberg, Bo, 17n17
Italy, 14, 80, 143n6

J

Jaspers, Karl, 10
Jessop, Bob, 77, 82, 86
Joas, Hans, 73
Jünger, Ernst, 118
Jurisprudence, 108
Justice system, 79

K

Kalerante, Evaggelia, 144
Kalfopoulos, Kostas Th., vi, 141
Kalitsounakis, Dimitrios, 6, 17
Kampouri, Nelly, 144
Kanellopoulos, Panagiotis, 6–18, 11n15, 26, 68n5
Kant, Immanuel, 72, 76n12, 96, 117, 123
Kantianism, 68n5
Kantzara, Vassiliki, 140
Karabatzaki-Perdiki, Helen, 113, 113n7
Karagiorgas, Sakis, 5n7, 96n29
Karakioulafi, Christina, 140
Karamanlis, Konstantinos, xi, xii, 50, 79
Karavidas, Kostas, 18n20
Karidas, Dimitris, 87, 88
Karyotakis, Kostas, 14
Kasimis, Charalambos, 154
Kassimati, Koula, 38, 125, 128, 144, 145n7
Kastellorizo, 136
Katharevousa (purist), 3, 144
Kathedersozialisten, 3
Katsambas, 32n12
Katsaros, Evangelos, 38
Katsas, Gregory, 144
Kavala, 36
Kavoulakos, Konstantinos, 90n24
Kavvadias, Georgios, 55
Kayser, Bernard, 35
Kelpanidis, Michalis, 145
Kelperis, Christos, 37
Kenna, Margaret, 35
Kennedy, Paul, 142, 143
Kevin Featherstone, 155n20
Khomeini, Ruhollah, 76
Kitromilides, Paschalis, 39
Knöbl, Wolfgang, 73
Kofler, Leo, 141

Kokkinia, 34
Kokosalakis, Nikos, 26, 64, 121n12, 124, 128, 153, 154n17, 156
Koliopoulos, John, ixn1
Kommounistiki Theoria kai Politiki, 81
Kondylis, Panagiotis, 65, 88–96, 90n24, 91n25, 93n26, 93n27, 96n31, 110, 113, 121, 137n1, 140, 141
Koniordos, Sokratis, vi, 5, 13, 26, 29n7, 109, 137, 140, 144–147, 152, 154, 159
Konstantinos Mitsotakis Foundation, 83
Kontiadis, Xenophon, 145
Kontiadis, 145
Koselleck, Reinhart, 89
Koty, John, 29, 29n8
Kourahanis, Nikolaos, 5
Kourvetaris, George, 6, 28, 29n7, 40
Kousis, Maria, 137, 142n5, 146
Koutoupis, Thalis, 2
Koutroulis, Spyros, 113
Kouvelis, Anastasia, 124
Kouzelis, Gerasimos, 96n30, 124
Kranaki, Mimika, 68
Kristeva, Julia, 115
Kultur, 11
Kulturkreis theories, 13
Kulturkritik, 71, 93, 95
Kyriazis, Nota, vi, 112, 112n4, 124, 125, 127n19, 145
Kyrtsis, Alexandros-Andreas, vi, 3, 5, 6, 10, 13, 14, 18n20, 64, 64n1, 89, 95, 128, 152, 152n13, 153, 156

L

Laboratory for Social Studies and Opinion Polls, 114
Laclau, Ernesto, 80, 80n17

Lagoumitzi, Georgia (author), 53n5, 144
Lakatos, Imre, 148
Lambiri-Dimaki, Joanna, 6, 13, 14, 29, 29n7, 32, 33, 37, 40, 40n29, 64, 65n2, 77n15, 106, 109n1, 110–112, 114, 125, 128, 141, 146, 151–152
Lamia, 108
Lasithi basin, 33
Lask, Emil, 68, 70, 91
Law 1268/1982, 125, 126n17
Law 4009/2011, 126n17
Layder, Derek, 153n14
Lazarsfeld, Paul, 141
Le Bon, Gustav, 16
Lebensphilosophie, 71, 94
Leclerc, Annie, 122n13
Lefebvre, Henri, 140
Lefort, Claude, 117
Left, 39, 82, 94, 126, 127, 137
Legein, 70, 71
Lekkas, Pantelis, 113n7, 124
Leledakis, Kanakis, 73
Lembesis, Evangelos, 7–18, 16n16, 17n17, 155
Lenin, Vladimir, 8n12, 76n14, 79
Leontsini, Mary, 145
Leros Psychiatric Hospital, 118
Leverrato, Jean-Marc, 145
Lévy-Bruhl, Henri, 140
Lianos, Michalis, 153n16
Libre, 88
Lienhardt, Godfrey, 56
Lineton, Michael, 35
Linguistics, 111, 116, 117, 118n10, 122
Linköping University, 153n16
L'Institut d'Études Politiques de Paris, 112
Lipowatz, Thanos, 109n1, 113, 124, 126, 140, 141, 145, 154

Lockwood, David, 148
London School of Economics (LSE), 64n1, 108, 110, 153n16, 155n20
Luhmann, Niklas, 72, 96n30, 114–116, 138, 143
Lukács, György, 53n4, 83
Lyotard, Jean-François, 117
Lyrintzis, Christos, 48n1
Lytras, Andreas, 145

M
Macedonian naming dispute, 138n2
Mackridge, Peter, 3n4
Macro-micro, 145, 148
Maglaras, Vassilis, 141
Magma, 70, 71, 75
Makarios, Archbishop, xi, 39
Manesis, Aristovoulos, 48
Mani, 35
Mann, Michael, 110, 136
Mannheim, Karl, 11, 12, 40n29, 88, 141, 152
Marantzidis, Nikos, 126
Maratou-Alipranti, Laura, 124, 146, 146n8
Marcuse, Herbert, 53n4
Markantonatou, Maria, 142
Marker, Chris, 71n7
Marketos, Spyros, 5, 7
Markides, Kyriacos, 39n25
Markis, Dimitris, 74, 75
Maroniti, Niki, 2
Marx, Karl, 10, 12, 16, 57, 58, 69, 71n7, 75, 76n12, 79, 80, 82, 83, 85, 86n21, 96, 96n30, 106, 112, 126, 140
Marxism, 58, 74, 78, 79, 81, 83, 86, 87, 95, 106, 107, 109, 122, 140, 152
The mass, ix, 15–17, 116, 119, 147
Mass democracy, 94, 95

Mass media, v, 80, 116, 121, 147, 156
Masson, Philippe, 65
Materialism, 86, 144
Materiality, 54, 82, 86
Maus, Heinz, 3, 28
Mavridis, Iraklis, 118n11
Mavrogordatos, George Th., 4, 125, 126n17
McCarthy, George, 113n7
Means of production, 84
Medical sociology, 156
Mediterranean, 31, 36, 78, 121, 125
Mediterranean Conferences, 31
Megara, 32
Meletopoulos, Meletis, 9, 9n13, 14, 68n5, 81n19, 113, 139
Menger, Carl, 96n30, 96n31
MeRA 25, 150n11
Merton, Robert K., 107, 112n5
Metapolitefsi, xi, 48, 48n1
Metaxas dictatorship, 13, 14
Metaxas, Ioannis, xi, 14, 17n17, 26
Metaxopoulos, Aimilios, 113
Methodenstreit, 58
Methodology of the social sciences, 156
Michailakis, Dimitris, 153n16
Michailidis-Nouaros, Georgios, 55
Michel, André, 56
Michels, Robert, 17
Middle-class, x, 94, 137
Miliband, Ralph, 79–81, 80n17
Milios, John, 56
Military *coup*, 81
Military League, x, 4, 4n5
Military sociology, 40, 156
Mills, C. Wright, 82
Minerva, 40
Modern European Civilization, 141
Modernity, 6, 12, 32, 36, 50, 51, 54, 74, 117, 119, 123, 138, 138n2, 143, 144, 146, 147, 149, 155

Modernization, xiii, 27, 30–41, 48–59, 95, 123, 125n16, 126, 127, 138, 138n2, 139, 171
Moebius, Stephan, 14
Moore, Barrington, 110
Morin, Edgar, 119
Mosca, Gaetano, 126
Moschonas, Gerasimos, 145
Moskos, Charles, 28, 29n7, 40
Moskov, Kostis, 87
Moussourou, Loukia, 30, 56, 124, 144
Moustaka, Calliope, 31–33, 38
Mouzakitis, Angelos, 73
Mouzelis, Nicos, 18n20, 37, 40, 48–50, 54–55, 64, 64n1, 65n2, 80n17, 106–108, 110, 111, 113, 121, 125–127, 137–140, 138n2, 143–159, 171
Münch, Richard, 139
Musil, Robert, 17n17
Mussolini, Benito, 14
Mylonas, Alexandros, 2

N

Nagopoulos, Nikos, 144
National and Kapodistrian University of Athens, 159
National Center for Social Research (EKKE), 30n11, 36n19, 39, 113
Nationalism, 95, 124, 136, 138n2, 154
National Kapodistrian University of Athens, 112n5
National Patriotic Alliance of Independent Greeks, 137
National Schism, x, 7, 7n11
NATO, 78, 136, 137n1, 139
Nazism, 78
Nea Koinoniologia, 95, 139

Nefeli Publishers, 141
Neohoraki, 28
Neo-Kantian philosophy, 68
Neoliberalism, 127n18, 136, 142, 143, 149
New Democracy, 112
Nicolaou, Litsa, 26, 29, 108
Nicos Poulantzas Institute, 86n22
Nietzsche, Friedrich, 14, 18, 96n31
Nihilism, 90, 91, 91n25
Nikolaidou, Celia, 124
Nikolaidou, Magda, 32, 33
Nikolakopoulos, Ilias, 145
Nikolaou, Litsa (as Nikolaou-Smokoviti, Litsa), 5, 6
Nikolaou-Smokoviti, L., 145
Nina-Pazarzi, Eleni, 145
Nisbet, Robert, 141
Non-sociology, 58, 122–123
Normativism, 138
Notaras, Gerasimos, 39
Noumas, 4
Nussbaum, Martha C., 155

O
OECD, 87
Oedipus, 75
Offer, Avner, 5
O Laos, 4
Olympic Airlines, 85
Olympic Games, 136
Ontology, 69, 73, 75, 76n12, 92, 95
Open Marxism, 81n18, 86, 86n21
Open University, UK, 159
O Politis, 81
Oppenheimer, Franz, 15
Optimism, 40, 119, 136, 152
Orientalism, 120
Ortega-y-Gasset, José, 16, 18
Over-education, 54n6

P
Panagiotopoulou, Roi, 145
Panagiotou, Aristeidis, 154n18
Panayotopoulos, Nikos, 140, 140n4, 141, 151n12
Panhellenic Socialist Movement (PA.SO.K), xii, 5n7, 50, 113, 125, 126, 127n19, 142, 154
Pantazis, Apostolos, 96
Panteion School of Political Sciences, 7, 13
Panteion University of Political and Social Sciences, 7
Papachristou, Thanasis, 125
Papadopoulos, Apostolos G., 144
Papadopoulos, Pavlos, 5n7
Papadopoulou, Teta, 74, 77
Papageorgiou-Lymperis, Panagiota, 124
Papaioannou, Skevos, 125, 145
Papakostas, Apostolis, 153n16
Papalexandrou, Konstantinos, 140
Papanastasiou, Alexandros, x, 2–5, 5n7, 7, 11n15, 26
Papanastasiou Society, 5n7
Papandreou, Andreas, 50, 77, 125, 126
Papandreou, George, 136
Papandreou, Georgios, 37, 48
Papataxiarchis, Efthymios, 111, 145
Papazisis, Victor, 139
Papilloud, Christian, 139, 139n3
Pappas, Takis, 145
Paradellis, Theodoros, 111
Parasite state, 53
Paraskinio, 74
Pareto, Vilfredo, 18
Paros, 31
Parsons, Talcott, 72, 76n12, 96, 96n30, 108, 116, 138, 141, 149
Parthenon, 75
Partitocrazia, 137

Pascal, Blaise, 119
PA.SO.K, *see* Panhellenic Socialist Movement
Passeron, Jean-Claude, 37, 38
Patočka, Jan, 117, 118
Patriarchy, 94
Patrikios, Titos, 82, 83, 83n20, 87
Patronage, 55, 111n3, 125, 147
Péchoux, Pierre-Yves, 33, 35, 36
Periskopio, 115n8
Peristiany, John, xi, 2, 6, 13, 26, 29n7, 30, 31, 34, 39
Perspectivism, 90n24, 91, 95, 96
Pessimism, 119, 126, 128
Petmesidou, Maria (Petmesidou-Tsoulouvi, Maria), 52, 125
Petmesidou-Tsoulouvi, Maria, 52
Petmezas, Thrasyvoulos, 2
Phenomenological sociology, 72, 110
Philosophical and Political Library, 141
Philosophy, 7, 9–11, 9n13, 18, 66, 67, 69, 69n6, 70, 74, 75, 76n12, 77, 88–90, 108, 109n1, 111, 113n7, 117, 146n9
Pierce, vi, 28
Piketty, Thomas, 136
Piraiki-Patraiki, 32, 32n12
Pireaus, 34
Piven, Frances Fox, 142
Plato, 76, 76n12, 113n7
Platt, Gerald M., 124n15
Pleios, George, 145
Plummer, Ken, 155n19
Pobia, 33
Polanyi, Karl, 85, 142
Polis, 143
Political parties, x, 3, 7, 9, 12, 80
Political society, 53
Political theory, 95
Politis, Nikolaos, 13
Polytechneion, xi, 49, 49n2
Polytechnic uprising, 79, 87, 152

Pomaks, 34
Pontic-Greek diaspora, 144
Popular Party, 4, 5
Poreia, 81
Portugal, 78, 79
Positivism, 8, 90
Post-modernism, 57, 122–123, 144, 152
Poulantzas, Nicos, xi, xiii, 40, 51–52, 57, 64, 64n1, 65, 65n2, 77–88, 88n23, 95, 106, 109, 113, 113n7, 122n13, 127n18, 142, 143n6, 152, 171
Power, x, xii, 11n15, 15, 26, 37, 50, 52, 59, 67, 74, 78, 81, 82, 85, 90n24, 93, 95, 113, 118, 120, 136, 137n1, 147
Pragmatism, 73, 107
Praxis, 70, 87, 150
Press, 17, 74n10, 77, 79, 81, 114, 137, 154
Prooptiki, 81
Protosociologists, 7–18, 28
Proto-sociology, 7n9, 75
Psalidopoulos, Michalis, vii, 96n29, 155
Psarras, Dimitris, 87, 88
Psathas, George, 141
Psimmenos, Iordanis, 125, 144, 146
Psimmitis, Michalis, 140
Psychoanalysis, 66, 67, 70, 74, 111
Psychopedis, Kosmas, 57, 65–66, 74, 75, 81n18, 83–86, 86n21, 88, 95–96, 96n30, 110, 121, 146n9
Public sociology, 56, 153n15
Pyrgiotakis, Ioannis, 145

R
Rational-choice theory, 90, 108
Rationalism, 10, 96, 154n17
Reactionary, 71, 144, 154n17

Reductionism, 54, 106, 107, 148
Reichelt, Helmut, 86n21
Reification, 83, 107
Relative autonomy, 53, 56, 78, 80, 106, 108, 116
Relativism, 70, 91, 146, 154n17
Religion, 106, 108, 116, 146
Rembetika, 78
Repressive apparatus of the State, 80
Research Centre of Social Morphology and Social Policy (KEKMOKOP), 114, 124, 145n7
Ressentiment, 15–18, 154, 155
Rethymnon, vii, 56, 74
Review of Social and Legal Sciences, 5
Revolution, 8, 15, 17, 74, 106
Revue Suisse de Sociologie, 139
Rickert, Heinrich, 10
Right, x, 3, 37, 49, 59, 79, 94, 124n15, 127, 127n19, 138, 142, 145
Rigos, Alkis, 86
Ritzer, George, 153n14
Robin, Corey, 13
Rojek, Chris, 153n14
Romanos, Vassilios, 118n10, 156
Rorty, Richard, 66
Roudometof, V., 153n16
Rural communities, 31, 33
Rural-urban continuum, 33
Russia, ix, 76n14, 150
Russian invasion, 76n14, 136

S
Safilios-Rothchild, Constantina, 29n7
Said, Edward, 120, 121
St. George, 28
Saint Mary's University, 153n16
Sakellariou, Alexandros, 145
Sakis Karagiorgas Foundation, 95, 96
Samatas, Minas, 124

Sarakatsani, 34
Scheler, Max, 15, 18
Schelsky, Helmut, 122n14
Schluchter, Wolfgang, 156
Schmitt, Carl, 92, 96n31
Schools, 28, 35, 38, 78, 80, 124n15, 157, 157n21
Schrecker, Cherry, 65
Schücking, Levin Ludwig, 141
Schütz, Alfred, 72, 141
Science and Society: Review of political theory and ethics, 140
Scott, John, 12, 65n2
Sen, Amartya, 155
Sennett, Richard, 141
Serafetinidou, Melina, 145
Serdedakis, Nikos, 145
Sighele, Scipio, 16
Sikoutris, Ioannis, 6, 6n8
Simitis, Kostas, 5n7, 113, 126
Simmel, Georg, 10, 12, 14, 16n16, 17n17, 18, 86n21, 139n3, 140, 141, 155
Simmel Studies, 139n3
Simopoulos, Kostas, 95
Siotis, Jean, 40
Sittlichkeit, 126
Sivignon, Michel, 35, 36, 36n19
Skamnakis, Christoforos, 144
Skepticism, 68
Skliros, Georgios, 27, 27n3
Skocpol, Theda, 110
Social Anthropology, 31, 114
Social Cohesion and Development, 140
Social crisis, 67
Social democracy, 139, 142, 148, 149
Socialisme ou Barbarie, 66, 77, 82, 117
Sociality, 8, 16n16, 58, 92, 117
Social media, 145
Social ontology, 89–93, 90n24, 96
Social opinions, 40, 40n26

Social psychology, 58, 88
Social research, xi, 28, 30–41, 112, 112n4, 146n8
Social science, 6, 13, 14, 28–31, 35, 39, 67, 68, 69n6, 77, 81, 88, 96, 109n1, 110, 114, 115, 125, 137, 155, 156
Social Science and Opinion Poll Workshop, 57
Social Sciences, 140n4
Social stratification, 37, 54, 83, 145
Social theory, 66, 67, 69, 73, 86, 88, 89, 96, 115n8, 121, 156
Social Welfare School, 28
Sociogram, 59
Sociological Library, 140
Sociological Research, 29, 38
Sociological Society, x, 2, 3n3, 5, 6
Sociological theory, 4, 67, 73, 78, 83, 88–96, 106–108, 112, 144, 147, 148, 154, 155, 171
Sociologism, 58, 91, 110
Sociology of agriculture and rural life, 145
Sociology of culture, 145, 156
Sociology of education, 37, 38, 124, 145, 156
Sociology of health, 156
Sociology of migration, 156
Sociology of organizations, 81
Sociology of religion, 145, 156
Sociology of work, 81, 156
Södertön University, 153n16
Solzhenitsyn, Aleksandr, 76n13
Sombart, Werner, 140, 141
Sophocles, 74
Sorel, Georges, 17, 17n19, 18, 141
Sotiropoulos, Dimitris, 126, 126n17
Sotiropoulos, Leonidas, 35n15
Sourlas, Pavlos, 113
Spain, 78, 143n6
Spengler, Oswald, 18

Spinelli, Calliope, 29
Spourdalakis, Michalis, 126
Stalin, Joseph, 76, 76n14
Stamatis, Giorgos, 56
State totalitarianism, 51
State University of New York, 142
Stavridi-Patrikiou, Rena, 3n4
Stewart, Alexander, 107
Stratigaki, Maria, 145
Streeck, Wolfgang, 136, 148
Structuralism, 77, 80, 81n18, 88n23
Structural Marxism, 78, 86, 95
Structuration theory, 72, 107
Structure, 8, 31, 36, 37, 39, 40, 50, 53–55, 57, 58, 75, 78, 81, 82, 86, 106, 107, 112, 122, 123, 125, 138
Student uprising, xi, 49, 49n2
Sunday Eleftherotypia, 76n14
Svoronos, Nikos, 26
Sweezy, Paul, 51
Switzerland, 108
Symbolic interactionism, 90
Synchrona Themata, 109n1
SY.RIZ.A, 86n22, 137, 150n11
Systems theory, 72, 90, 115, 126, 138

T

Ta Nea, 81
Tarde, Gabriel, 16
Tatsis, Nicholas, vi, 30, 56, 112n6, 126, 144, 155, 156
Tatsoglou, Evangelia, 153n16
Taylor, Charles, 89
Teleology, 15, 91, 107, 148
Tenbruck, Friedrich, 122n14
Teperoglou, Afroditi, 124
Tepstra, Marin, 89
Terlexis, Pantazis, 56, 57, 113, 114, 126

Teukein, 70
Thanopoulou, Maria, 144
Themata, 74
Theodorakopoulos, Ioannis,
    9n13, 10n14
Theory and Society, 113
Theory of the state, 77, 80, 82–84,
    86, 86n21
Theotokas, Georgios, 14
There is no alternative' (TINA), 136
Thesis Eleven, 66
Thessaloniki, xi, 7, 73n9, 74,
    85, 119
Thompson, Kenneth, 35, 35n16
Thourios, 81
Thrace, 34, 145
To Dendro, 77n15
To Mellon, 4
To Vima, 81, 137
*To Vima ton Koinonikon
    Epistimon*, 57, 113
Tönnies, Ferdinand, 10–12
Torrance, John, 15
Touraine, Alain, 73, 139, 143
Tourist industry, 85
Trade unions, 3, 79
Trauma, 2, 7, 27, 48, 136, 144, 150,
    151, 154
Triantafyllopoulos, Konstantinos, 2
Trotskyist, 77
Tsakonas, Dimitrios, 26, 27,
    27n2, 27n5
Tsalikoglou, Foteini, 115
Tsangaris, Michalis, 145
Tsaoussi, Aspasia, 145, 147
Tsaoussis, Dimitrios, 29, 56, 58,
    112n6, 114, 124, 140, 147
Tsartas, Paris, 125
Tsatsos, Konstantinos, 9n13, 68n5
Tsiganou, I.
Tsinorema, Stavroula, 96
Tsirigotis, Dionysios, 137

Tsivakou, Ioanna, 90n24
Tsoukalas, Constantinos, 26, 39, 40,
    48, 49, 53–54, 85–87, 109n1,
    113, 115, 116, 119–122,
    126n17, 127, 127n18, 137,
    140, 142–159, 142n5,
    143n6, 171
Turkey, 121
TV, 114–123, 115n8, 122n13,
    142–143, 145

U
UBI, 143
Ukraine, 76n14, 136
UNESCO, 30, 31, 39
United Kingdom (UK), 106, 108,
    112, 112n6, 121, 152, 159
United States (US), 78, 85, 112n6,
    114, 120, 142, 143, 149, 151,
    154n17, 159
Universities, xii, 7, 13, 29, 37, 39n24,
    40, 55, 56, 65n2, 68n5, 79, 89,
    110n2, 111, 112, 117n9, 118,
    118n10, 124, 124n15, 125,
    126n17, 157–159, 172
University of Crete, vii, xii, 73n9, 74,
    142n5, 153n14, 156
University of Cyprus, 39n24, 153n16
University of Edinburgh, 112
University of Glasgow, 154n18
University of Ioannina, 113n7
University of Leicester, 108
University of Milan, 153n16
University of Northampton, 153n16
University of Oxford, 31
University of Rouen, 153n16
University of the Aegean, xii,
    111, 115
University of Thessaloniki, 7, 73n9, 74
University of Thessaly, 57, 114
USSR, 70, 85, 119

V

'Value-rational' and 'instrumental rational' action, 93
Values, 4, 10–15, 18, 32–34, 40, 57, 58, 85–87, 90n24, 92, 95, 96, 114, 119, 120, 127, 138, 146, 147, 149, 152, 155
Varoufakis, Yanis, 150n11
Vasilika, 35
Vaternelle, Roger, 35
Vegleris, Phaedon, 26n1
Velouchi (Tymphristos), 28
Veltsos, Yiorgos, 57, 58, 73, 83, 87, 109n1, 115, 115n8, 117–119, 118n10, 121–123, 142, 171
Venizelos, Eleftherios, x, 5, 155n20
Verein für Socialpolitik, 6
Veremis, Thanos, ixn1
Vergopoulos, Kostas, 18n20, 51–52, 83, 84, 87, 109n1, 115
Vernier, Betrand, 34
Verstehen, 10, 75, 90
Vezanis, Demetrios, 9
Vlachos, E.C., 37
Volos, 74
von Stein, Lorenz, 11
von Wiese, Leopold, 10
Voulelis, Nikos, 39
Vrettos, Louis, 28, 29

W

Wagner, Peter, 73
Waldmann, Peter, 156
Wallerstein, Immanuel, 52, 142, 148
Wallimann, Isidor, 126
Walzer, Michael, 142

Waters, Malcolm, 78
Weber, Alfred, 6, 10–12
Weber, Max, 6, 10–12, 14, 27n5, 67–69, 75, 79, 81, 91, 92, 96, 96n30, 96n31, 107, 110, 113, 116, 126, 140–142, 156
West, 50, 74, 121, 127, 136
Western Enlightenment, 89
Will-to-power, 96n31
Working-class, x, 3, 79, 83–85, 124
World Bank, 143
World system theory, 142
World Value Survey (WVS), 146, 147
World War II (WWII), 13, 14, 78, 80, 119
WTO, 143

X

Xypolitas, Nikolaos, 140

Y

Yale University, 142
Young Women's Christian Association (YWCA), 28
Yugoslavia, 119, 139

Z

Zachou, Chryssa, vii, 144
Zagori, 31
Zamparloukou, Stella, 137
Ziegler, Jean, 113, 139
Zisis, Petros, 11n15
Zito, George, 126
Zivilisation, 11

GPSR Compliance
The European Union's (EU) General Product Safety Regulation (GPSR) is a set of rules that requires consumer products to be safe and our obligations to ensure this.

If you have any concerns about our products, you can contact us on

ProductSafety@springernature.com

In case Publisher is established outside the EU, the EU authorized representative is:

Springer Nature Customer Service Center GmbH
Europaplatz 3
69115 Heidelberg, Germany

www.ingramcontent.com/pod-product-compliance
Ingram Content Group UK Ltd.
Pitfield, Milton Keynes, MK11 3LW, UK
UKHW021251180426

11946UKWH00004B/77